Suicide and Self-Harm in Prisons and Jails

Suicide and Self-Harm in Prisons and Jails

Second Edition

Christine Tartaro

LEXINGTON BOOKS
Lanham • Boulder • New York • London

Published by Lexington Books
An imprint of The Rowman & Littlefield Publishing Group, Inc.
4501 Forbes Boulevard, Suite 200, Lanham, Maryland 20706
www.rowman.com

Unit A, Whitacre Mews, 26-34 Stannary Street, London SE11 4AB

British Library Cataloguing in Publication Information Available

Library of Congress Cataloging-in-Publication Data Available

ISBN: 978-1-4985-5872-3 (cloth : alk. paper)
ISBN: 978-1-4985-5873-0 (electronic)

♾™ The paper used in this publication meets the minimum requirements of American National Standard for Information Sciences—Permanence of Paper for Printed Library Materials, ANSI/NISO Z39.48-1992.

Printed in the United States of America

Contents

Acknowledgments

I would like to first thank David Lester, my co-author on the first edition of this book. I never would have had the confidence to try to take on such a project without having him as a partner. David has had a tremendous influence on my career, and I am forever grateful to him for agreeing to work with me. I will do my best to pay it forward and help my younger colleagues succeed.

The staff at Lexington Books has been wonderful. I would like to thank Carissa Marcelle for her help securing the contract and working on the early phases of manuscript preparation. Sarah Craig and Becca Rohde helped with the later stages of the work. All were so patient and helpful.

I had some great support at Stockton University and at home during the two years that it took to do this second edition. I was fortunate to have not one, but two smart and efficient graduate assistants. Kathryn Martucci helped to hunt down statistics, and Jillian Kutner served as a wonderful reader and sounding board. Paula Duntley was kind enough to use her creativity to design the book cover. Chris DeSantis was available anytime I needed to "talk shop." My immediate family dealt with two years of listening to me vent and being patient when I had to say no to social events so I could stay on schedule. My parents, Jen, Dena, and Abbi took the time to listen to me, even though they have absolutely no interest in this topic. Speaking of moral support, of course I have to thank Gus, Jake, Camille, Templeton, Sully, Petey, and Todd for always listening and helping.

Chapter One

Incarceration and Suicide

Incarceration, whether it is used simply to detain someone awaiting trial or as the sentence itself, is likely to take a psychological toll on the people who are subjected to it. Some politicians and members of the general public carry the misperception that incarceration is easy, consists of "three hots and a cot," and is just an opportunity to get free health care and other services. Those who have lived or even worked in corrections know otherwise. In one of the earliest studies of the prison environment, Gresham Sykes (1958) researched the impact of incarceration and argued that it involved harms beyond having to be locked inside a building. Specifically, Sykes identified five "pains of imprisonment": deprivation of liberty, deprivation of goods and services, deprivation of heterosexual relationships, deprivation of security, and deprivation of autonomy. Of particular importance for this book are the deprivations of liberty and autonomy. The deprivation of liberty restricts inmate movement to not just inside the walls or fences of the institutions but also to specific parts of those facilities. The deprivation of autonomy strips adults of their control over most of life's daily activities. This lack of freedom and autonomy prevents people who are incarcerated from having control over aspects of their lives, including some related to health and safety (Sharkey, 2010). The deprivations of goods and services, heterosexual relations, and security add to the stress and discomfort of incarceration and, in some instances, contribute to inmates' desire to escape their circumstances. Sometimes, that desire to escape manifests itself in the form of a suicide attempt.

Incarceration prevents those who are locked up from being able to take oneself to an emergency room or any other doctor's office when they need help. Inmates generally lack the freedom to even visit the institution's infirmary without a pass. While in custody, those who need to see a doctor must fill out a request and then wait for the medical and custody staff to arrange

1

for care. It could take hours or days for the inmate to be taken to medical or for a professional to visit the inmate in the housing area. Depending on the facility and security level, inmates may have limited access to telephones to call suicide hotlines. Regardless if someone is detained by police for an hour or is imprisoned for life, the incarcerating authority is morally and legally obligated to ensure that the individual receives timely and adequate medical care. This includes mental health care and steps to prevent physical harm to the inmate, even if that physical harm is self-inflicted.

The difficulty of coping with incarceration is exacerbated by the presence of individuals who are at greater risk of self-harm than most people in general society. While the previously described deprivation model supported by Sykes (1958) points to the conditions of confinement as an explanation for inmate behavior, another theory—the importation model—suggests that, since humans are not "blank slates," they import their values and behavioral patterns into the institutions (Irwin & Cressy, 1962). As will be discussed throughout this book, men and women who are incarcerated are disproportionately involved in drug and alcohol abuse, have higher rates of mental illness, and often have higher levels of aggression and impulsivity than the general public. In other words, people who are incarcerated are at a higher risk for self-harm even before they are exposed to the stressful custodial environment. It is this combination of the presence of high-risk individuals and the stressful, confining, and possibly dangerous environment of the correctional facilities that makes surviving incarceration difficult, and even unbearable, for some (Dye, 2010, 2011; Sanchez, Fearn, & Vaughn, 2018).

One writer who helped to explain the difficulty of adapting to the prison culture, staying safe while living among maximum security inmates, and struggling to find an appropriate niche to make life palatable while incarcerated was Victor Hassine. Hassine was charged with first-degree murder shortly after graduating from law school. After being found guilty, he began a journey through several prisons in Pennsylvania over 27 years. Hassine chronicled his experiences in four editions of his book, *Life without Parole*. In his books, Hassine shared stories about the shock of entering his first maximum security prison, coping with all of Sykes's (1958) pains of imprisonment, and trying to find meaning to his life knowing that he was facing a long term of incarceration. The fifth and final edition of Hassine's book (Hassine, Johnson, & Tabriz, 2011) was edited by others, since Hassine was found hanging in his cell in 2008. He committed suicide shortly after learning that his request to have his sentence commuted was denied.

The focus of this book is the care and management of people who become suicidal or experience a mental health crisis while in police or correctional custody. Specifically, I will examine suicides and acts of deliberate self-harm in three settings: the prison, the jail, and the police lockup. Most readers are probably already familiar with the functions of these three different types of facilities, but for those who are not, I will provide a brief overview in this chapter. It is important to understand the characteristics of each of these types of institutions, since each presents unique challenges to suicide prevention.

TYPES OF CORRECTIONAL FACILITIES

Prison

The United States is the birthplace of the modern prison system, and it continues to rely on incarceration as a response to crime. The incarceration rate increased dramatically starting in 1980, peaked in 2010, and has been slowly decreasing in the second decade of the 2000s. Despite the slight decline in the incarceration rate, the United States remains the world's leader in the use of imprisonment. The Bureau of Justice Statistics (BJS) reported that there were approximately 319,600 inmates held in state and federal prisons at midyear 1980 (U.S. Bureau of Justice Statistics, 2007). By the end of 2016, state prisons held 1,316,200 inmates, while the Federal Bureau of Prisons (BOP) incarcerated approximately 189,100 additional individuals. The incarceration rate in 2016 was 450 per 100,000, down from 501 per 100,000 in 2006 (Carson, 2018).

Prisons are distinct from jails in that prisons are places where long-term inmates serve their sentences. Generally, inmates go to prison, rather than jail, if they are serving sentences that are over a year long. Prisons are built at minimum-, medium-, maximum-, and occasionally supermaximum-security levels, and they are governed by either a state or the federal government. Each state has its own department of corrections and houses inmates charged with state-level crimes, such as murder, manslaughter, rape, robbery, kidnapping (within the state), burglary, theft, assault, child abuse/neglect, and other offenses. These departments are part of the executive branches of each state government. Some states construct and operate all of their prisons, while others send some of their inmates to other states or contract with private companies to build and/or operate facilities.

The Federal BOP began operation as the central office for federal prison operations in 1930, but there were some federal prisons in the United States prior to this time. The original purpose of the BOP was to centralize administration of the 11 federal prisons that existed in 1930. There are currently 122 federal prisons and federally run detention centers throughout the United States and Puerto Rico. The bureau is currently responsible for 184,000 inmates, but 15% are residing in state, local, or privately run corrections institutions and juvenile facilities (Federal Bureau of Prisons, n.d.).

With regard to doing time in prison, there are advantages and disadvantages when compared to remaining in jails. State and federal prisons (especially federal prisons) tend to have more activities and programs available to inmates than jails. Since inmates are there for longer periods of time, prison administrators tend to allow inmates to accumulate some personal belongings to make them feel more comfortable and to help them pass the time. Rules regarding accumulation of belongings vary depending on the inmates' security level and the state and federal policies governing inmates' living conditions. One disadvantage to doing time in a prison is that these facilities can be far from inmates' homes. Federal inmates could be transferred to a facility thousands of miles from their homes. State prisoners might also be sent to an institution within the state but far from their loved ones. Making matters worse is that most prisons are located in rural areas with no access to public transportation, thereby complicating visits from relatives and friends residing in urban areas. Some inmates in both state and federal prisons must endure years of separation from their families, and they must try to adjust to a world that, for some, is unlike their usual surroundings.

Jail

Although the state and federal governments typically run prisons, most jails are generally controlled by counties. While the governing of jails varies by state, many states have at least one jail in each county. Six states have set up regional jail systems where multiple counties share a single facility. The BJS reported that, at midyear 2016, there were 740,700 inmates being held in city and county jails (Zeng, 2018). Jails vary greatly in their size. There are 30 jurisdictions that hold an average of at least 2,500 inmates per day. Most jails, however, are much smaller. In 2016, 54% of jails in the United States held fewer than 100 people, on average, each day. These small jails only hold 10% of the total jail population throughout the United States, while the 30 largest jurisdictions house 20% of the population (Zeng, 2018). As I will discuss later in this book, jail size and facility location present unique challenges when dealing with inmates who are mentally ill and/or suicidal.

The role of jails in the criminal justice system is more complex than that of prisons. As was noted earlier, prisons typically house sentenced inmates. Jails house inmates who are serving shorter sentences as well as those who are awaiting arraignment, bail, trial, or sentencing. These institutions are also responsible for holding state and federal inmates when prisons become overcrowded and for incarcerating probation and parole violators while they await their revocation hearings.

Alleged offenders who are arrested will either go to the police station for booking, or they will go directly to jail to be processed. Those who are initially taken to the police station but need to face a judge for a bail hearing will spend a short time in the police lockup and then be transported to jail. Either way, jail employees must receive offenders who, just hours or even minutes ago, were on the streets where they might have been abusing alcohol or drugs. This presents a problem for jail administrators that is not generally faced in the prison system: a sizable proportion of offenders enter jail while intoxicated or under the influence of drugs. Drug and alcohol intoxication and withdrawal can influence one's perception of life's circumstances and decision-making abilities. Intoxication and withdrawal may also necessitate medical interventions and can increase the risk of a suicide attempt.

The jail staff must also manage individuals who are mentally ill and are entering the jail after living in the community without medication or other treatment. The widespread deinstitutionalization and shutdown of psychiatric facilities that began in the 1970s was not followed by a commensurate growth in community-based mental health services necessary to stabilize those who were released. There were 559,000 patients residing in psychiatric facilities in the United States in 1955, but this number declined to 69,000 by 1995 (Felix, Barber, & Lesser, 2001), and was estimated to be about 35,000 by 2012 (Torrey, 2016). The combination of deinstitutionalization and the unavailability of community-based services results in many mentally ill individuals being released with no follow-up care.

When the community mental health treatment providers were unable to treat and monitor all those suffering from psychiatric disorders, it became necessary for another government agency to address the issue. By default, the criminal justice system became responsible for many of those whose behavior became too abnormal or threatening for them to remain in the community (Torrey, Kennard, Eslinger, Lamb, & Pavle, 2010). This is referred to as the criminalization of mental illness. Lamb, Weinberger, and Reston-Parham (1996) define this as "placing mentally ill persons who have committed minor crimes into the criminal justice system instead of into the mental health system, in psychiatric hospitals, or other psychiatric treatment facilities" (p. 275). Whether the behavior that precipitated the arrest was directly related to a psychiatric problem or the individual has psychiatric problems in addition to being involved in illegal activities, jails have become home to people who are at a higher risk for suicide and other self-harming behaviors. Jails, however, were never intended to serve as de facto psychiatric institutions, and most jail settings can be difficult, and even dangerous, environments for individuals with mental illness.

Police Lockup

Police departments vary in whether they book arrestees at the police station or at the jail. The departments that conduct bookings at the station have small detention areas. The detention areas can consist of one cell or a few cells and are supposed to be used for short periods of time. People placed in those cells can be precharge suspects, meaning that they have been taken into custody by the police but have yet to be charged with a crime. Individuals who have already made an initial court appearance but need to be held somewhere for a few hours may also be placed in a lockup (Hounmenou, 2010). Jail and police lockup personnel share the same problems of having to work with people who are coming from the streets under the influence of drugs and alcohol and who may be mentally ill and/or experiencing symptoms of mental illness. Since running lockups is not the primary mission of police, and these areas are used for such short periods of time, there tends to be little oversight of standards. Only a few countries have independent agencies that focus on monitoring conditions specifically in police lockups (Huonmenou, 2010). Additionally, there is very little existing research on lockups.

TERMINOLOGY

Suicide

The terminology used to describe self-inflicted injury and death continues to vary across the literature. One possible definition of suicide is a person intentionally committing an act that results in death. This definition still is a bit ambiguous. Most people would agree that intentionally drinking large quantities of alcohol or taking high doses of drugs could result in a self-inflicted death. Should all drug overdoses and fatal cases of alcohol poisoning be considered suicide? Just about everyone knows that heroin, crack, and alcohol are unhealthy, and that consumption of excessive amounts leads to death. Even people who are addicted are aware that using drugs or drinking can lead to death, but in most cases, they are not using with the intent to die. Instead, they are more often chasing a high or attempting to escape emotional or physical pain without a specific plan to extinguish life. For this book, I adopt the World Health Organization's (1986) definition of suicide, which is a conscious or deliberate act that ends one's life. In other words, I will not consider overdoses or other risky behavior to be suicide unless there is evidence to indicate that the intent was death.

Official statistics on suicide, and especially suicides in custody, have been criticized for their potential inaccuracies. For example, Liebling (1994) and

Loucks (1997) found that suicides of female inmates were more likely than male suicides to be labeled as "misadventure," "open," or "lack of care." Suicides may be covered up and misclassified so as to place the correctional facility and staff in a better light (Ruiz, Wangmo, Mutzenberg, Sinclair, & Elger, 2014; Welch & Gunther, 1997) and to reduce the threat of litigation. Some suicides are recorded as taking place in the hospital where the inmate was transferred, and ultimately died following the attempt, even though the actual attempt occurred in the corrections environment (Ruiz et al., 2014).

Governments in several countries have been working to collect data on mortality in custody, including the number of suicides. Until the early 2000s, tracking inmate suicides in the United States was largely handled by individual researchers and organizations interested in the subject. The federal government in the United States recognized the importance of tracking suicides in custody by passing the Death in Custody Act of 2000 (Pub. L. 106–297). This act mandates the quarterly collection of inmate death data from local jails, state prisons, juvenile facilities, and law enforcement centers (U.S. Department of Justice, 2002). The U.S. BJS is responsible for this data collection activity. BJS also collects and publishes aggregate suicide data. This was called the Deaths in Custody Reporting Program but was renamed Mortality in Correctional Institutions in 2018. BJS reports data involving deaths in adult prisons and jails on an annual basis,[1] including deaths that stemmed from an injury or illness while individuals were in custody, regardless of whether they were actually declared dead (U.S. Bureau of Justice Statistics, 2018a).

Nonfatal Self-Harm

Researchers and practitioners have used a variety of definitions when writing about suicide attempts and non-suicidal self-injury (NSSI). These are more difficult to define than suicide. Is swallowing a foreign object a suicide attempt? What if someone cuts his/her arm or leg near an artery? Should the seriousness of the injury matter when distinguishing a suicide attempt from another type of nonfatal self-injury? What about the individual's intent?

There are no uniform definitions of self-harm, self-mutilation, parasuicide, and attempted suicide (Fagan, Cox, Helfand, & Aufderheide, 2010; Lanes, 2011). Researchers have not agreed on what to call this type of behavior, with some using the term "deliberate self-harm," while others choose "self-mutilation," "self-injury," "parasuicide," or "non-suicidal self-harm." Even if researchers do use the same terms, they might not define them consistently. There tends to be general agreement that these acts involve intentional harm to one's body in the form of poisoning, cutting, burning, or other destruction of body tissue, but there are also occasional arguments that the definition should be expanded to include high-risk behaviors, such as risky sexual conduct and substance abuse (Canadian Centre on Substance Abuse, 2006). There is less agreement about whether motive should be part of the definition. Some researchers include a statement in their definition of self-harm that the behavior qualifies as intentional self-harm regardless of the degree of suicidal intent or motive for the act (Hawton, Linsell, Adeniji, Sariaslan, & Fazel, 2014; Morgan & Hawton, 2004), while others specifically exclude any injury where there is evidence of conscious suicidal intent (American Psychiatric Association, 2016; Fagan et al., 2010; Ross & Heath, 2003; Wichmann, Serin, & Abracen, 2002). A good example of the difficulty comparing studies can be found with the use of the term "parasuicide." Some researchers consider parasuicide to be an umbrella term for all types of intentional self-harm (Chapman, Gratz, & Brown, 2006), but others define parasuicide as self-injury specifically lacking fatal intent (Crighton & Towl, 1997).

In addition to researchers using various definitions for self-harm, correctional administrations may also lack consistency in how they define and measure this. Applebaum, Savageau, Trestman, and Baillargeon's (2011) survey of medical directors for the state and federal departments of corrections found that only one-third of the departments had a formal definition of self-injurious behavior. Thirteen percent of systems either had no definition or encouraged staff to use "clinical judgment" in identifying self-injury, while the remaining departments had unwritten definitions. Three-quarters of the responding systems distinguished between behaviors thought to be suicidal and those considered NSSI (Applebaum et al., 2011), but in the absence of formal, written definitions, reporting and data collection might be uneven. This, and the other aforementioned methodological issues, should be kept in mind during the overview of the available research on self-harm.

Suicidologists cannot reach an agreement about whether to view self-harm on a continuum of suicidal behavior or as distinct actions brought about by different psychological states and motivated by different desired outcomes. The research suggests that a substantial number of self-harm incidents are not merely failed suicide attempts but are performed for purposes other than seeking death or escaping life. Outside of corrections facilities, the intent of self-harm (to be fatal or not), has important implications for treatment responses. While the same can be said for therapeutic responses in correctional custody, the nature of the custodial environment provides additional challenges to framing supervision and management approaches for a few reasons. First, self-harm, even if it is meant to be nonfatal, is a strong predictor of later suicide attempts and completed suicides (Austin, van den Heuvel, & Byard, 2014; Favril, Wittouck, Audenaert, & Laenen, 2018; Hawton et al.,

2014; Klonsky, May, & Glenn, 2013; Loucks, 1997; Matsumoto, Yamaguchi, Asami, Okada, Yoshikawa, & Hirayasu, 2005; Penn, Esposito, Schaeffer, Fritz, & Spirito, 2003; Serin, Motiuk, & Wichmann, 2002; Victor & Klonsky, 2014). Second, even when intended to be nonfatal, such action can accidentally become deadly inside prison, jail, or police cells (American Psychiatric Association, 2016). Nock and Kessler (2006) use the term "suicidal gesture" to describe NSSI where there is no motivation to die, yet the individual makes the act look like a suicide attempt. An example of this would be using the most common method of custodial suicide—hanging or asphyxiation—without the intent to die. A person may make a gesture by simply creating a noose, but others might go further and actually simulate hanging or strangulation for attention-seeking purposes. People can lose consciousness faster than they expected, and the anticipated officer or nurse rounds might be delayed, resulting in the expected rescue arriving too late.

For this book, I will use the term "non-suicidal self-injury" (NSSI) to describe nonfatal incidents involving purposeful injury to oneself, including cutting, burning, ingestion of foreign objects, jumping a distance with the intent to harm oneself, or intentional overdoses, regardless of motive. In other words, this definition encompasses suicide attempts, incidents with minor injuries, and those where there was either no motive to die or the motive was unclear. I do this, because NSSI should be managed similarly to suicide attempts in custody. Even if these incidents were not intended to be fatal, correctional and mental health staff must consider these people as having a high risk for suicide and monitor them accordingly. I will use the term "suicide attempts" to describe nonfatal acts of self-harm where it appears that the individual intended for the act to be fatal.

Additional Terms

Suicidal behavior and "at-risk" are two additional terms that appear in writings about suicide. Suicidal behavior encompasses a wide range of actions, including writing suicide notes, sharing suicidal thoughts and plans, carrying out suicidal gestures and minor acts of self-injury, attempting suicide, and suicide (Blaauw, 2005; Camilleri & McArthur, 2008). Dexter and Towl (1995) define at-risk prisoners as those "who were distressed, depressed, or finding it difficult to cope and experiencing thoughts or feelings of a suicidal nature, and/or prisoners identified as at-risk by prison staff with a suicide risk referral form" (p. 46). The Victoria Department of Justice Correctional Services Task Force (1998) defines at-risk simply as those with an increased probability of attempting suicide or self-harm. Each correctional facility has its own criteria for what is considered to be an at-risk inmate. While some facilities might explicitly define what their administrations consider to be at-risk in their suicide prevention policies and suicide screening checklists, others do not and leave this distinction up to the discretion of the corrections staff and available mental health personnel.

UTILIZING A PUBLIC HEALTH APPROACH

Hanson (2010) applied a public health framework to suicide prevention behind bars. This framework is a useful way of viewing the different types of suicide prevention practices that are necessary in custodial institutions. First, there are the tertiary intervention practices. The focus here is to prevent death in the wake of a suicide attempt. Next is secondary prevention. In public health, secondary prevention involves early intervention to block or slow the progression of a disease. Applying this to suicide prevention, secondary prevention includes screening and identifying people who are at risk and then providing an intervention to prevent the suicide attempt from occurring. This can include observation, special housing assignments, restricted access to items that can be used for self-harm, and therapeutic interventions. Finally, primary prevention involves taking steps to prevent people from needing secondary or tertiary prevention. Primary prevention includes broader environmental and management changes rather than therapeutic interventions for a particular individual. Applied to suicide in custody, primary prevention methods include altering the overall facility environment. Changes to the environment and management structure can result in an institution with less violence, more constructive activities, and less of a need to utilize restrictive housing. Just as a population's good diet and exercise practices can reduce the need for treatment of diseases, effective primary suicide prevention techniques are likely to reduce the need for interventions at the individual level with inmates in crisis. This book will include recommendations for suicide prevention at all three levels.

WHAT IS NEW IN THIS EDITION

I met up with an old college friend when I was about halfway through this project. When she asked me what I was researching these days, I told her I was working on a second edition. Ever the cynic, my friend said to me "So, you are changing three words from the first edition so that you can sell more copies." I laughed, partially because I wish that I actually wrote a book that sold lots of copies and just needed a minor tweaking every few years. I also laughed because I know that can be the perception of second editions, but in this circumstance, it is far from true. Many of the headings are the same as they were in the first edition, and there is an occasional paragraph from the first edition that seemed to fit well here. For example, the differences between federal civil rights claims versus state tort claims that David Lester and I included in the first edition has not changed, so there was no need to redo that section (Chapter 9). Almost everything else has changed.

I felt that there was a need for a second edition of the book for several reasons. First, I thought it would be useful to have an update on how the United States and other countries are doing with preventing suicides and suicide attempts. As will be discussed in Chapter 3, there have been some changes in trends regarding when suicides tend to occur in jails. There has also been an uptick in suicide rates in some states and countries. Second, there continues to be debate about how to view and classify NSSI in the corrections setting. I present updated research on that topic in Chapters 4 and 6. As I already mentioned, there is evidence that some acts of NSSI are meant to be nonfatal. What I have personally witnessed in my work as a consultant is that some mental health and correctional staff members become so fixated on the motives of NSSI, particularly when they suspect that the motive is to manipulate staff, that they dismiss the possibility that the inmates may actually become suicidal or may "up the ante" with their self-harming behavior and perform a suicidal gesture that turns fatal. Such incidents serve as reminders that corrections officials must approach even apparently non-suicidal incidents of NSSI as warning signs of possible future suicidal behavior.

Third, departments' approaches to restrictive housing have changed considerably in the past decade. Around the time that my former co-author and I were putting together the first edition, several states were either in court or preparing to respond to lawsuits about their reliance on restrictive housing for juveniles and individuals with mental illness. Since publication of the first edition, some states and counties have made commitments to reduce the use of restrictive housing. Such housing has historically been used for inmates who are difficult to manage, including those who are suffering from mental illness. The U.S. Department of Justice (2016) announced that the Federal BOP would seek alternatives to restrictive housing for juveniles and offenders whose mental illness would likely preclude them from being able to withstand that type of environment. Several state and local corrections departments are currently implementing plans to place inmates who are at a heightened risk of self-harm in environments that are more treatment-oriented and less focused on isolation and sensory deprivation. Housing, unit, and facility-level initiatives are discussed in Chapters 6 and 7.

Fourth, research on community alternatives for individuals with mental illness and reentry services for those who do go into custody has advanced. The prevailing belief in criminal justice-related mental health services used to be the direct-cause model, meaning that individuals with mental illness became justice-involved solely because of their mental illness (Skeem, Winter, Kennealy, Louden, & Tartar, 2014). If that is the case, rehabilitation need only consist of mental health treatment. Recently, researchers have presented evidence that, while a small percentage of justice-involved individuals with mental illness are likely to become law abiding again with just mental health treatment, the majority of offenders with mental illness also have the same risk factors found among most offenders. Specifically, most offenders with mental illness have counterproductive attitudes, exposure to criminal peers or relatives, familial dysfunction, and educational deficits. It is still important to treat mental illness, as symptoms emanating from mental illness may interfere with an offender's ability to address criminogenic risk factors, but those risk factors must also be addressed for there to be reductions in recidivism (Skeem et al., 2014). Chapter 8 includes a discussion of addressing mental health and criminogenic needs through diversion and reentry programs.

Fifth, in the first edition, my co-author and I discussed how the manipulation of facility design, combined with management strategies, can work to reduce suicides. In this edition, I discuss some behavioral management strategies that can be of use to jurisdictions that are unable to afford renovating existing structures or constructing a new facility (Chapter 7).

Sixth, this edition includes more detailed information about screening and mental health assessments, including examples of screening forms that have been used successfully by some corrections departments (Chapter 5). Finally, it also includes updates on suicide case law, including the possibility of an important change in federal court (Chapter 9). Whenever appropriate, I included discussions of current accreditation standards pertaining to suicide prevention in custody, especially standards written by the American Correctional Association (ACA) and the National Commission on Correctional Health Care. In sum, there are many additions to this book.

As with the first edition, this book will provide readers with an overview of who attempts and commits suicide while in custody, where, when, and how these incidents occur, and whenever possible, I will address why the suicides occurred. I use research on correctional populations throughout the world to inform readers about the state of suicide screening and prevention practices for people in custody in various correctional settings. Since adult males make up the majority of the incarcerated population, much of what is presented here involves the care and custody of males, but I sought to include research on females and juveniles as often as possible.

CONCLUSION

There will be instances where (1) inmates show no signs of being distressed or suicidal, (2) the criminal justice and mental health personnel handle screening properly, and (3) inmates are housed and supervised appropriately, and yet suicides still occur. These, however, are rare occurrences, and there is much that corrections administrations can do to identify people who are at risk, provide appropriate monitoring during the crisis, and employ therapeutic interventions. Establishing and properly implementing a multifaceted suicide prevention program can help foster safer facilities for inmates, reduce staff members' exposure to the trauma associated with inmates' self-harm and suicide, and protect the administrations from legal liability. There are certain housing assignments that are associated with disproportionate numbers of inmate suicides, but there are other settings inside facilities that help to reduce tension, self-harm, and suicide. Despite the overreliance on mass incarceration in the United States, jurisdictions have developed evidence-based approaches to diverting less-serious offenders with mental illness from prison and jail and have found ways to help incarcerated people successfully navigate reentry. I hope that this book will provide ideas to practitioners, both frontline and management, as well as inform scholars about some of the best practices and more recent developments in the field.

NOTE

1. BJS reports on this subject are currently backlogged. At the time of this writing (late 2018) the most recent suicide data available for the United States are from 2014.

Chapter Two

Who Commits
Suicide While Incarcerated?

Incarceration is obviously a very stressful event for anyone who experiences it. What makes survival in custody more challenging is that many people who must face it are at a higher risk for self-harm and suicide than people in the community. Who commits suicide in prisons, jails, and police station detention areas? The present chapter provides answers to this question. This chapter is divided into two parts. Part one includes a discussion of static factors, meaning characteristics of inmates that cannot be changed. Examples are demographic characteristics and historical factors. Part two addresses dynamic factors, which are fluid characteristics, such as individuals' *current* mental health status. Both sets of factors play a part in understanding who is at risk for suicide.

STATIC CHARACTERISTICS

Gender

One consistent finding outside of custodial institutions is that male suicide rates are higher than those for females. The World Health Organization (WHO) (2018) publishes periodic suicide statistics for specific countries as well as regions of the world. In every region, males had higher suicide rates than females in 2016. Regional rates varied from as much as a fourfold difference between males and females in Europe (24.7 per 100,000 vs. 6.6 per 100,000 respectively) to very little difference in the Western Pacific (10.9 per 100,000 for males and 9.4 per 100,000 for females). Males had higher suicide rates in 185 out of the 191 countries studied by WHO. Females had higher suicide rates only in Bangladesh, China, Granada, Lesotho, Morocco, and

Pakistan. Unfortunately, data on suicides in these countries' prison systems are not available, so it is not possible to see if this difference in suicide rates also exists among the population in custody.

Outside of prisons and jails, the suicide rate in the United States was 15.3 per 100,000 for both genders combined in 2016. The male suicide rate was over three times higher than the female rate (23.6 per 100,000 for males and 7.2 per 100,000 for females) (World Health Organization, 2018). Dye (2011) compared suicide statistics from 2,000 for males and females in the United States both inside and out of correctional facilities. The suicide rate per 100,000 individuals for males in the community was higher than the rate for males in state prison (22.09 in the community and 15.69 in custody). For females, however, suicide rates in the community were much lower than they were for incarcerated women. The suicide rate per 100,000 was 5.03 for women in the community but 12.9 for females in state prison. Rates of suicide for male and female state prisoners were similar (15.69 vs. 12.9 per 100,000), and the differences were not statistically significant, whereas the differences in the community (22.09 for men, 5.03 for women) were significant. Why such differences? One possibility is that the years of publicity and research on the majority of suicides in corrections—involving males—has prompted greater vigilance among corrections staff working with males. As will be discussed shortly, females in and out of institutions are more known for suicide attempts and other forms of self-harm rather than completed suicides. Three possible reasons for the higher suicide rates among institutionalized females compared to those in the community are (1) the very high prevalence of mental illness and past traumas along with reliance on non-suicidal self-injury (NSSI) as a coping mechanism among female inmates; (2) the combination of restricted availability of less lethal methods for self-harm and the availability of a very lethal method (hanging/asphyxiation) in prison; and (3) possible lack of vigilance among correctional staff who might not expect female inmates to commit suicide.

Newcomen (2014a) studied deaths in prisons in the United Kingdom in 2013 and reported that the prison population was 95% male, and 96% of the custodial suicides were committed by males. Humber, Piper, Appleby, and Shaw (2011) studied suicides in England and Wales from 1999 through 2007 and found that, while the male to female prison population ratio was 17 to 1, the ratio of male to female custodial suicides was 10 to 1. In Australia, 92% of prisoners from 1999 through 2013 were male, and 93% of self-inflicted deaths[1] involved males (Willis, Baker, Cussen, & Patterson, 2016). In Germany, the incarcerated male suicide rate was twice that of females from 2000 through 2011 (Opitz-Welke, Bennefeld-Kersten, Konrad, & Welke, 2013; Radeloff et al., 2015). While women make up about 6% of the prison population of Switzerland (World Prison Brief Data, 2018), only 2% of suicides in Swiss prisons involved women (Gauthier, Reisch, & Bartsch, 2015). To summarize, in the United States, Great Britain, and Australia, the suicide rates for incarcerated females are proportionate to their representation behind bars or somewhat higher than expected. In other countries, incarcerated female suicide rates are substantially lower compared to their male counterparts.

While comparisons of male and female suicides in custody vary by country, findings regarding suicide attempts are much more consistent, with females being more likely to attempt suicide or commit NSSI in and out of prison (Meltzer, Jenkins, Singleton, Charlton, & Yar, 2003; Newcomen, 2014a; Stoliker, 2018). The Ministry of Justice reported a self-harm rate of 46,700 per 100,000 inmates for incarcerated males in England and Wales from March 2017 through March 2018.[2] Female inmates, however, had a rate of 224,000 incidents of self-harm per 100,000 inmates during the same time. Smith and Kaminski (2010) used the 2000 Census of State and Federal Adult Correctional Facilities to study self-injury among state prisoners in the United States. They found that facilities housing only females tended to have a higher prevalence of self-injury. In a survey of over 18,000 inmates in the United States, females were 2.12 more likely to have a lifetime history of suicide attempts compared to males (Stoliker, 2018). Abram et al. (2014) observed that incarcerated female juveniles were more likely to have a history of attempted suicide than males of the same age group.

Women's rates of attempted, but not completed, suicides are likely higher than men's at least partially due to women's preference for less violent and less lethal methods of suicide (Haw, Hawton, Houston, & Townsend, 2003; Hjelmeland et al., 2000; Moore, Gaskin, & Indig, 2015; Sarchiapone, Mandelli, Iosue, Andrisano, & Roy, 2011). Since women are more likely than men to use overdoses of drugs and poisons, it is easier for life-saving interventions to occur than when firearms are used. These less violent methods are also slower to kill, thereby permitting individuals to change their minds and seek assistance. As I will discuss in Chapters 3 and 4, these less violent methods, such as overdoses, can be difficult to access in prisons and jails, whereas the more violent and lethal method of hanging/asphyxiation is more readily available.

Race and Ethnicity

The racial patterns of prison and jail suicide parallel trends in the general population. The suicide rate in 2014 for white males outside prison in the United States was 17.6 per 100,000 people, 17.5 for American Indians/Alaskan Natives, 6.3 for Asian/Pacific Islanders, 5.6 for Blacks, and 5.9 for Hispanics

(Suicide Prevention Resource Center, 2017). Between 1999 and 2016, 84% of suicides in the United States involved non-Hispanic whites (Stone et al., 2018). For the incarcerated population, the average suicide rate among state prisoners in the United States from 2000 through 2013 was 25 per 100,000 for whites, 19 for "others" including American Indians, Alaskan Natives, Asian and Pacific Islanders, and Native Hawaiians, 16 for Hispanics, and 8 for Blacks (Noonan, Rohloff, & Ginder, 2015). The Office of Juvenile Justice and Delinquency Prevention also found whites to be overrepresented among correctional suicides, with white juveniles making up 38% of the incarcerated population but 68% of the suicides, compared to African Americans making up 39% of the incarcerated population but just 11% of suicides (Hayes, 2009). Racial differences also exist in lifetime history of suicide attempts, with whites being 35% more likely to report at least one suicide attempt in a nationally representative study of male and female prison inmates in the United States (Stoliker, 2018).

Researchers who have conducted smaller studies in specific regions of the United States have found similar racial and ethnic patterns. Kovasznay, Miraglia, Beer, and Way (2004) studied 40 inmate suicides that occurred in New York State correctional facilities and found that whites were disproportionately represented in those deaths. Whites made up only 16% of the New York correctional population from 1993 through 1999, but they made up 28% of custodial suicides. White inmates were also disproportionately involved in attempted and completed suicides in other studies conducted in correctional facilities in the United States (Abram et al., 2014; Baillargeon et al., 2009a; Charles, Abram, McClelland, & Teplin, 2003).

Racial differences in suicides are not exclusive to the United States. Researchers from Great Britain, Canada, and Australia have also reported that whites tend to be overrepresented among prison suicides (British Home Office, 1999; Serin, Motiuk, & Wichmann, 2002; Shaw & Turnbull, 2009). The racial differences in suicide and attempted suicides are also present in both sexes (Borrill et al., 2003; MacKenzie, Oram, & Borrill, 2003). The exception to the fairly consistent findings of whites being overrepresented among prison suicides is the study conducted by Humber, Webb, Piper, Appleby, and Shaw (2013) on suicides in England and Wales. Humber et al. reported that nonwhite inmates were more likely to commit suicide. Data included suicides over a three-year period, and the authors speculated that their findings were a result of a temporary increase in the number of foreign nationals incarcerated in England and Wales due to a refugee crisis.

Rodgers (1995) attempted to explain the racial differences in suicide rates among incarcerated populations by drawing on Durkheim's (1897 [1951]) theory of anomie. Durkheim believed that suicides rose in times and places where there was a disturbance in the regular order of society. These periods would be characterized by individuals losing their sense of integration with society. The demographic makeup of the prison population and the nature of the prison culture tend to resemble urban areas characterized by poverty and the street culture. Rodgers believed that racial and ethnic minorities would already be familiar with that environment and would be less likely to experience culture shock upon incarceration. White inmates, however, would be more likely to feel socially isolated in the corrections setting, as they are more likely to be accustomed to suburban or rural culture. While white inmates may feel socially isolated, if for no other reason than they are likely to be the racial minority in the institution, this explanation does not account for why the same disparities in suicide rates occur outside of correctional facilities.

Researchers studying suicide in the community have explored differences in suicide rates between African Americans and whites. One possible explanation is a "survival strategy" among African Americans that is an outgrowth from years of facing discrimination. Part of this survival strategy involves strong ties to family and the church, as strong religious beliefs and church involvement tend to be associated with disapproval of suicide (Stack, 2000). Harris and Molock (2000) also found that family support was associated with reduced suicidal ideation among African American college students.

While black inmates in the United States appear to have lower rates of suicidal ideation, suicide attempts, and completed suicides, some other racial minorities are at high risk for suicide. The national statistics for U.S. residents break out Native Americans and Alaskan Natives, but the Bureau of Justice Statistics (BJS) data for incarcerated suicides lump these groups into the "other" category along with Asians, Pacific Islanders, and Hawaiian Natives. For that reason, it is difficult to compare incarcerated and nonincarcerated groups. In a national study of suicide among incarcerated juveniles, Hayes (2009) found that American Indians were only 2% of the incarcerated juvenile population, but they were 11% of suicides in the late 1990s. In the United States, Native Americans can find themselves incarcerated in a county or regional jail or in one of the 76 jails located in Indian Country (Minton, 2016). One inmate committed suicide in an Indian Country jail during the midyear 2014–2015 recording period, and there were 53 suicide attempts. Attempted suicides in these facilities have decreased since the 2002 peak of 230. This decrease is an encouraging sign, especially given that the inmate population grew between 2002 and 2015, so one would have expected a corresponding increase in suicide attempts (Minton, 2003, 2015).

The aforementioned reduction of suicides among Native Americans might be a result of greater attention being paid to indigenous incarcerated people in places like the United States and Australia. The World Health Organization

(2007) identified indigenous people as high risk for suicide and suggested that more steps need to be taken to protect them in custody. The National Institute of Justice (2004) in the United States and the Victoria Department of Justice Correctional Services Task Force (1998) in Australia published reports recommending the implementation of specialized screening procedures for Native Americans, Aborigines, and Torres Straight Islanders, respectively. Recently, there have been some promising findings out of Australia. While the indigenous population in Australian prisons increased from 20% to 27% of the total incarcerated population between 1999 and 2013, they represented only 16% of self-inflicted deaths in custody during this same time (Willis et al., 2016).

Age

Age is related to individuals' social and psychological development. Since juveniles' brains have yet to fully develop, they may have trouble coping with difficult situations. Suicide tends to be the leading cause of death for juveniles in custody, partly because there are very few instances of young people dying from illness, which is the leading cause of death for adult inmates. In the United States, the BJS reported that suicide accounted for 45% of juvenile deaths in custody from 2002 through 2005 (Noonan, 2007). In Australia, 61% of juvenile custodial deaths from 1979 to 2011 were attributed to suicide. Fortunately, there were zero juvenile suicides in Australia between 1999 and 2011 (Lyneham & Chan, 2013). Radeloff and colleagues (2015) published a comparison of juvenile suicide rates in custody to suicide rates in the community in Germany. Adolescents in detention had a suicide rate of 113 per 100,000 individuals, compared to 4.9 in the community.[3] In a study of incarcerated adults in the United States, Stoliker (2018) found that increased age of the correctional population was associated with decreased chances of suicide.

One reason people find themselves incarcerated is their difficulty with approaching problems in a constructive manner. For example, while one person walks away or verbally responds to an insult, someone else may respond to that same provocation violently. Some juveniles have difficulty managing problems in a constructive manner and are especially prone to impulsive and counterproductive behavior, since their brains are still in the process of developing. Juveniles in custody need to be monitored for coping deficits and self-destructive behavior. Toch (1992a) found that incarcerated juveniles were more likely than older inmates to experience a "self-destructive breakdown" associated with some form of self-harm.[4]

As part of the "get tough" movement in the United States in the 1990s, several states made it easier to waive juveniles to adult court, and this resulted in some juveniles being incarcerated in adult facilities.[5] Lambie and Randell (2013) reported that juveniles who are incarcerated in adult prisons have higher suicide rates than juveniles placed in settings specifically designed to hold juveniles.

There are three potential problems with placing juveniles in adult facilities. First, those juveniles might differ from others their age and be more in need of programs and services. Murrie, Henderson, Vincent, Rockett, and Mundt (2009) compared juveniles incarcerated with adults in Texas to a national sample of juveniles housed with other juveniles. The former scored higher on the *Massachusetts Youth Screening Instrument—2* for the angry-irritable, depressed-anxious, thought disturbance, and suicide ideation domains. Given that this was not a longitudinal study, it is not possible to determine whether the juveniles incarcerated with adults differed from other juveniles prior to their latest incarceration or if the results of this test are a product of juveniles' response to the stress of being incarcerated with adults. Regardless of whether the juveniles imported those problems into the prison or they developed in response to the deprivations of adult incarceration, these individuals are at a higher risk for self-harm and suicide. The second potential problem is that adult facilities are rarely equipped with the personnel or programs to work with juveniles who may be struggling with developmental issues. Third, juveniles in adult institutions might experience more isolation than if they were housed with other juveniles. Juveniles in adult facilities may be separated from adults in "sight and sound" partly for their safety, meaning that the juveniles are not supposed to be able to hear or see the adult offenders (American Psychiatric Association, 2016). The result of this policy could prompt administrators to house juveniles in more remote parts of the facilities, thereby increasing their sense of isolation and abandonment as well as increasing opportunities for suicide attempts. The American Psychiatric Association (APA) warns that limiting juveniles' contact to just other incarcerated juveniles who are likely impulsive, immature, and even violent can foster adoption of even more maladaptive behaviors and prompt emotional crises.

Just as juveniles pose a risk for suicide in custody, so do elderly inmates. Opitz-Welke and colleagues (2013) found that older inmates, specifically males aged 50 through 55, had the highest rates of suicide in German prisons. Mumola (2005) studied correctional suicides in the United States and found the highest suicide rates among jail inmates under 18 (rate of 101 per 100,000) and inmates 55 and older (58 per 100,000). In comparison, inmates aged 18 to 24 had the lowest suicide rates (38 per 100,000), followed by inmates 25 to 34 (47 per 100,000). Inmates who were 35 to 44 had rates that were closer to their elderly counterparts (55 per 100,000). The American Psychiatric Association (2016) noted that elderly inmates (50+) are vulnerable, since their confinement is likely to be especially difficult. Older inmates may feel not only estranged from their own families but from the younger inmate culture. They may also have trouble defending themselves from predatory inmates, and they have to face the possibility that they will never be free again. For these reasons, the elderly may feel more motivated to take control and end their lives on their own terms.

Offense Type

Some researchers have found that violent offenders, particularly those accused of rape or homicide, are more likely to commit suicide in custody (Duthe, Hazard, Kensey, & Ke Shon, 2013; Kovasznay et al., 2004; Opitz-Welke et al., 2013; Rabe, 2012). Forty-three percent of correctional suicides in the national study conducted by Hayes (2009) were charged with a violent-person offense, and inmates who committed suicide in Austria were more likely than those who did not to be in prison for a violent offense (Frottier, Konig, Matschnig, Seyringer, & Fruhwald, 2007). Byrne, Lurigio, and Pimentel (2009) found a high risk of suicide among pretrial defendants held for suspicion of sex offending in federal facilities. One third of prisoner suicides in England and Wales from 1999 through 2007 involved someone with a charge for a violent crime. In Australia, 65% of self-inflicted deaths in prison were committed by someone with a history of violence (Willis et al., 2016).

Not every study found a relationship between violent offense charge/conviction and suicide. Shaw, Appleby, and Baker (2003) studied suicides or suspected suicides in England and Wales and found that only 26% of suicides had been charged with or convicted of a violent offense. It is important to consider that charges and convictions for violent offenses are limited in what they reveal about an individual's levels of violence and aggression. People may be violent, but it is possible that their arrest history could consist of only nonviolent offenses. More useful information would be measures of current violence, such as behavior while in custody, and measures of aggression and impulsivity derived from classification tests. Marzano et al. (2016) conducted a systematic review of articles analyzing near lethal suicide attempts in custody and found that, while offense type was not associated with serious attempts on one's life, high levels of self-reported aggression, impulsivity, and hostility were.

Researchers have identified sentence length as a predictor of suicide risk. The World Health Organization (2007) noted that the risk for long-term inmates seems to increase with length of stay, and life sentences have the highest risk. Duthe et al.'s (2013) research of inmate suicides in France found support for this, with sentence length being associated with death by suicide.

Inmates serving 15 years to life were more likely to commit suicide than other inmates. Additional researchers have found evidence that people with life sentences are at greater risk for suicide (Barker, Kolves, & De Leo, 2014; Liebling & Ludlow, 2016; Newcomen, 2014a; Pompili et al., 2009). It is not clear whether it is the sentence length itself, the characteristics of people who have such long sentences, or both that prompt the suicides.

History of Self-Harm

One of the strongest predictors of suicide is history of previous suicide attempts and NSSI, regardless of whether they occurred in custody or in the community (Austin et al., 2014; Frottier et al., 2007; Hawton et al., 2014; Humber et al., 2013; Klonsky, 2007; Klonsky, May, & Glenn, 2013; Marzano et al., 2016; Penn et al., 2003; Victor & Klonsky, 2014). Shaw et al. (2003) reported a history of prior self-harm among 53% of prison suicides in England and Wales, and Austin and colleagues (2014) found a history of previous self-harm in 40% of Australian custodial suicide cases. Favril et al. (2018) reported that 50% of suicides in prison in Belgium had a history of prior suicide attempts. Seventy percent of juveniles who died by suicide while in custody in the United States had a history of suicidal behavior (Hayes, 2009). Sixty-two percent of suicides in California prisons from 1999 through 2004 had documented histories of suicidal behavior and/or statements (Patterson & Hughes, 2008).

Prior acts of self-harm mark an important point in demonstrating the ability to overcome one of the most basic human instincts—self-preservation (Joiner, 2005). Liebling (1994) stated that, "Once an injury is inflicted, an important threshold has been crossed. . . . People who injure themselves are far more likely to go on to commit suicide at some later stage, without help, or without some change to their life situation" (p. 6). Joiner (2005) calls the ability to harm oneself the acquired capability for suicide (ACS) and argues that it can take time for people to develop the ability to lethally injure themselves. Since fear and pain are part of humans' evolutionarily developed survival system, it is a hurdle that people must overcome to commit suicide (Joiner, 2005; Smith, Selwyn, D'Amato, Ganato, Kuhlman, & Mandracchia, 2016). Smith and colleagues surveyed incarcerated men to assess their ACS levels, defined as fearlessness about death and the ability to tolerate physical pain. They found that high pain tolerance and general fearlessness among inmates were associated with suicidal thoughts and behaviors. In another study, Smith, Worlford-Clevenger, Mandracchia, and Jahn (2013) did not find acquired capability to differentiate suicide attempters from nonattempters in a sample of male inmates. There are two possible explanations for this. One is that the capability to overcome fear of pain and death is a separate issue from actually wanting to die. The other is that the survey that was used was originally designed for the general community and not the prison environment. The hypermasculine ideals of the prison setting might have impacted inmates' answers to questions regarding fear of violence and death.

Psychiatric History

Inmates who commit suicide often have documented histories of mental illness and/or records of mental health treatment. Shaw and colleagues (2003) found that 72% of prison suicides in England and Wales had histories of at least one psychiatric diagnosis at reception, and 29% had previously received inpatient psychiatric care. In a later study of prisoners in England and Wales, Humber et al. (2013) found that previous psychiatric treatment was a significant predictor of suicides even after controlling for other risk factors. Eighty-seven percent of suicides in Belgium prisons had histories of at least one mental disorder (Favril et al., 2018). Hayes (2010) found that 38% of adult inmates in the United States who committed suicide had a history of mental illness, and 20% had a history of taking psychotropic medication. Seventy-three percent of suicides in the California prison system had a history of prior mental health treatment (Patterson & Hughes, 2008).

Psychiatric history is not distributed evenly across the entire correctional population. Mundt, Kastner, Mir, and Priebe (2015) examined rates of histories of psychiatric interventions among prisoners in European countries and found that males tended to be less likely to have either inpatient or outpatient treatment records than females. If incarcerated females do have higher rates of serious mental illness, it has obvious implications for understanding suicide and self-harm among incarcerated women. Liebling (1999), however, questioned the validity of such reported differences, arguing that the claims of higher rates of psychiatric disorder for women is at least somewhat a product of labeling, since females have historically received greater psychiatric attention than males.

There is the possibility that mental illness in general is overreported in suicides after the fact. Hindsight may prompt us to overestimate the proportion of suicides that were cases of mental illness, since mental illness seems like a logical explanation for why one has taken his or her own life. In retrospective studies, in which the names of suicides were linked to records of psychiatric facilities, an average of 29% of all suicides were found to have a psychiatric record. In contrast, psychological autopsy studies, in which psychiatrists diagnose suicides after their death, find that an average of 90% of the suicides had a psychiatric disorder, most commonly an affective (depressive) disorder

(61%), followed by substance abuse (41%), anxiety disorders (10%), and schizophrenia (16%). In addition, 42% had a personality disorder. Many of the suicides received more than one diagnosis (Tanney, 2000). Hindsight bias tends to be somewhat less of a problem in studies of inmates, given the high prevalence of psychiatric problems among inmates that have already been documented in previous incarcerations, psychiatric hospital stays, court hearings, or mental health screenings in custody.

PAST TRAUMA

Past, unresolved trauma can make coping with present problems especially difficult. It is estimated that approximately 10% of the population of the United States has posttraumatic stress disorder (PTSD). PTSD is characterized by four sets of symptoms: (1) Repetition, when people experience the traumatic event over and over again in flashbacks, dreams, or in some other form; (2) Avoidance, which involves trying to avoid people, places, activities, or feelings that remind them of the traumatic event; (3) Numbing, or diminished interest or participation in life events; and (4) Increased arousal, meaning people have a difficult time sleeping, have outbursts of anger, have difficulty concentrating, and exhibit hypervigilance (Kokorowski & Freng, 2001).

In a study of over 5,000 African Americans, Anderson, Geier, and Cahill (2015) found that people with a history of incarceration reported more incidents of potentially traumatic events than those with no history of incarceration. Specifically, those with a history of incarceration were more likely to have experienced assault, being robbed, being in an accident, serving in combat, witnessing someone else being seriously injured, or having done something to injure or kill another person. Since this was a cross-sectional study, the authors were unable to determine whether the traumatic events occurred prior to, during, or after incarceration. Some researchers have studied trauma among current inmates and have found that many come into custody already having been exposed to traumatizing events. Seventy percent of youth in residential placement in 2003 reported experiencing "something very bad or terrifying," and 67% personally saw someone being injured or killed (Sickmund & Puzzanchera, 2014).

Experience with trauma is related to suicidal behavior. Hochstetler, Murphy, and Simons (2004) found that previous trauma predicted the presence of depressive symptoms among inmates. Researchers have found histories of trauma among inmates who have attempted or committed suicide. Inmates in Spain who made near-lethal suicide attempts in custody had more extensive histories of childhood emotional abuse and parental substance abuse than other inmates (Sanchez et al., 2018). It can be argued that a great majority of inmates, suicidal or not, have dysfunctional family backgrounds. However, Blaauw, Arensman, Kraaij, Winkel, and Bout (2002) compared a group of inmates at high-risk for suicide with those who were at low risk and reported that the high-risk group experienced substantially more traumatic life events than their low-risk counterparts. Furthermore, suicide risk was related to life events that took place at varying points in the inmates' lives, ranging from traumatic events occurring during childhood to events occurring during the current detention period. Smith, Selwyn, Wolford-Clevenger, and Mandracchia (2014) found a relationship between secondary psychopathic traits, which are thought to be primarily a product of severe neglect, abuse, and trauma, and multiple suicide attempts. Individuals with secondary psychopathic traits tend to have higher levels of anxiety, poor interpersonal functioning, and less emotional stability than those with primary psychopathic traits (Skeem, Johansson, Andersheed, Kerr, & Louden, 2007).

The challenges of past traumas are not exclusive to adult inmates. Even juvenile detainees are often faced with having experienced trauma during their short lives. Forty-four percent of juvenile suicides in custody in the United States had a history of emotional abuse, 34% had a history of physical abuse, and 28% a history of sexual abuse (Hayes, 2009). Moore and colleagues (2015) used the 2009 Young People in Custody Heath Survey (United States) to analyze data from juveniles housed in nine different facilities. They found that female juveniles had more extensive histories of childhood abuse, trauma, and bullying when compared to males.

While there seems to be a relationship between past trauma and suicides, corrections personnel may not be successful at using this information to gauge suicide risk for two reasons. First, history of abuse and trauma is fairly common among the correctional population, so using this as a primary indicator of suicide potential would likely be problematic. Second, information about inmates' pasts are unlikely to be readily available unless the inmates have incarceration histories that involved detailed classification efforts. Even if that is the case, trauma history is unlikely to be among the first things that the corrections staff will look up as recidivists are being processed back into custody.

DYNAMIC FACTORS

Dynamic factors are characteristics such as current mental health symptoms, current drug and alcohol problems, and current coping skills, which are among some of the most important issues that need to be monitored as potential warning signs of suicide. All dynamic factors can change over the course of time spent in custody.

CURRENT MENTAL HEALTH SYMPTOMS

It is difficult to determine the precise number of incarcerated people who are mentally ill, and researchers have presented some very different estimates. Prins (2014) explained that there are two factors that may affect the types of statistics that researchers collect. The first factor is measurement issues, such as how the data collectors define mental illness. The second is selection issues, as the study results will depend on the populations living in the selected jurisdictions, criminal codes, availability of mental health and substance abuse services outside of prison, etc. The BJS reported that over half of the prison and jail population experienced some sort of mental health problem (James & Glaze, 2006). Some sort of "mental health problem," however, is a rather broad category and included anyone with symptoms of a mental health problem within the 12 months preceding the interview. Steadman, Osher, Robbins, Case, and Samuels (2009) estimated the prevalence of serious mental illness among jail inmates to be 14.5% of men and 31.5% of women. Steadman and colleagues did not include counts of inmates with a primary diagnosis of anxiety disorders, PTSD, and some Axis II disorders, including borderline personality disorder (BPD), in their estimates. Fazel and Seewald (2012) reviewed studies estimating the prevalence of major depression and psychotic disorders among inmates housed in the general populations of prisons in 24 countries from 1966 through 2010. For the studies that measured major depression, mean prevalence rates were 10% for males and 14% for females. Prevalence of psychosis, schizophrenia, manic episodes, and schizophreniform disorders was 3.9% in females and 3.6% in males.

Mental illness is an important risk factor for suicide (Baillargeon et al., 2009a; Suto & Arnaut, 2010; World Health Organization, 2007), especially if the individuals are currently experiencing symptoms. Studies of inmates who died by suicide provide strong evidence of this. Kovasznay and colleagues (2004) accessed files of inmates who committed suicide in New York and found that two-thirds had seen a mental health professional in custody within two weeks of the suicide. In England and Wales, Humber and colleagues (2011) found that 58% of suicides in custody from 1999 through 2007 had an open mental health care plan at the time of death. Baillargeon and associates (2009a) studied suicides among inmates in the Texas prison system and found a rate of 61 per 100,000 for severe depression, 49 for bipolar disorder, 91 for schizophrenia, and 144 for nonschizophrenic psychotic disorders. Additionally, 23% of inmates who committed suicide had a mood disorder and 22% a psychotic disorder. These findings were surprising given that individuals with major depressive disorder and bipolar disorder generally have higher rates of suicide in the community compared to those with other disorders. One possible explanation for this is that the Texas Department of Criminal Justice (TDCJ) might have been more watchful over inmates with disorders known to be better predictors of suicide, and that vigilance might have prevented some deaths.

Diagnoses of depression are usually associated with increased risk of suicide (American Psychiatric Association, 2016; Cook & Davis, 2012; Encrenaz et al., 2014; Hayes, 2009; Joiner, 2005; Marzano, Fazel, Rivlin, & Hawton, 2010; Rivlin, Ferris, Marzano, Fazel, & Hawton, 2013; Sanchez et al., 2018). People who are experiencing severe depression may find that their current living situation has become too difficult to withstand, and they see suicide as a way to escape the pain. Rivlin and colleagues (2013) found that 87% of the near-fatal suicide cases in the prisons in their sample had a diagnosis of depression at the time of their first in-custody suicide attempt. Even people who appear to be emerging from a depression might not be clear of danger. The American Psychiatric Association (2016) and Cook and Davis (2012) warned that people who are in the process of recovering from depression should continue to be monitored for suicidal risk. It is not uncommon for someone whose mood seems to have improved to commit suicide. Joiner (2005) suggested that this heightened risk might be due to people gaining the energy and cognitive clarity to act on suicidal ideas as the depression starts to clear but does not completely dissipate.

There is one psychiatric diagnosis that may be undercounted among custodial suicides. Newcomen (2016) suspects that personality disorders might go undetected among some deceased inmates, as he found that only 10% of self-inflicted deaths in custody had such a diagnosis. These disorders may be misinterpreted by corrections staff members as behavioral problems instead of a mental health condition. A personality disorder is not a mental illness. Mental illness is characterized by changes to a person's personality that, if treated, can be addressed with the person's "normal" personality reemerging. A personality disorder, however, relates to the psychological construct of a person whose personality characteristics, such as mood swings or avoidance of conflict, are on the extreme end. These disorders are associated with increased risk of suicide and self-harm (Lester, 2000; Packman, Marlitt, Bhangar, & Pennuto, 2004). Treatment can merely seek to manage the abnormal aspects of the personality to help people function well enough to minimize the negative impact of the disorder. Some personality disorders, such as BPD, can be difficult to treat and are characterized by impulsivity and suicidal behaviors. Hefland (2011) estimated that about 17% of female jail inmates and 13% of males have BPD, compared to only 0.5% of the general population.

Just as females have more extensive histories of mental health diagnoses and treatment, females tend to be more likely than males to be identified as experiencing a current problem. Mothers in state and federal prisons in the United States were approximately 1.5 times more likely than fathers to have current medical or mental health problems (Glaze & Maruschak, 2008). Researchers who studied files of over 200,000 inmates in Texas found higher rates of major depressive disorder and bipolar disorder among females but higher rates of schizophrenia in males (Baillargeon et al., 2009a). A U.S. Department of Justice study found that female offenders tend to have higher rates of depression and anxiety disorder, while men have more antisocial disorders (Thompson, 2008).

Organic brain dysfunction can also be a predictor of suicide. Vadini and associates (2018) found neurocognitive impairments to be the strongest predictor of lifetime suicide attempts and current high risk for suicide among prison inmates. Problems with cognitive functions remained the strongest predictors of suicide risk and attempt history even after controlling for psychiatric disorders, history of psychopharmalogical treatment, presence of a substance use disorder, impulsivity, and comorbidity.

Substance Abuse/Addiction

Substance abuse is a common problem among incarcerated individuals. In 2007, 26% of victims participating in the National Crime Victimization Survey reported that the offender was using drugs or alcohol at the time of the crime (U.S. Bureau of Justice Statistics, 2018b). When asked, 32% of arrestees in Australia believed their drug use contributed to their continued criminal behavior, while 41% attributed alcohol to impacting their offending (Payne & Gaffney, 2012).

It is important to remember that inmates in police lockups and in some jails are entering custody directly from the streets, so they may be under the influence. In a study of 333 deaths in police custody in England and Wales, the most common reason for staff's inability to screen detainees was the arrestees' severe intoxication. Drug/alcohol intoxication is the third leading cause of death in U.S. jails, comprising 7.2% of all jail deaths in 2013 (Noonan et al., 2015). In a national study of jail suicide, Hayes (2010) found that 20% of jail inmates and police detention facility detainees who committed suicide were intoxicated when they died.

Incarceration is a traumatic event, even for people who are sober. The combination of this distressing change of circumstances, along with withdrawal from the altered state of mind that accompanies the use of drugs or alcohol, might increase the risk of suicidal behavior. Individuals suffering from addiction have the additional stress of not knowing when or where they will get their next fix now that they are incarcerated. Not only are addicted inmates likely to be anxious about finding more drugs, they also have the problem of losing the numbing influence of drugs and alcohol. Gibbs (1992) argued that offenders on the street are so preoccupied with obtaining drugs and the high from the drugs themselves that it precludes them from seriously contemplating the implications of their crimes and other harmful behavior. With the absence of drugs during the initial incarceration period comes the opportunity for these inmates to embark on "the process of taking a personal inventory in which one's deficiencies as suggested by the situation [incarceration] are compared with one's contributions to the world, and a determination of self-worth is made" (Gibbs, 1992, p. 187). After studying near-fatal suicide attempts, Rivlin et al. (2013) included attempts associated with drug or alcohol withdrawal as a category in their typology of suicidal prisoners. The World Health Organization (2007) lists substance abuse problems as a known risk factor for suicide while in custody. Stoliker (2018) found that inmates who were frequent drug users were 23% more likely to attempt suicide at some point in their lives. Inmates who used alcohol daily prior to incarceration were 38% more likely to have a lifetime history of suicide attempts.

Obtaining drugs upon initial entry to a facility is likely to be challenging, but once inmates become acclimated and are exposed to other inmates, it is possible to acquire them. Drugs are available, albeit at much higher prices than on the street. Leese, Thomas, and Snow (2006) found that facilities in England and Wales that had higher levels of positive drug tests in the early 2000s also had higher rates of suicide (Leese, Thomas, & Snow, 2006). These data, however, are not conclusive proof that drug use was associated with suicide. Leese and colleagues only studied entire institutions instead of individual inmates. The correlation here between drugs and suicides might be an indicator that both are related to something else, such as poor management and institutional instability.

Coping with Incarceration

Due to the nature of incarceration, facilities are largely inhabited by people who have approached or reacted to situations in an inappropriate manner. They made money in ways that were against the law. They reacted to provocations or threats violently, or they might have even been completely responsible for the initiation of violence. It should be of little surprise that some inmates react to stressful or upsetting situations in maladaptive ways. Inmates are very likely to import their inappropriate problem-solving skills into prisons and jails.

Dear, Thomson, Hall, and Howells (1998) interviewed inmates who had self-injured in the prior three-day period. Compared to inmates who had not harmed themselves, the self-injurers reported higher levels of distress and rated their coping responses as less effective in reducing their distress. They were less likely to use coping styles that would help them redefine the negative situation and/or accept it. Histories of handling issues impulsively and with anger are predictive of suicide attempts, as these are examples of poor coping strategies (Rudd et al., 2006; Victoria Department of Justice Correctional Services Task Force, 1998).

The lack of one's personal safety is one of the toughest challenges facing inmates (Sykes, 1958), especially males and juveniles. Not only are inmates dealing with the stress associated with legal troubles and separation from family, but they have to cope with an environment that, depending on the security level, can be characterized by exploitation and threats of violence. Dutch prisoners who were found to be at a high risk for suicide reported experiences of being bullied while in custody more often than the inmates at low risk for suicide. The results of their multivariate analysis showed that bullying had the strongest relationship with suicide, followed by time in jail. Most of the suicidal inmates reported being bullied by fellow inmates, while some reported being victimized by the corrections officers (Blaauw, Winkel, & Kerkhof, 2001). More recent research has supported the Dutch findings. Twenty-one percent of suicides in England and Wales were victims of bullying while incarcerated (Shaw et al., 2003). In a study of self-harming behaviors among females, one of the most common themes during their interviews was harming due to the stress and danger of being incarcerated (Doty, Smith, & Rojek, 2012). Encrenaz et al. (2014) ran a multivariate statistical model to compare inmates in France who attempted suicide during imprisonment to those who did not. Being a victim of either physical or sexual violence during that incarceration period increased the odds of a suicide attempt, even after controlling for lifetime history of suicide attempts.

For studies that involve suicide ideation, attempts, and other self-harm, it is not always possible to tell what came first, the bullying/violence or the suicidal behavior. For example, Stoliker (2018) studied lifetime suicide attempts and incarceration and found that people who attempted suicide at some point in their lives were also 38% more likely to have been victimized in prison than nonattempters. Inmates who make suicidal gestures in correctional facilities are considered vulnerable and easy targets by other inmates. It is possible that the suicidal behavior prompted the bullying, and further re-search is necessary to understand the exact nature of the relationship between suicide and bullying.

A study by Reeves and Tamburello (2014) provided additional support for the relationship between difficulty coping with incarceration and suicide. They found that inmates who tended to find themselves in segregation due to disciplinary infractions were more likely to have poor coping skills. Placing people with poor coping skills in an environment where they have limited ac-cess to activities but extra opportunity to commit self-harm without detection can increase the incidence of self-harm. Shaw et al. (2003) and Sanchez et al. (2018) also found a relationship between disciplinary action and suicidal be-havior, and this suggests that poor coping skills that prompt sanctions might also signal that these individuals lack the ability to address problems, includ-ing emotional crises and depression, in a prosocial manner. The work of Se-rin et al. (2002) lends additional support to the importance of taking note of inmates' adjustment to incarceration and their coping abilities. In a study of Canadian inmates, the researchers found that, when compared to inmates who refrained from attempting suicide, the suicide attempters were more likely to be characterized by disciplinary infractions, escape attempts, and overall poor institutional adjustment, all of which are indicators of maladaptive coping skills. As with the relationship between in-facility victimization and suicidal behavior that falls short of death, time-order is an issue. It is unclear what comes first, the suicidal behavior or the disciplinary actions. It is also possible that the suicidal behavior is being treated by some correctional administra-tions as infractions (Applebaum et al., 2011; Smith & Kaminski, 2010).

The research demonstrates that life challenges, whether they are related to in-facility conflict, legal issues, or problems external to the corrections environment, such as family relationships, present hurdles that some inmates interpret to be insurmountable. Kovasznay and colleagues (2004) reported that 65% of suicides in the New York Corrections System followed inmates' receipt of "adverse information," such as legal, disciplinary, or family news.

When attempting to understand how women cope with incarceration, per-haps one of the most important considerations is separation from family. As of 2004, 62% of female state prisoners and 56% of females incarcerated in federal prisons in the United States were mothers of minor children (Glaze & Maruschak, 2008). The forced separation brought about by incarceration tends to weigh more heavily on women, who are far more likely than men to have been caring for their children prior to incarceration. Forty-two percent of incarcerated males in the United States were living with their minor chil-dren just prior to their incarceration, compared to 64% of women (Glaze & Maruschak, 2008). Negative news from the "outside" has been found to be precursors to self-harm for incarcerated females (Doty et al., 2012). Liebling (1994) found that, while male inmates reported that boredom, bullying, or debts were the most difficult aspects of incarceration, female inmates cited separation from family as the most difficult. These findings have important treatment implications for women. If females have more trouble coping with the separation from their families rather than with the issues relating to life inside prison or jail, it is important to take measures that facilitate better access to the outside world (including contact with their families) in addition to helping them cope with the stress of life in prison.

The way people cope with adversity has an impact on their feelings and outlook for the future. The American Psychiatric Association (2016) identified the following high-risk periods that may present inmates with coping challenges: admission to a facility, new legal problems, receipt of bad news, experiencing humiliation or rejection, placement into specialized housing (particularly administrative segregation), worsening of mental health symptoms, and early stages of recovery from depression. As noted earlier, drug and alcohol withdrawal can also make coping with incarceration especially difficult (Brown, 2016; Newcomen, 2014a; Rivlin et al., 2013).

Thwarted Belongingness and Burdensomeness

Two perceptions that inmates may struggle to cope with during incarceration are burdensomeness and thwarted belongingness. Even among people who are not incarcerated, such feelings are associated with suicidal thoughts (Joiner, 2005; Mandracchia & Smith, 2015; Van Orden et al., 2010). Incarceration forcibly removes people from their homes, families, and friends. They miss milestones, such as birthdays, weddings, and funerals as life outside prison seemingly goes on without them. Thwarted belongingness, defined as feeling alienated from valued social circles (Ribeiro & Joiner, 2009), can be difficult for incarcerated individuals.

Inmates may also come to see themselves as a burden to others. Men and women who used to provide money or housing to relatives, whether through legal or illegal means, may experience guilt from the inability to contribute. Inmates may also suffer as they watch their families struggle to find the time and money to visit and the money to make phone calls to the prison. Correctional facilities, particularly in the United States, tend to be very austere institutions, and inmates are provided minimal food and supplies for survival. Inmates frequently want goods from the commissary, and those can be purchased with money in inmates' accounts. While inmates may earn some commissary money through in-facility jobs or through hustling, they may also depend on friends and relatives for money (Mandracchia & Smith, 2015). Inmates may view their continued existence as a burden to family who struggle with the financial and social ramifications of having an incarcerated relative.

According to the Interpersonal Theory of Suicide, suicidal ideation occurs when people develop a sense of both thwarted belongingness and perceived burdensomeness. Van Orden and colleagues (2010) noted that loneliness, the absence of reciprocally caring relationships, and pleasant and positive interactions with the same individuals are a few characteristics of belongingness. Joiner (2005) suggested that the need for humans to belong can be so powerful that it can prevent suicide even when people believe that they have become a burden to others. People can come to believe that they have become a burden to others in a number of ways, including losing one's job or home or becoming seriously ill. Another way is to become incarcerated (Mandracchia & Smith, 2015). Mandracchia and Smith (2015) found a that inmates with suicidal ideation were more likely to report experiencing both thwarted belongingness and perceived themselves as being a burden. Inmates must find ways to cope with the separation from loved ones and their guilt over becoming dependent on relatives, but some might find this too difficult to do.

USE OF PROFILES AND TYPOLOGIES

There have been efforts to attempt to identify the "typical" suicidal inmate. One of the earliest studies on suicidal inmates presented readers with information about what their research found to be the "typical" suicide. According to the National Center on Institutions and Alternatives (NCIA), the typical suicide was a twenty-two-year-old, white, single, male, who was arrested for public intoxication (Hayes, 1989). This individual was intoxicated or high at the time of arrest, and there was no significant history of prior arrests. The inmate was placed in isolation for his own protection or surveillance and was dead within three hours of incarceration. The method used for suicide was hanging (Hayes, 1983, 1989). Profiles based on inmate demographics and offense types have been criticized for leading to false-positives and false-negatives. In other words, the profiles identify people who are not suicidal (false-positives) and miss those who are (false-negatives) (Pompili et al., 2009). False negatives are the bigger concern, as the inmates who are truly at risk do not get the necessary assistance and may be put in positions where they have the opportunity to harm themselves.

Newcomen (2014a) researched self-inflicted deaths in custody and noted that demographic profiles of those who commit acts of nonfatal self-harm differ from those who commit suicide in custody. Adult males tend to be most likely to commit suicide, but younger inmates and females tend to be most at risk for nonfatal self-harm. Use of a suicide profile based on demographics would likely miss those at risk for nonfatal self-harm. That is problematic, since such behavior is a strong risk factor for later suicide, and an undetected nonfatal act can accidentally become fatal if the injury is serious enough and too much time elapses.

What tends to be more helpful than demographics are inmates' histories of self-harm and mental illness and the *current* state of the individuals. Some researchers have created typologies of inmate suicides that emphasize the importance of the inmates' current state of mind. Liebling (1999), using suicide data from prisons in England and Wales from 1987 through 1993, identified three groups of inmates with specific treatment needs. The first group consists of inmates who are serving life or long sentences, including pretrial inmates who are facing long sentences. These inmates are older than the average inmate population and tend to be serving time for violent offenses. They are likely to take their lives much later into their incarceration stay than others. The second set of inmates are those who are psychiatrically ill. They tend to commit suicide earlier in their stay and are overrepresented in jails. The final group are the "poor copers" who tend to have similar demographic characteristics as the general inmate population, but they are having difficulty adapting to their current life situation. This is the largest of the three groups. Note that it would be impossible to detect anyone from the second and third groups using only demographic and offense profiles.

Rivlin and colleagues (2013) adopted some of Liebling's (1999) groups but decided that the typology of suicidal prisoners should include five categories rather than three. Rivlin et al. kept the poor coper category that Liebling used. Poor copers, according to Rivlin and associates, are individuals who have been unable to cope with day-to-day prison life, particularly interactions with staff members and fellow inmates. These inmates tend to attempt suicide due to pressure from having to manage prison life while simultaneously dealing with another stressor, such as a breakup, death in the family, or some other trauma. Rivlin and colleagues' second group is similar to Liebling's psychiatrically ill group, only Rivlin et al. specify that this group is motivated by psychotic symptoms rather than a broader mental health diagnosis. These inmates are usually either in the process of being transferred to a psychiatric hospital or are awaiting that transfer. The third group attempts suicide for instrumental reasons, such as trying to influence a housing assignment. These inmates have difficulty managing in prison and are habitually bullied. Such inmates tend to be in regular physical altercations with both inmates and staff and tend to be socially isolated. The fourth group consists of "unexpected" attempters. They tend to be well-adjusted and lack a history of self-harm or any psychiatric issues besides depression. Inmates in this category may become temporarily overwhelmed by a problem and impulsively make a suicide attempt. The attempt itself will be viewed by staff and even the inmates themselves as out of character, so these individuals are very unlikely to have been considered by staff to be at risk. The final group consists of those who attempt suicide around the time of a drug or alcohol withdrawal. Rivlin and colleagues noted that, in their research, withdrawal from heroin appeared to be the type of withdrawal most likely to precede a suicide attempt. Brown (2016), who interviewed counselors inside Texas jails, supported this finding. One Texas jail counselor commented "but what also scares me the most are heroin folks, because they've been comfortably numb for a while and now they're in a setting where they can't self-medicate and now they've got this onslaught of reality and lots of problems and not having the coping skills" (Brown, 2016, p. 80).

Facilities whose staff members utilize profiles of the "typical" suicide based only on the static factors of demographics or offense type would likely miss the distinction between these aforementioned groups, as many inmates attempted suicide due to more immediate problems and, with the exception of the "unexpected attempters," were generally having difficulty coping with some aspect of their lives. This has important implications for screening and monitoring, as will be discussed in detail in Chapter 5.

CONCLUSION

The research presented in this chapter demonstrates that people who are incarcerated exhibit many static and dynamic factors that put them at risk for suicide and self-harm. To make matters worse, the stressful environment associated with corrections also has the potential to help precipitate a suicidal crisis. It appears that both the importation and deprivation models are relevant when understanding suicide in the correctional environment. This has important policy implications for staff who work with people in custody, as it demonstrates the need for screening upon entry into custody to collect information on both static and dynamic factors. Additional, repeated screening and monitoring is then necessary to continue to gauge any changes to dynamic factors that are associated with suicide risk.

As will be discussed in greater detail in Chapter 5, *current* mental health symptoms, particularly suicidal ideation, are among the most important predictors of suicides and attempts. Since moods change and crises can arise after initial screening, it is important to monitor inmates for significant mood changes, particularly around times when they might be in receipt of bad news or are under more stress than usual. There are screening instruments that have shown promise in terms of their reliability (consistency) and validity (accuracy), and I recommend exploring the use of those types of tools. Some of these instruments have been developed specifically for ease of use in corrections facilities.

NOTES

1. The Australian data included self-inflicted deaths, including accidental overdoses.

2. The Ministry of Justice used rates per 1,000 inmates, but I converted them to rates per 100,000 inmates to be more consistent with rates displayed throughout this book.

3. This dramatic difference may be at least partially attributable to the way the suicide rate was calculated for juveniles in detention. See Chapter 3 for a discussion of calculating suicide rates.

4. Toch did not distinguish between suicide attempts and other incidents of non-fatal self-harm in his research.

5. Judicial waivers peaked in 1994 in the United States. This practice has become less popular in recent years. The number of cases waived to adult court in 2013 was 31% less than 1985 (Hockenberry & Puzzanchera, 2015).

Chapter Three

When, Where, and How Suicides in Prisons and Jails Occur

Suicides are not evenly distributed across correctional facilities or even housing areas within each institution. This chapter addresses the frequency of suicide in the different types of correctional facilities and detention centers and discusses high-risk areas and times within each type of facility. Throughout this chapter, I will discuss how the deprivations of the correctional environment may provide not only motive, but opportunity, for inmates to commit suicide. Knowing when and how inmates are given opportunities to commit suicide can help correctional staff work on plans to protect inmates. I also consider the most frequently used method for suicide in custody and the role that restricting access to methods to commit plays in prevention programs.

TYPES OF FACILITIES

Suicide Rates in Prison

From 2001 through 2014, suicide was the cause of death for 6% of state and 4% of federal prisoners in the United States. Suicide was the second leading cause of death behind illness, which accounted for 89% of state and 88% of federal prisoner deaths (Noonan, 2016a). By comparison, suicide was the 10th leading cause of death outside of prisons and jails in the United States from 2001 through 2016 (Stone et al., 2018). According to the National Center for Health Statistics (Curtin, Warner, & Hedegaard, 2016; Minino, Heron, Murphy, & Kochanek, 2007), the overall suicide rate in the general population of the United States has stayed between 10.4 and 13.4 per 100,000 residents per year from 1960 through 2014. The mean suicide rate from 1978 through 2014 was 11.94 per 100,000 residents in the community. During those same years, the suicide rate in state prisons fluctuated between a low of 12.22 and a high of 26.67, with a mean of 17.43 (Noonan, 2016a; U.S. Bureau of Justice Statistics, 1981–2001). Figure 3.1 illustrates the differences between the state prison and community populations. The prison systems experienced a substantial reduction of suicides between the late 1970s and early 1990s. This is likely due to the increased attention given to custodial suicides during this time, as researchers disseminated information about risk factors, and courts became more willing to define some staff action or inaction as civil rights violations. The state prison suicide rate dropped under 20 per 100,000 people in 1986 and remained below that level for over two decades. Unfortunately, there has been an upward trend recently. The state prison suicide rate reached 20 per 100,000 people for the first time in 25 years in 2014. There is a similar, recent trend with rising suicide rates in British correctional facilities. Suicide rates started to rise in the United Kingdom in 2016 (Liebling & Ludlow, 2016), but they did drop between 2017 and 2018 (Ministry of Justice, 2018). At the time of this writing, data for the United States are only available through 2014.

The suicide statistics for the community provided in Figure 3.1 include both men and women. While women make up about half of the people living outside of custody, they consist of only about 10% of the correctional population. Since women tend to have low suicide rates, it is difficult to compare

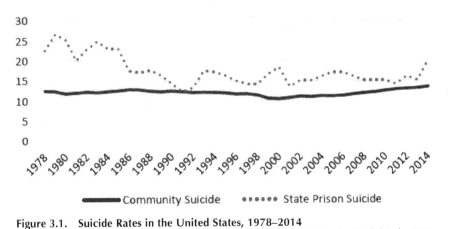

Figure 3.1.   Suicide Rates in the United States, 1978–2014
Sources: Kochanek, K. D., Murphy, S. L., Xu, J., & Tejada-Vera, B. (2016). Deaths: Final data for 2014. *National Vital Statistics Report, 65*(4). Hyattsville, MD: United States Department of Health and Human Services, Centers for Disease Control. Noonan, M. E. (2016a). *Mortality in state prisons, 2001–2014— Statistical tables.* Washington, DC: United States Department of Justice, Office of Justice Programs, Bureau of Justice Statistics. United States Bureau of Justice Statistics (1981–2001). *Correctional populations in the United States.* Washington, DC: United States Department of Justice, Office of Justice Programs, Bureau of Justice Statistics. United States Census Bureau (2000). *Statistical abstract of the United States, 2000.* Washington, DC: Census Bureau.
Notes: Mean suicide rate for state prison inmates = 17.43 (SD = 3.70). Mean suicide rate for the United States = 11.94 (SD = 0.72).

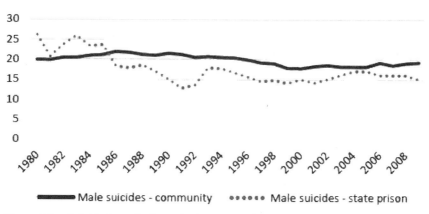

Figure 3.2. Suicide Rates in the United States, Males 1980–2009
Sources: Kochanek, K. D., Murphy, S. L., Xu, J., & Tejada-Vera, B. (2016). Deaths: final data for 2014. *National Vital Statistics Report,* 65(4). Hyattsville, MD: United States Department of Health and Human Services, Centers for Disease Control. Noonan, M. E. & Ginder, S. (2013). *Mortality in local jails and state prisons, 2000–2011—statistical tables.* United States Department of Justice, Office of Justice Programs, Bureau of Justice Statistics. United States Bureau of Justice Statistics (1981–2001). *Correctional populations in the United States.* Washington, DC: United States Department of Justice, Office of Justice Programs, Bureau of Justice Statistics. United States Census Bureau (2000). *Statistical abstract of the United States, 2000.* Washington, DC: Census Bureau.
Notes: Mean suicide rate for male state prison inmates = 17.48 (SD = 3.64). Mean suicide rate for the United States = 19.77 (SD = 1.28).

prisons to the rest of society, as the largely male-populated prisons should be expected to have a higher suicide rate than the mixed-gender community. Figure 3.2 includes suicide rates only for males in prison and males in the community. When the two male populations are compared, the prison suicide rates were actually lower than rates for males in general from the mid-1980s through 2009 (mean of 17.48 for male inmates versus 19.77 per 100,000 residents for males in the community). A few possible explanations for this are the lack of desirable suicide methods available to people in custody, the greater supervision of inmates compared to people in the free community, and the disproportionate minority representation among the correctional population. Chapter 2 provided information about the demographic characteristics of people who commit suicide. Suicide rates tend to be low among African Americans, and African Americans are overrepresented in the corrections system. Correctional suicide data broken down by gender beyond 2009 are not available at the time of this writing, so Figure 3.2 does not show the increase in suicide rates both in the community and the prison system that started in 2010.

It can be difficult to compare custodial suicide rates from country to country. Some countries, such as the United States, distinguish between facilities housing pretrial/remand inmates and those that house only sentenced prisoners. Facilities holding pretrial inmates often have higher suicide rates than those responsible for sentenced inmates. Most other nations combine institutions holding pretrial and sentenced inmates in their suicide reports, resulting in prison suicide rates that are higher than what are seen in U.S. prisons. As was noted earlier in this chapter, the suicide rates in prisons in the United States have been between 13 and 20 per 100,000 people since the mid-1980s. The suicide rate for prisoners in Germany, however, is 75.6 per 100,000 people (Radeloff et al., 2017). The average suicide rate for inmates in the general population of Italian correctional facilities is 97 per 100,000 (Roma, Pompili, Lester, Girardi, & Ferracuti, 2013) and 156 per 100,000 in Belgium (Favril et al., 2018). Fazel, Grann, Kling, and Hawton (2011) reported on custodial suicide rates in 12 countries from 2003 through 2007. The country with the highest suicide rate was Denmark with 147 suicides per 100,000 inmates. Sweden and Norway had the next highest suicide rates with 128 and 127 suicides per 100,000 inmates, respectively. The country with the lowest suicide rate was Australia with 58 suicides per 100,000 inmates. Willis et al. (2016) studied prisoner deaths in Australia from 1999 through 2013 and found an average rate of 67.8 deaths by suicide per 100,000 inmates during this time. These statistics represent suicides among both pretrial and convicted offenders, which likely explain why they are so much higher than suicide rates for prisoners in the United States.

To illustrate the difference in suicide rates among convicted and pretrial inmates, Opitz-Welke and colleagues (2013) reported on custodial suicides in Germany from 2000 through 2011. The pretrial inmates had suicide rates that were much higher than sentenced inmates. The average suicide rate per 100,000 inmates was 55.8 for sentenced males, 291.5 for pretrial males, 22.9 for sentenced females and 136.4 for pretrial females. Does this mean that pretrial inmates are naturally at higher risk than those who are sentenced? Not necessarily. A possible explanation for the high suicide rates in some of these countries is that facilities that hold pretrial inmates tend to have high population turnover. The large turnover of inmates will result in a much larger number of potential suicides. If the rate of suicides in a facility with a high turnover of inmates is calculated using the average daily population as the denominator, the suicide rates may be inflated. I will address this issue in greater detail later in this chapter.

Where Prison Suicides Occur

Researchers have identified specific prison settings that are associated with high suicide rates. A common finding across prisons, jails, and police lockups is that inmates tend to attempt suicide when they are alone (Hayes, 2010; Humber et al., 2011; Patterson & Hughes, 2008; Reeves & Tamburello, 2014;

Shaw et al., 2003; Shaw, Baker, Hunt, Maloney, & Appleby, 2004). Being alone gives suicidal inmates, and inmates who are looking to commit a non-fatal act of self-harm, the opportunity to do so. When inmates are in view of staff members and even other inmates, gestures indicative of an impending suicide attempt or another act of self-harm are likely to be stopped either before an injury occurs or before the incident turns fatal. In Belgium, 61% of prisoner suicides occurred in single-cell housing. Twenty-four percent took place in shared cells, but 63% of suicides in shared housing occurred at times when the roommates were outside the cells (Favril et al., 2018). In the United Kingdom slightly over 60% of suicides took place in single cells. For suicides in shared cells, 52% happened in the absence of the roommate (Shaw et al., 2003).

Given the opportunity for self-harm that single-cell housing presents, such placement can be very problematic, especially for individuals who are at high-risk. On the other hand, single cells do have benefits for some inmates, as being housed alone allows them to have their own space (Molleman & van Ginneken, 2015). Toch (1992a), for example, found that some inmates prefer to be alone, so single cell housing would likely reduce anxiety among those who seek solitude and privacy. Molleman and van Ginneken argued that multiple-occupancy cells and the frequent presence of a roommate might undermine the development of prisoner-staff rapport. Additionally, single-cell housing does have the advantage of preventing inmate on inmate exploitation that is often difficult for corrections officers to see and prevent. A challenge, however, is that 87% of prison suicides throughout the United States in 2001 and 2002 occurred in inmates' cells (Mumola, 2005), as this is where inmates are most likely to find the opportunity to commit suicide without being seen. The incarceration boom of the 1980s, 1990s, and early 2000s in the United States has made space a rare commodity, so unless there is a security or medical need for single-cell housing, inmates who are able to be housed in multi-occupancy cells or dormitories are generally housed with other inmates.

There is an important distinction between regular single cell housing, which might be preferable to some inmates, and restrictive housing, which often has negative repercussions for inmates' quality of life. Inmates in single cells outside of restrictive housing are unlikely to have limitations imposed on their access to programming, recreation, or visitation beyond what their security level mandates. Restrictive housing is different, and the U.S. Department of Justice (2016) identified three characteristics that distinguish this setting from other living areas. First, restrictive housing involves inmates being removed from the general population. Second, inmates are placed in a locked room or cell, either alone or with another inmate. Third, inmates are unable to leave that room or cell for the vast majority of the day. Restrictive housing can be used for disciplinary purposes, to prevent inmates from assaulting other inmates or staff, in response to an act of self-harm or the threat of it, or as a form of protective custody.

Reeves and Tamburello (2014) researched the relationship between housing type and suicide in New Jersey state prisons. Of the 26 suicides that occurred from 2005 through 2011, only one occurred in general population. That person was housed in a two-person cell, but the suicide occurred outside the cell. The other 25 suicides occurred in locations that qualified as restrictive housing. Single-cell detention units, where inmates were allotted the fewest privileges and could be held on disciplinary lockup for at least 15 days, had the most suicides. Other areas that experienced suicides were protective custody units, the infirmary, administrative segregation areas, and inpatient units. The only type of restrictive, single-cell housing that did not have any suicides during the study period was the stabilization unit, as those units are designed with cells specifically equipped to prevent suicide attempts. Inmates on the stabilization unit also receive extra psychiatric care. This Department of Corrections responded to these findings by introducing double cell housing for inmates in detention in an effort to reduce suicides.

Researchers in Europe have also studied the relationship between restrictive housing and suicide. Results there provide additional evidence that inmates housed in isolation have higher suicide rates than the general prison population. The suicide rate for the general prison population of Italy was 97 per 100,000 inmates compared to 353 in isolation units and 233 in temporary isolation units (Roma et al., 2013).

Restrictive housing is not the only setting that has high suicide rates. Higher security units, particularly maximum-security, have higher suicide levels than medium and minimum security wings (Duthe et al., 2013; Dye, 2010; van Ginneken, Sutherland, & Molleman, 2017). The locations of suicides are telling about the impact of housing type both on opportunity structures and on the motivation for self-harm. Inmates who are in maximum security or segregation units experience greater levels of deprivation than people doing time in more open, less restrictive settings. Maximum security inmates generally have less access to programs, work assignments, or other activities that would allow them to focus on something more positive or simply give them something to do. While imprisonment itself isolates an inmate from his or her family and friends, being housed in a maximum security prison is even more isolating because of the lack of educational and recreational programs found in these facilities. Additionally, visitation programs are likely to be more restrictive in higher security settings. The absence of prosocial activities is unlikely to improve one's psychological state and may make matters worse. Inmates in higher security settings might also be facing longer sentences. As was mentioned in Chapter 2, those with life sentences are at particular risk for suicide, and people with such long prison terms tend to be housed in maximum security.

With regard to opportunity, inmates who are in lockdown or who are incarcerated alone in a cell are in a precarious position, since there is no one present in the cell who can attempt to intervene or call for help. Officers are required to make rounds and check on each inmate, but the length of time between checks can be enough time for an inmate to commit a nonfatal or fatal act of self-injury. Hanging/strangulation/asphyxiation is the most common method of suicide among incarcerated populations. Stone (1999) reports that death from hanging or strangulation can occur within about five to ten minutes after the cutoff of oxygen or blockage of blood flow to the brain and that the mortality rate of this method is close to 80%. Use of this method allows those who have high suicidal intent to complete the act before officers begin their next check, and it also puts those who are trying to make suicidal gestures at risk, since they might lose consciousness before help arrives.

Is housing type itself a risk factor, or are inmates who are placed in more restrictive housing settings already at higher risk for suicide prior to entering that area? One possible explanation for increased suicides in maximum security and some types of restrictive housing could be the characteristics of the inmates who reside there. There are two ways that inmates can be assigned to high security housing. First, the seriousness of offense and the sentence length strongly influence classification decisions. As was discussed in Chapter 2, offense type and inmate aggression levels are related to the probability of suicides in prisons and jails, with violent offenders often found to be overrepresented among suicides. Second, inmates can "earn" their way into maximum security or restrictive housing through poor institutional adjustment. Inmates who commit numerous or serious infractions can be reclassified and transferred from less secure prisons or lower security units of jails. In Chapter 2, I noted that poor institutional adjustment and disciplinary infractions are associated with suicides. Inmates who are placed in a restrictive unit due to their need for protection from other inmates are also at a higher risk for suicide, as was also discussed in Chapter 2. Being victimized in custody is a risk factor for suicide and suicide attempts, and the need for protective custody may also be a sign of inability to cope with incarcerated life.

Frottier and associates (2007) tested the assumption that inmates placed in solitary confinement might have characteristics that place them at a higher risk of suicide, independent of housing placement. The researchers compared inmates who died by suicide while in isolation to people who committed suicide while housed in a shared cell. Researchers classified both groups using the Viennese Instrument for Suicidality in Correctional Institutions (VISCI).

The research team compared the two groups on risk factors for suicide, such as offense type, history of self-harm, psychiatric diagnosis, previous incarcerations, mental health treatment history, use of psychopharmacological medication, addiction history, and involvement in prison programs and visitation. There was no difference in VISCI scores between inmates who committed suicide while in a solitary cell and those who died by suicide in shared cells. Frottier and colleagues concluded that "it was evident that solitary confinement as a risk factor was not due to the possibility that inmates with higher risk had been selected for solitary confinement" (p. 230). These results suggest that, at least in Austria, the inmates placed in solitary were at no higher risk for suicide than those in the shared cells at the time of their placement in those cells. This would suggest that the housing assignment itself is a risk factor for suicide.

A study of near-fatal suicide attempts in Spain is among the few bodies of work that did not find a relationship between housing assignment and suicide risk. Sanchez and associates (2018) considered housing assignment in their multivariate model. Inmates' presence in solitary confinement was not a significant predictor of the likelihood of a near-fatal attempt. More research in this area is necessary to fully understand the relationship between housing and suicides. Most of the research on this topic points to isolation or restrictive housing having an impact on residents' motivation and/or opportunity to attempt suicide.

A particularly difficult place to do time is, not surprisingly, death row. Tartaro and Lester (2016) studied suicides on death row in U.S. prisons from 1978 through 2010 and found higher rates of suicide for death row inmates compared to the prison population in general. The mean suicide rate on death row during that time was 129.7, per 100,000 with a median of 104.9. Suicide rates in state prisons, however, averaged 17.41 per 100,000 inmates, with a median of 16.18. Suicide rates on death row did gradually decline between 1978 and 2000, but they increased somewhat in the first decade of the 2000s. Death row suicide rates are susceptible to large fluctuations given the small size of its population (mean = 2,413 from 1978 through 2010), so readers must use caution when interpreting trends, as the increase or decrease of a single suicide in a year could result in a large change in rates.

One would expect that death row prisoners would receive high levels of supervision, given the seriousness of their offenses and their perceived dangerousness. A likely explanation for the disproportionately high suicide rates is the combination of high levels of both motivation and opportunity for death row inmates. Inmates on death row have experienced at least one traumatic event in their past (the murder or, if they are innocent, the conviction), face a difficult present, and a bleak future. Conditions on death row can be difficult for inmates, particularly those who struggle with isolation. While most states lack statutes mandating that inmates sentenced to death be placed in segregation or isolation (Aldape et al., 2016), there is evidence that, in practice, these inmates tend to be isolated and given very little access to programming that could occupy their time (Cunningham, Reidy, & Sorensen, 2015). What is particularly challenging about this housing situation is that the length of time spent on death row has risen over the years, with the average time spent reaching 16.5 years in 2011 (Snell, 2013). In California, inmates are likely to be on death row and housed in that setting for 25 years before execution (*Jones v. Davis,* 2015). Inmates housed in areas with little or nothing to do each day can only occupy themselves with their minds, but many on death row lack literacy skills or the intellectual capacity to occupy themselves in a productive manner (Cunningham et al., 2015). Death row inmates may find their living situations to be particularly unbearable given that they are to be released from it via execution. People in that situation might decide to take matters into their own hands and die on their own terms rather than wait for the state to do it. The extended periods of isolation these inmates experience present the opportunity for the attempt to come to fruition.

Defendants who lack competency to stand trial and inmates who are too psychiatrically unstable to be housed in a correctional facility may be housed in a hospital on either a temporary or long-term basis. Jones, Hales, Butwell, Ferrier, and Taylor (2011) researched high security hospital patients in England and Wales from 1972 through 2000 and found suicide rates of 129 per 100,000 patient-years for men and 310 per 100,000 for women. The suicide rate for German forensic psychiatric hospitals from 2000 to 2004 was 123 per 100,000 patients (Voulgaris, Kose, Konrad, & Opitz-Welke, 2018).

When Prison Suicides Occur

Most researchers who have searched for temporal patterns among suicides in prisons have not found any significant differences in monthly or seasonal distribution. Favril et al. (2018) did find a temporal pattern in suicides in Belgium prisons, with 43% occurring between 9pm and 6am. The Victoria Department of Justice Correctional Services Task Force (1998) also reported higher instances of suicides at night while inmates are locked down in their cells, which is not surprising given that inmates are under less supervision and have more opportunity to prepare and carry out a suicide attempt. Joukamaa (1997), Fruehwald, Frottier, Eher, Gutierrez, and Ritter (2000), and Mumola (2005), however, did not find such temporal patterns among prison suicides in Finland, Austria, and the United States, respectively.

Prison inmates have been found to commit suicide at a variety of points in their sentences. Studying prisons in the United States, Mumola (2005) found that only 7% of prisoners committed suicide within the first month of incarceration in prison. Nearly two-thirds (65%) committed suicide after their first year in prison, while 33% committed suicide after five. Mumola also found that the time of death differed by race, with 50% of suicides involving white inmates occurring in the first 21 months in prison, compared to 40 months for blacks and 49 months for Hispanics. In Belgium, 51% of inmate suicides happened in the first 6 months, 22% in the first month, and 8% in the first week. Half of all self-inflicted deaths in Australian prisons occurred in the first three months of incarceration, with 29% taking place in the first month. It is important to note, however, that the Australian data includes all self-inflicted deaths, including accidental overdoses. When considering only suicides in prisons in the southern part of Australia, Austin and associates (2014) found 39% of suicides took place in the first month. Both of the Australian studies and the research from Belgium included facilities that hold both pretrial and sentenced inmates. This is noteworthy, given differences in temporal patterns in suicides between pretrial and sentenced inmates. As will be discussed shortly, facilities that specialize in housing pretrial inmates tend to report higher proportions of suicides occurring shortly after entry into custody.

Periods preceding and following transfers are also high-risk times for suicides. MacKenzie, Oram, and Borill (2003) found that 69% of females who committed suicide in facilities in England and Wales did so within four days of being transferred from their cells. Seventeen percent of suicides in prisons throughout England and Wales occurred within 72 hours of a transfer to a new cell or a change of cellmate (Newcomen, 2014a), while 22% of inmate suicides in Belgium happened within a week of a transfer. Inmates subject to transfer may have to work to reestablish their reputations and deal with being tested for their mental and physical toughness all over again. Transfers that take inmates farther away from home may be difficult, particularly if they were receiving visitors at their previous institution. Interfacility transfers might also involve a change in security level or at least new protocols that might make doing time more difficult. While transfers within and between institutions are necessary, corrections departments should aim to move inmates previously identified as at risk for suicide as infrequently as possible (New South Wales Corrections, 2005). When transfers are necessary, additional screening and supervision may be warranted.

The National Commission on Correctional Health Care's (NCCHC) standards (NCCHC, 2015) identified additional high-risk periods for inmates: immediately after adjudication, following an inmate's return to the facility from court, following the receipt of bad news regarding family or himself/herself, and after suffering humiliation or rejection. It is important for correctional staff to be aware of how inmates are coping with these stressors. Newcomen (2014a) noted that the period following an appointment with medical staff is a high-risk time, with 32% of suicides occurring after such appointments. While it is possible that a few inmates might have received some discouraging health news, the more likely explanation is that the medical visit was related to either a self-reported mental health problem or a psychological issue that prompted a referral. Awareness of self- or staff-reported problems is essential in the correctional setting, especially since 18% of deceased inmates in Newcomen's analysis had a written Assessment, Care in Custody, and Teamwork (ACCT) plan opened within 72 hours of suicide, meaning that staff was already aware that those inmates were at risk. An additional 11% of suicides in Newcomen's study either self-harmed or expressed suicidal feelings to staff within the 72 hours preceding the suicide.

Jails Suicide Rates

Jails and detention areas inside police stations have problems that are unique to these types of facilities. First, jails and police lockups are frequently faced with handling people who are under the influence of alcohol/drugs or going through withdrawal. Second, these facilities tend to have very high turnover rates, and this complicates the work of custodial and mental health staff who have to screen and monitor the constant influxes of people. Third, jails and police detention areas are particularly affected by the consequences of the deinstitutionalization movement for psychiatric patients that resulted in an increase of mentally ill inmates in the criminal justice system (Torrey et al., 2010). Fourth, local jails are also burdened by crowding at the state level, especially when the state establishes a policy whereby jails become responsible for inmates serving some state sentences[1] (Gerlinger & Turner, 2015).

Individuals enter police lockups, and even some jails, from right off of the street, and many of these individuals are under the influence of drugs and/or alcohol. Hannan, Hearnden, Grace, and Bucke (2010) found that only 49% of inmates who died in police custody in Great Britain were actually assessed for physical and mental health risks. The most frequently cited reason for failure to assess was that the inmates were too intoxicated to participate in the process. Of those who were assessed, the most commonly noted concern for health and safety was intoxication. Newcomen (2014a) found that 8% of suicides in facilities in England and Wales occurred within three days of substance use or the start of withdrawal.

Jails have received special attention in the custodial suicide literature, since suicides occur more frequently in jails than they do in prisons. For example, in 2013, there were 192 suicides in state prisons and 327 suicides in jails in the United States (Noonan et al., 2015). This tends to make one wonder if there are fundamental differences between prison and jail inmates or if prisons are simply much more adept at preventing suicides? There certainly are some differences between the two populations, with the most striking being the potential for jail inmates to enter the facility from the streets while intoxicated and requiring a detoxification period. Jail staff and inmates must also deal with turnover, or churn. The U.S. Bureau of Justice Statistics (BJS) reported that the average jail stay in the United States is 21 days compared to two years for prison inmates (Noonan, 2016b), so jails usually have much higher turnover rates than prisons.

The rotation of inmates in and out of facilities not only consumes more time and resources of staff, but it makes it more difficult for staff and even well-intentioned inmates to learn about what type of behavior and emotions are typical versus worrisome for individuals who may be in crisis. Van Ginneken and colleagues (2017) conducted a multivariate statistical analysis and found that turnover rates were actually a better predictor of suicides than the function of the institution (housing for pretrial or sentenced). Baggio et al., (2018) also found turnover rates to be a significant predictor of self-harm in Swiss pretrial facilities.

Whenever criminologists compare numbers across jurisdictions, we tend to use rates to account for differences in population sizes. After all, a facility with more inmates should be expected to have more suicides. A review of jail suicide statistics reveals consistently higher rates for jails than for prison. In 2013, the jail suicide rate was 46 per 100,000 inmates compared to 15 for state prisons in the United States (Noonan et al., 2015). The differences in suicide rates between the types of institutions, however, are not as drastic as they might appear. To understand why, it is necessary to remember how suicide rates for prisons and jails are derived. The most commonly used equation is as follows:

(Number of suicides in jails / average daily population in jails) * 100,000

The use of this equation has been widespread and has framed jails as having substantially higher suicide rates when compared to prisons and the general community. The problem is that using the average daily population to measure jail suicides dramatically underestimates the number of inmates for whom jail personnel are responsible for supervising each year. For example, while the average jail population in the United States was about 740,000 in 2016, jails admitted 10.6 million people from midyear 2015 through midyear 2016. This means that jail populations turnover at a much greater rate than populations do in prisons. This issue also affects individual jails differently.

In 2016, jails with a capacity of 49 or fewer inmates had an average stay of 11.2 days with a weekly turnover rate of 123%. The largest jail jurisdictions, with average daily populations of at least 2,500 inmates, had an average length of stay of 34 days and a weekly turnover rate of 40% (Zeng, 2018).

O'Toole (1997) explained how using the average daily population to calculate suicide rates can be problematic by comparing some key prison and jail statistics. Take two facilities, one jail and one prison, each with a rated capacity of 1,000. Each facility has an average daily population of 1,000. So far, the facilities look identical. The problem arises when looking at the number of admissions to each facility over a year. While the prison might have 1,500 admissions each year, the same size jail might have 23,000 admissions that same year. In this situation, the total number of inmates to pass through the hypothetical prison is 1,500 over the one-year period. In comparison, that jail sees over 23,000 inmates during the same time. This dramatically increases the number of potential suicides in the jail, since the number of inmates coming into the jail is substantially higher. O'Toole argued that if we attempt to calculate the national jail suicide rate with an average daily population, but the jails admit 10 to 20 times that, the result is a greatly inflated suicide rate for jails.

Crighton and Towl (1997) provided further evidence of the impact that equations have on suicide rates and how this affects jails compared to prisons. Using data from 1988 through 1990 and 1994 through 1995 for prisons in England and Wales, the researchers calculated suicide rates for pretrial and sentenced inmates separately. The suicide rate for sentenced prisoners, using average daily population as the denominator of the equation, was 54 per 100,000. When using the number of facility receptions as the denominator of the equation, the suicide rate for sentenced prisoners was 27 per 100,000. For pretrial inmates, the suicide rates had a much greater fluctuation, dropping from 242 per 100,000 inmates to just 37 per 100,000 when the researchers took facility admissions into consideration.

As O'Toole (1997) and Crighton and Towl (1997) demonstrated, other facility-level factors, such as reception rate and length of stay in the facilities, have a substantial impact on suicide rates. Recognizing this, some researchers have developed equations to present suicide statistics that take the aforementioned factors into consideration. Winfree (1988) developed a useful equation for determining jail suicide rates, with a focus on estimating the time of exposure to risk (length of stay in the jail) for each member of the jail population. Winfree's study involved male suicides, so the calculation included only male inmates. The equation involves (1) calculating the number of days it would typically take a given fixed jail population to reproduce itself, (2) determining the average daily male population of each jail divided by the number of male inmates released on an average day (The resulting figure is the average stay in days), (3) taking the average stay in days and multiplying it by the sum of the average daily population plus the yearly admissions, and (4) dividing the figure derived from Step 3 by 365.

The BJS (Mumola, 2005) took a slightly different approach to calculating jail suicide rates. The BJS estimated the "population at risk" by combining the population of each jail on January 1 of each year with the number of admissions at each facility for a given year. The jail suicide rate dropped by 90% when using the at-risk figure instead of average daily population. For the 50 largest jail jurisdictions, the at-risk statistic accounted for the 2,827,133 inmates who passed through large jails that year rather than basing the rate on just the 207,471 average daily population for those facilities. Gastwirth (2005) criticized the BJS at-risk calculation for counting each admission of someone who is jailed several times and cautioned against using this method for comparison to community suicide rates.

The question of how to calculate jail suicide rates remains a controversial issue debated in the suicide literature. The co-author to the first edition of this book (David Lester) disagreed with the argument advocating for more sensitive measures of jail populations and supported the use of average daily population as an estimate for the number of jail inmates potentially at risk for suicide (Lester & Yang, 2008). Lindsey Hayes of the National Center on Institutions and Alternatives argued that the use of Average Daily Population (ADP) makes jail suicide rates more easily comparable to suicide rates in the community (Hayes, 2010).

This discussion should not be interpreted as dismissal of the fact that suicides do occur and are a problem that needs to be addressed. The point to this is to present readers with an understanding that some of the jail suicide statistics that have appeared in publications may not account for the number of people who pass through jails each year. If a rate is supposed to consider the proportion of people who commit suicide versus the total number of people in that population, it makes little sense to use figures that undercount the population by millions. After all, every person who enters jail has the potential to be involved in a jail suicide.

When Jail Suicides Occur

Earlier correctional suicide publications reported that the first few hours or days in jail were the highest-risk period for inmates (Hayes, 1983, 1989). While the initial period of incarceration in jail and police lockups remains a high-risk period, fewer suicides in jails now occur in the first hours or days than in the past (Hayes, 2010). Hayes compared data from 1985 and 1986 to

2005 and 2006 and found that 51% of suicides occurred within the first 24 hours of custody in jail or a police lockup in the 1980s but, by the early 2000s, only 23% of suicides took place in the first day. In England and Wales during the early 2000s, 32% of suicides occurred within the first seven days, with 11% occurring in the first day (Shaw et al., 2004).

While there are no definitive explanations for why this change has occurred, one possible reason is the increased awareness of the initial incarceration period as a high-risk time. Jail suicides, and the lawsuits that have been filed in the wake of such events, have been covered in practitioner publications, such as *American Jails.* Accrediting bodies, such as the National Commission on Correctional Health Care and the American Correctional Association, have spread awareness of the need for suicide prevention policies. Jails are likely changing their practices in light of court orders or the administrations' desire to be in line with current best practices in the field.

In addition to awareness of jail suicides, corrections agencies have become more mindful of the dangers posed by the intoxication of incoming inmates. The first week in jail can be an especially difficult time for people addicted to drugs or alcohol. The change in the percentage of suicides occurring early in incarceration could be a product of facilities improving their intoxication and detox protocols. Hayes (2010) found that 60% of the suicides in jails and detention centers occurred while individuals were intoxicated in the mid-1980s, but that number decreased to just 20% in 2005 and 2006.

While suicides are now less common upon inmates' immediate entry into the jail, admission remains a high-risk period for inmates. Gibbs (1982) researched inmates' adjustment to confinement and identified four associated challenges. First, inmates must find a way to withstand the shock of entry to the jail. The jail has its own noises, smells, and atmosphere, and inmates must find a way to acclimate. Second, inmates will be concerned with maintaining links to the outside. There are likely people whom the inmates will want to contact, and the inmates will be concerned about not being able to see their family and friends. Those who held jobs in the community will worry about being fired. Third, inmates must secure their stability and safety. Fourth, they have to find activities to fill their time. Gibbs notes that coping with these issues can be considered irritants for some inmates, but they can be viewed as major crises for others. Gibbs (1987) studied the effect that jail entry had on stress levels of inmates. He interviewed inmates from three New Jersey jails within the first 72 hours of their confinement and then interviewed them again five days later. The newly admitted inmates experienced high levels of depression and anxiety and overall high levels of psychopathology during their initial admission to the jail, but there was a modest decline in such feelings five days later.

Gibbs (1982, 1987) did not specifically address suicide, but his research is interesting considering research on patterns of jail suicides. Frottier and colleagues (2002) studied suicides in Austria from 1975 through 1996 and found that the first 20 days of incarceration was a particularly high-risk time for inmates. The rates then declined, only to rise again after the inmates had spent over sixty days in jail. The authors speculated that, following the initial shock of incarceration, inmates adjust, but the stress of incarcerated life becomes tiresome and unbearable for some inmates after a long time spent in jail. More recently, Mumola (2005) detected a similar trend in U.S. jail suicides. Nearly half of all suicides in the United States from 2002 through 2005 occurred during the first week of incarceration. This was followed by a decrease in deaths, and then an additional 14% of suicides occurred between two and six months of incarceration.

There are additional high-risk periods for jail inmates. Hayes (2010) found that, in the early 2000s, 35% of jail suicides took place close to a court date. Phone calls and visits are typically considered to be positive events for inmates, but contact with home can sometimes involve the communication of bad news, such as death or divorce. Twenty-two percent of jail suicides occurred around the time of contact with home (Hayes, 2010).

Time of day does not appear to have a substantial impact on when jail suicides occur. In U.S. jails, 32% of suicides in 2005 and 2006 occurred between 3pm and 9pm, while 24% took place between midnight and 6am (Hayes, 2010). Looking at data from 2000 through 2002, Mumola (2005) found 28% of jail suicides occurred between 6pm and midnight, and 28% between midnight and 6am. Slightly more than half of all suicides occurred between 6pm and 6am.

Where Jail Suicides Occur

As with prisons, suicides in jail tend to occur when inmates are housed alone (Hayes, 2010; Mumola, 2005). Hayes (2010) did find some changes regarding suicides in isolation. During 1985 and 1986, 67% of inmate suicides occurred while inmates were in isolation, but by 2005 and 2006, that percentage was down to 38%. Part of this change is likely due to fewer suicides occurring within the first few days of a jail stay. Jails may choose to place inmates in isolation upon initial entry into jail until a full physical screening can be done and it is clear that the inmate is free of serious contagious diseases. The increased awareness of initial incarceration as a high-risk period is likely associated with the demonstrated reduction of suicides among newly admitted inmates and, perhaps, even newly admitted inmates who are still housed alone. Additionally, the role of isolation in inmate suicides has been highlighted by accrediting agencies and researchers who have worked to disseminate information about correctional suicides. While fewer jail suicides are occurring while inmates are placed in conditions considered isolation, inmates who commit suicide in jails are still more likely than not to have been assigned to a single-occupancy cell at their time of death (Hayes, 2010).

Suicides are not evenly distributed across jails. For example, Mumola (2005) found that the 50 largest jail jurisdictions in the United States had an overall lower prevalence rate of suicide compared to smaller facilities. Whereas suicides accounted for 41% of deaths in smaller jails, they only accounted for 17% of deaths in the 50 largest facilities. One possible explanation is that jail size has been found to be associated with the extent to which mental health and screening are provided to inmates. Rural jails, which are often smaller than those in urban jurisdictions, are less likely to have on-site medical services, are slightly less likely to offer mental health services (Applegate & Sitren, 2008), and are less likely to be able to do comprehensive assessments and have suicide prevention services than larger jails (Borum & Rand, 2000). More research is necessary to determine whether screening and availability of services are responsible for the prevalence of suicides in different size jails.

Are Pretrial or Sentenced Inmates at a Greater Risk for Suicide?

The conventional wisdom has been that pretrial inmates are at a greater risk for suicide than those who are sentenced. It is important to remember, however, that there are many more pretrial inmates than there are sentenced inmates each year. Many people will be arrested and placed in a lockup or a jail and then will be freed and have their charges dropped or be acquitted, fined, placed on probation, or given another type of nonincarceration sentence. As discussed earlier, the number of people who pass through a jail or police lockup each year is far greater than the number of sentenced inmates. Given how suicide rates have been calculated for years, practitioners and some researchers have been under the impression that pretrial inmates are at much higher risk for suicide than their sentenced counterparts.

When suicide rates for jails are calculated with the average daily population as the denominator, researchers and practitioners assume that the high rates in facilities can be explained by the presence of pretrial inmates. As I demonstrated earlier, more conservative calculations that account for the number of people who enter facilities each year reveal that the suicide rates for jails and prisons are actually similar. Towl and Crighton (1998, 2002) compared pretrial inmates to sentenced inmates in Scotland and found that pretrial inmates were at a similar risk of suicide as inmates serving short sentences (less than 18 months). Inmates serving longer sentences were actually at a higher risk for suicide than pretrial inmates. Van Ginneken and colleagues (2017) found that the population being held in prisons (pretrial or sentenced) was associated with suicide rates only until inmate turnover levels were considered. Once turnover was included in the statistical analysis, the purpose of the facility was no longer associated with suicide rates.

Juvenile Facilities

As was noted in Chapter 2, suicide is the leading cause of death among juveniles in custody, but this is at least partially due to the rarity of juveniles dying from illness or natural causes. Juveniles housed with adults are at higher risk for suicide for reasons that were discussed in the previous chapter. For facilities reserved exclusively for juveniles, 42% of suicides from 1995 through 1999 occurred in training schools or other types of secure facilities used for adjudicated juveniles in the United States. Thirty-seven percent of suicides occurred in preadjudication detention centers, 15% in residential treatment facilities, and the remaining 6% in reception and diagnostic institutions (Hayes, 2009). As with adult suicides, incidents of juvenile suicides were most likely to occur in single-occupancy rooms (75%, Hayes, 2009).

METHODS OF SUICIDE FOR INMATES

Outside of custody, death by firearms continues to be the leading method of suicide in the United States, but preference for type of suicide method differs by gender. In 2014, 55% of male suicides in the United States involved a gun. Women, however, were slightly more likely to use poison (34%) than a firearm (31%) (Curtin, Warner, & Hedegaard, 2016). This variation in approach is a product of the freedom afforded to people in the community to select methods that satisfy certain requirements. While men may feel comfortable with a very violent, lethal form of suicide, women tend to opt for methods less likely to be disfiguring and more easily reversible. Other options for suicide in the community are jumping/falling, drowning, suffocation, hanging, cutting, fire, and using a form of transportation to sustain a fatal injury (Konchanek et al., 2016). Most of these methods involve either going someplace or obtaining one or more items to use as tools. Inmates lack freedom of movement, and they face varying degrees of restricted access to items. Inmates are not permitted firearms for obvious reasons. They have very limited access to prescription or street drugs that could be used for poisoning themselves. Prescription drugs are distributed to inmates under supervision, and medical staff have the option of giving liquid doses to prevent the stockpiling of pills. Nonprescription drugs are worth ten to fifteen times their street value behind bars, so it is difficult to obtain enough for a suicide attempt. There is some documentation of rare inmate suicides through medication overdoses (Bartoli et al., 2018), but this remains a rather exceptional occurrence. People in the community may choose to jump from a building, parking garage, bridge, or cliff. The only viable option for jumping while in custody may be from an upper floor of a tier or pod, and that is only if the institution has not placed screens or bars across the tiers to prevent inmates from jumping or throwing others over the rails. Drowning and use of transportation for suicide are not feasible for those who are incarcerated.

Opportunities for cutting are limited, especially in jails, police lockups, or any form of restrictive housing in prison. Inmates placed in cells inside police departments lack any sharp objects, since they were already frisked, and the cells tend to be bare. Jail inmates are not permitted to accumulate many personal belongings, and this is especially true for inmates in their first 48 to 72 hours in the facilities. Since prison inmates may reside in the same facility for years, they can acquire and stockpile more items. This affords prison inmates the opportunity to have a choice, albeit a limited one, when they are seeking a method for suicide. Cutting or stabbing may be possible, but it is only fatal about 5% of the times that it is attempted (Stone, 1999). They might be able to overdose, but as already noted, it may be difficult to hoard medication. This leaves one common method of suicide left as a viable option for most inmates—hanging/asphyxiation (Austin et al., 2014; Favril et al., 2018; Gauthier et al., 2015; Humber et al., 2013; Kiekbusch, 2017; Newcomen, 2014b; Serin et al., 2002; Willis et al., 2016; Wobeser, Datema, Bechard, & Ford, 2002). Hanging/asphyxiation is highly fatal and relatively quick.

It is likely that inmates either choose hanging because it is the only method of self-harm available to them or because they have the ability to cut but are looking for something faster and more lethal than that. There is evidence that many people in custody have utilized forms of self-harm other than hanging prior to incarceration. Newcomen (2014a) found that 45% of inmates who committed suicide in England and Wales from 2007 through 2013 previously committed acts of self-harm through cutting or scratching, but only 3% of suicides in custody were attributed to cutting. In contrast, while nearly 75% of suicides discussed in Newcomen's study were a result of hanging, only 9% of those individuals previously used hanging or self-strangulation as an act of nonfatal self-harm. Twenty-eight percent of individuals who later committed suicide in custody were found to have constructed a ligature as a suicidal gesture or interrupted suicide attempt prior to the final suicidal act.

It is difficult to tell if the displacement from cutting to hanging is due to a desire for a quicker, more lethal method of suicide, if it is due to the desire for inmates to make a suicidal gesture at times when they may not have access to cutting, or they do not deem cutting to be a serious enough act to manipulate staff or adequately communicate their levels of distress. Stone (1999) notes that hanging and strangulation "are highly lethal methods and cannot be done safely as a suicidal gesture" (p. 322). While some who are truly suicidal do cut, cutting deep enough to cause death is painful and will likely require some knowledge of how to make the cut lethal.[2] Most incidents of cutting behind bars, however, are either (1) not intended to be fatal, (2) do not produce serious enough injuries to lead to death, or (3) are detected before the injury turns fatal.

As is evidenced by the behavior of suicidal individuals in the community, suicidal inmates would likely choose other options, such as firearms or poisoning, if they were available. Even in European countries where access to firearms is limited and where hanging is the most common form of suicide, only half of all suicides involve hanging, while the other 50% involve a variety of methods, including poisoning, jumping, or firearms (Sarchiapone et al., 2011). In contrast, hanging/asphyxiation is the cause of death for the clear majority of correctional suicides (Gauthier et al., 2015; Humber et al., 2013; Willis et al., 2016).

There are times when inmates have very few personal belongings, and some of these time periods are also increased periods of stress. Periods of initial incarceration, transfers, or movement to restrictive housing are all high-risk periods, and all are times when inmates have few personal belongings at their disposal. A suicide by hanging/asphyxiation requires little in the way of tools. All that is necessary is for inmates to have access to something that can be used to make a ligature and a tie-off point. Inmates who have access to bedding can do this while remaining fully clothed, and this is likely why researchers have found bedding to be the most common material used for a ligature (Gauthier et al., 2015; Hayes, 2010; Humber et al., 2013; Lyneham & Chan, 2013; Willis et al., 2016). In the absence of bedding, clothing can be used. While it is common practice to remove arrestees' belts, ties, and shoelaces, 27% of hangings in custody in Australia were accomplished with some other form of clothing, such as shirts, pants, underwear, or socks (Lyneham & Chan, 2013). For tie-off points, Lyneham and Chan (2013) found that 36% used cell bars, 13% shower fixtures, 9% bed bunks, and the other 36% used various fittings inside the cells, such as door handles and vents. There is some variation in reported use of different tie-off points, with Hayes (2010) finding that the bunk was used as a tie-off point in 30% of suicides in American jails, while Shaw and colleagues (2004) found that 48% of the custodial hangings in England and Wales involved the use of window bars, 18% cell fittings, and 11% the beds themselves to attach the ligature. In Belgium, 67% of people who committed suicide by hanging attached the ligature to cell window bars (Favril et al., 2018). It is not necessary for inmates to suspend their bodies off the ground in order to cut off oxygen. In fact, 72% of people who died by hanging in a pretrial facility in Switzerland maintained contact with the floor (Gauthier et al., 2015). This is important to note, as staff need to remember that low tie-off points in a cell are just as dangerous as ones that are high off the ground.

While hanging/asphyxiation is consistently the most frequently used method of suicide for people in custody, there are occasional suicides with other methods. With the advent of multitiered cell blocks came occasional jumping, particularly in areas where it is not possible to string people catchers across the tier. If jumping off of a tier is an option, for example, it is usually a jump from a second floor that will be deadly only if the inmate positions himself or herself to fall head-first. Such a maneuver needs to be done quickly to prevent anyone from grabbing the inmate as he or she climbs the rail and jumps, and it requires that the inmate resist survival instincts that would prompt most people to attempt to fall feet-first.

CONCLUSION

The information discussed in this chapter has important implications for suicide prevention. Previous research on suicides tells us about potentially high-risk times for inmates in various correctional settings. Additionally, there is evidence that some areas within facilities, particularly different housing units and security levels, have disproportionately high levels of suicide. While this could be a product of the types of inmates held there, as these inmates might be more disturbed and have fewer prosocial coping mechanisms, it could also be that certain environments are particularly challenging to manage and present greater opportunities for inmates to self-harm. It is important for correctional staff to be aware of settings that have had disproportional percentages of suicide, take precautions when managing and supervising inmates housed there, and be mindful of putting especially vulnerable inmates in these housing units.

As I have discussed in this chapter, the number of suicides and the times when they occur differ by facility type. This is important to consider when designing suicide prevention programs for each institution. For all corrections facilities, the periods around an inmate transfer or movements to and from court have been identified as high-risk periods. The time of initial incarceration is a common at-risk period for jail and lockup inmates. All institutions can benefit from increased vigilance upon inmates' entry to the facilities and during all of the aforementioned time periods.

Inmates in all types of facilities lack the tools to commit the most common acts of self-harm. This leaves those incarcerated with only a few viable options, such as hanging and, for prison inmates, cutting. Jails and lockups have restricted the availability of cutting tools, thereby limiting that option for most offenders in custody. Hanging/asphyxiation remains the only commonly used, highly lethal method of suicide in prisons and jails. This has important ramifications for suicide prevention, as facility staff can help to focus on ways to prevent hanging. This should not, however, be the extent of suicide prevention strategies. Stripping an inmate naked and putting him or her into a bare cell will very likely prevent suicide, but at what cost? It is not feasible to keep people in that condition for the length of incarceration, nor is it in line with standards of care in civilized society. Using environmental design strategies to reduce the opportunity for suicide attempts is important and useful, but it should not be the entire prevention strategy. This will be discussed further in Chapter 7. It may be necessary to initially place a heavy focus on opportunity reduction to guide inmates through a suicidal crisis, but there also needs to be a plan to have the individuals complete their period of incarceration in a safe and productive way and to prepare them for return to the community. The second half of this book will provide suggestions for prevention plans, some of which target individual inmates, while others seek broader changes to facility administration.

NOTES

1. For an example of this, see California's plan for realignment.
2. Cross-cutting a wrist or arm has low lethality, while cutting along the arm, over the artery, has a high lethality, but few people are aware of this.

Chapter Four

Suicide Attempts and Non-Suicidal Self-Injury

Until now, the focus of this book has primarily been on completed suicides. For every completed suicide, there are numerous suicide attempts that are interrupted by staff members, by other inmates, or even by the self-harming individuals themselves. There are also incidents that involve non-suicidal self-injury (NSSI) that are not meant to be fatal and are, instead, designed to achieve some other purpose. All of these, regardless of motive, are significant security threats that can be psychologically damaging to the individuals as well as other inmates on the pod or block. They can also stress and overextend the staff, and responses to these incidents might require resources that may be beyond what the facility can offer.

One question that clinicians and researchers have debated for years is how much consideration should be given to the motives for the destructive behavior? In the community, there seems to be more support for closely examining the motives for self-harm in order to inform the appropriate response and treatment. Some in the corrections field have advocated for the same approach behind bars, while others have cautioned against doing so, arguing that failure to consider all cases of self-harm on a suicidal spectrum is extremely risky. The former group cites evidence that some self-harmers have reported that they were not trying to kill themselves. The latter group draws on research showing that one of the strongest predictors of suicide is previous acts of deliberate self-harm and argues that even gestures that are meant to be nonfatal can accidentally result in death in the custodial setting.

The purpose of this chapter is to discuss attempted suicides and acts of deliberate self-harm where the intention may or may not be to cause death and to consider the pros and cons of making the distinction between NSSI and attempted suicide in the correctional setting. The issue of malingering will also be addressed.

SUICIDE ATTEMPTS

Outside of the custodial setting, 3.9% of adults in the United States contemplated suicide in 2014, while 0.6% attempted suicide (Centers for Disease Control, 2015). Muehlenkamp (2005) estimated an attempted suicide rate in the community of approximately 100 per 100,000 for the United States, about 10 times the national suicide rate. Butler, Young, Kinner, and Borschmann (2018) estimated that the incarcerated population of Australia had suicide ideation prevalence that was ten times higher than what is found in Australian free society. Correctional populations have higher prevalence rates of people who have both contemplated and attempted suicide (Abram et al., 2014; Austin et al., 2014; Charles et al., 2003; Daigle & Cote, 2006; Favril et al., 2018; Mandracchia & Smith, 2015; Shaw et al., 2003). As was noted in Chapter 2, the corrections setting houses a disproportionate percentage of individuals with mental health and substance abuse problems. The challenges of incarceration might be especially difficult for certain categories of inmates, particularly those who are suffering from mental illness, drug or alcohol addiction or withdrawal, those serving life sentences, or inmates who lack appropriate coping mechanisms. For these groups, suicide may seem like an attractive option while in custody, and self-harm that is not intended to be fatal might be utilized as a coping mechanism.

While doing research on prisoners in England, Jenkins and colleagues (2005) found that 3.8% of male and 8.4% of female sentenced prisoners had had thoughts of suicide in the past week compared to less than 0.3% of men and 0.5% of women outside of prison. For prisoners on remand, 11.9% of males and 23.0% of females reported suicidal thoughts in the past week. Favril, Vander Laenen, Vandeviver, and Audenaert (2017) reported that 43% of male prisoners in Belgium had a lifetime history of suicidal ideation, with 23% contemplating suicide in the past year. Twenty percent of inmates in Belgium had a lifetime history of suicide attempts. Researchers studying inmates in Australia, Ireland, and the United States found similar results, with inmates having much higher lifetime prevalence of suicidal thoughts than people outside of custody (Daeid & Lynch, 2000; Larney, Topp, Indig, O'Driscoll, & Greenberg, 2012; Schaefer, Esposito-Smythers, & Tangney, 2016; Stoliker, 2018). While most researchers have reported gender differences in prevalence of suicidal ideation, specifically with women being more likely to have contemplated suicide, Larney et al. and Schaefer et al. did not find any gender differences.

Inmates are under supervision while incarcerated, although that supervision is rarely constant. The supervision that does exist has resulted in numerous suicide attempts being detected and stopped before their completion. Tartaro (2000) surveyed 646 jails in the United States and found approximately 22 suicide attempts for every one completed suicide. Tartaro and Ruddell's (2006) later work on small jails in the United States produced a similar finding, with 23 attempts for every one suicide.

Who Attempts Suicide

Gender

Outside of the correctional environment, American males have suicide rates that are four times higher than females, but women tend to contemplate and attempt suicide more often than men (Centers for Disease Control, 2015). As was discussed in the previous chapters, females tend to attempt suicide rather than commit suicide more often, likely because the methods that they use, such as poisoning or cutting, are of low lethality.

A common feature among female inmates is a history of physical and/ or sexual abuse, more so than among male inmates (Chen & Gueta, 2017; Glaze & Maruschak, 2008; Greenfield & Snell, 1999; Moore et al., 2015). In addition to the difficulty of living with the memories of past abuse, female inmates may be triggered during their interaction by staff members, particularly males. Many incarcerated women must also face the pain of separation from children. As I discussed in greater detail in Chapter 2, separation from children tends to weigh more heavily on female inmates than on males, given that female offenders were more likely to serve as caregivers for their children prior to incarceration than male inmates.

Research on incarcerated women has shown that many have a history of prior suicide attempts. Meltzer and colleagues (2003) studied prisoners in England and Wales and found that over one-quarter of the male inmates on remand had a previous suicide attempt at some point in their lives, but half of their female counterparts had a lifetime history of suicide attempts. One-fourth of the women had attempted suicide in the year preceding research participation. Jenkins et al. (2005) also studied inmates in England and Wales but compared men and women on recent suicide attempts. For attempted suicide in the past week, sentenced prisoners had a prevalence of 0.4% for men and 1.4% for women, while prevalence in remand was higher, with 1.8% of men and 2.1% of women.

Daigle and Cote (2006) compared suicide attempts and lethality among both male and female inmates in Quebec, Canada. Twenty-one percent of female inmates and 24% of male inmates were judged to be at risk for suicide, with 2% and 8%, respectively, at serious risk. While 41% of the female inmates reported previous suicide attempts, 28% of the males also had a history of attempts. The lethality of the attempts was lower among women, but 70% of the women and 77% of the men reported that they intended to die when they previously attempted suicide. Daigle and Cote attempted to classify the suicidal incidents as suicide attempts or instrumental behavior using intent to die, lethality of the means used in the attempt, and lethality of the attempt itself. Instrumental behavior was defined as an act of self-harm where there was no suicidal intent, low lethality of means, and the act itself was of low lethality. After their classification, Daigle and Cote concluded that 12% of women and 16% of men in their sample made genuine suicide attempts. Daigle and Cote's conclusion that such a small percentage of these incidents were genuine suicide attempts should be interpreted with caution, given the high percentage of inmates who stated that they had at least some lethal intent.

Age

Juveniles tend to be at an elevated risk for suicide attempts relative to adults. Abram and colleagues (2014) studied suicidal behavior among incarcerated youth in the United States and found that 11% had attempted suicide at least once and had made an average of two attempts. There were gender differences found in this study, with females being more likely than males to attempt suicide. Similar to race and ethnicity patterns in the community, White, non-Hispanic individuals were more likely to have attempted suicide than Hispanics or African Americans. Hales, Davison, Misch, and Taylor (2003) found a lifetime prevalence of 20% attempted suicide and NSSI among incarcerated juveniles in England and Wales. In Australia, 28% of young incarcerated females and 4% of males had suicidal thoughts at some point in their lives. Young females were three times more likely to have a lifetime history of suicide attempts (23%) compared to young males (8%), and 13% of females and 4% of males attempted suicide in the past 12 months (Moore et al., 2015).

Juveniles have had less time and opportunity than adults to develop positive coping skills. The American Psychiatric Association (2000) warns that juvenile offenders are likely to have high impulsivity that tends to come with young age, and this can be problematic during emotional crises. Juveniles who are in legal trouble tend to exhibit more signs of coping problems than boys and girls their age who are not delinquents. When comparing incarcerated juveniles in Japan to teenagers outside of such facilities, incarcerated boys had more suicide attempts, instances of self-injury, suicide ideation, and illicit drug use. Incarcerated females had more extensive histories of self-injury, suicidal ideation, and suicide attempts than girls in the community (Matsumoto et al., 2009).

As discussed in Chapter 2, juveniles who are placed in adult facilities require extra attention, as rates of suicide tend to be higher for juveniles in such settings (Lambie & Randell, 2013). If it is necessary to house juveniles in adult institutions, those facilities should be staffed and equipped to provide programming appropriate for juveniles and make that programming available as frequently as it is in the juvenile facilities.

Risk Factors for Attempted Suicide

Similar to inmates who commit suicide, those who attempt suicide tend to have histories of psychiatric problems (Gates, Turney, Ferguson, Walker, & Staples-Horne, 2017; Goss, Peterson, Smith, Kalb, & Brodey, 2002; Marzano et al., 2016; Moore et al., 2015; Rivlin et al., 2013; Sanchez et al., 2018; Serin et al., 2002), as well as current symptoms of depression (Daeid & Lynch, 2000; Encrenaz et al., 2014; Suto & Arnaut, 2010). Swooger, Walsh, Maisto, and Conner (2014) found that offenders who exhibited signs of reactive aggression, meaning that they become aggressive in response to a perceived threat that involves affective arousal, had a history of suicide attempts, whereas those who utilized proactive aggression did not. People use proactive aggression in a premeditative way to achieve a goal. The authors did note that these findings contradicted those of other researchers who used non-offenders in their sample. A possible explanation is that the offender sample might have included a high percentage of individuals with psychopathic traits. Smith and colleagues (2014) studied male inmates with psychopathic traits in an effort to understand the relationship between those traits and suicide. They found that primary psychopathic traits, thought to be a product of genetic influence, were positively related to depressive symptoms and suicidal ideation. Secondary psychopathic traits, thought to arise from environmental influences such as trauma and neglect, were associated with likelihood to attempt suicide multiple times. This should not be surprising, given that secondary psychopathic traits are associated with sensation seeking and impulsive behavior as well as negative emotions. Daeid and Lynch (2000) also found that inmates with histories of attempted suicide in Ireland were more likely to have psychotic or personality disorders. Gates et al. (2017), however, did not find psychotic disorders to be predictive of suicide attempts. Instead, they cited depression and depression along with bipolar and anxiety disorders to be associated with suicide attempts among state prison inmates in the United States.

Current mental health symptoms also distinguish incarcerated suicide attempters from the general population. Encrenaz and colleagues (2014) studied suicide attempts among French prisoners. Current depressive or anxious symptoms were significant predictors of suicide attempts during imprisonment. Sanchez et al. (2018) also found that inmates who were currently being treated for depression, schizophrenia, or bipolar disorder were more likely to make near-lethal suicide attempts than others. Marzano et al. (2010) compared female inmates who made near-lethal suicide attempts to inmates with no such history and found that 87% of attempters were suffering from depression compared to 22% of the comparison group. Marzano and associates (2016) conducted a systematic review of research on near-lethal suicide attempts in prison and reported that diagnoses of co-occurring disorders were commonly identified as being associated with serious suicide attempts.

Histories of substance abuse problems tend to be found among inmates who attempt suicide (Daeid & Lynch, 2000; Gates et al., 2017; Meltzer et al., 2003; Rivlin et al., 2013). Such history can be a product of inmates with mental illness self-medicating. Drug use is also associated with impulsivity (de Wit, 2009), which is a predictor of suicide attempts. As noted in Chapter 2, Rivlin et al.'s (2013) typology of male prisoners who made near-fatal suicide attempts included a category for those who are experiencing withdrawal. Stoliker (2018) reported that inmates who used drugs at least weekly and/or alcohol daily prior to incarceration were more likely to have a history of at least one lifetime attempted suicide compared to offenders who did not use substances as often.

Inmates' coping abilities are also associated with suicide attempts (Liebling, 1999; Rivlin et al., 2013). Serin and associates (2002) studied inmates in a Canadian federal prison and noted that the inmates who were having difficulty coping with incarcerated life were more likely to attempt suicide. Sanchez and colleagues (2018) found that inmates who made near-lethal suicide attempts were more likely than others to have records of in-prison disciplinary action. Encrenaz et al. (2014) found history of in-prison victimization, specifically physical and/or sexual violence, to be associated with in-prison suicide attempts.

Other risk factors that are associated with completed suicides are also relevant when identifying those at risk for suicide attempts. Multiple studies have identified inmates' feelings of hopelessness as a predictor of suicide attempts (Gooding et al., 2017; Marzano et al., 2016; Stoliker, 2018). Marzano et al. (2016) identified impulsivity, aggression, and hostility as predicting near-lethal suicide attempts in a systematic review of the literature of attempts in prison.

Single versus Multiple Attempters

A suicide attempt might come at a particularly difficult time in life, and that brush with death might help people consider their lives and decide that death is not the solution they are seeking. For others, an initial attempt can be a first step in resorting to this behavior in times of crisis. Joiner's (2005) work on suicide and discussion of acquired capability is relevant here, as people with at least one previous suicide attempt have already crossed the threshold of being able to overcome the human instinct for self-preservation and engage in an act that threatens life.

One persistent finding in research on attempted suicides and self-harm is that there are a few people who are responsible for a disproportionate number of these acts. The British Home Office (1999) found that 85% of inmates who attempted suicide while in prison in England and Wales in 1996 and 1997 did so just once, but the remaining 15% attempted suicide 2 to 19 times. Hakansson, Bradvik, Schlyter, and Berglund (2011) studied repeat suicide attempts among Swedish offenders. Those who had repeated attempts were more likely to report having a chronic medical condition, histories of emotional, physical, and sexual abuse, and a history of difficulty getting along with other people. Repeated suicide attempts were also more common among younger inmates who had trouble controlling their violent behavior.

Triggering Events for Attempted Suicide

High-risk times for suicide in custody are also high-risk times for suicide attempts. The time of initial incarceration, the days preceding and following court dates, and the days before and after a transfer to a different institution or unit are high-risk periods for inmates. Additional difficult times depend on individual inmates, as there may be additional personal and legal problems that can trigger a crisis. Newcomen (2014a) defines triggers as "an event that has or may have an adverse impact on the individual's level of risk" (p. 8), and these triggering events tend to be highly specific to each individual. Suto and Arnaut (2010) identified relationship problems with family and friends outside prison and interpersonal problems inside prison as triggers for suicide attempts. For some inmates, finding out that a spouse is filing for divorce may be the event that triggers a crisis, while for another, it may be struggling with threats from other inmates. Inmates who are facing the choice of either being victimized by other inmates or fighting them may see that as an impossible choice, particularly since even winning the fight can result in a pyrrhic victory (the immediate problem is solved, but now the inmate is facing extra prison time or segregation). Suto and Arnaut also found that inmates attempted suicide due to problems with some staff members, as suicide may be considered a way for inmates, who have very little control over their lives, to show officers that they still do maintain some control.

Methods Used for Attempted Suicide in Custody

As was discussed in Chapter 3, people outside of prisons and jails have the freedom to search for and choose from a variety of methods to end their lives. Abram and colleagues (2014) studied detained juveniles and found that their suicide attempts preincarceration included cutting (27%), drug overdoses (24%), and jumping from high places (21%). Cutting and drug overdoses are possible, but difficult, while in custody and are more likely to occur either in a prison setting where inmates have been able to accumulate more belongings or in a jail setting after being incarcerated long enough to acquire items. The feasibility of jumping depends on the design of the facility, but some multistory wings have been designed in ways to prevent jumping. Rivlin and colleagues (2013) found hanging or use of a ligature to be the most frequently used method (67%) for in-custody suicide attempts, followed by cutting (20%), self-asphyxiation through use of something other than a ligature (5%), overdose (5%), ingestion of foreign objects (2%), and self-immolation (2%). All of the inmates included in Rivlin et al.'s study committed near-fatal suicide attempts, and this likely explains the widespread use of hanging in their sample. Serin and colleagues (2002) compared in-custody suicide attempts to completed suicides and found that attempters were much more likely to use the less lethal methods of cutting or overdosing, while those who committed suicide were more likely to use hanging/asphyxiation. Marzano et al. (2010) restricted their study to female inmates who made near-lethal suicide attempts and found that, while the majority of the inmates who nearly died used hanging or asphyxiation (63%), 12% used cutting, and 12% overdosed. The remaining 1% involved a self-induced diabetic coma.

Moore, Gaskin, and Indig (2015) found sex differences in types of suicide attempts among young offenders. Respondents were asked about all the methods that they used to attempt suicide in the past 12 months, regardless of whether they were in custody at the time. They were asked to give multiple responses if they had multiple attempts. The two most frequently used methods for females were poisoning/overdose and stabbing/slashing, both of which were used by 44% of females. Only 22% of women attempted hanging at any time in custody. Males, however, were much more likely to attempt hanging or asphyxiation (90%), while rarely using stabbing/slashing (19%). The methods used by the majority of males were much more likely to be lethal than what the females chose.

NON-SUICIDAL SELF-INJURY

Motivations for Self-Injury besides Suicide

The debate concerning whether to consider self-harm as part of a suicidal spectrum or something unique has been taking place for several decades. Menninger (1938) conducted some of the earliest work on the topic of intentional self-mutilation and argued that such acts were a manifestation of some level of suicidal desire, albeit perhaps an unconscious desire. Menninger even took some forms of self-harm that are rarely labeled intentional, such as alcoholism, and labeled them *chronic* suicide, since the addicted persons were shortening their lives by their substance abuse. In contrast, Walsh and Rosen (1988) and Wichmann and colleagues (2002) contend that intentional self-harm is distinct from suicide, as suicide involves extinguishing life while NSSI aims at making life more tolerable. The nature of the acts also tends to differ, with NSSI occurring more often and usually with a variety of methods.

Ross and Heath (2003) reviewed theories of why adolescents in the community self-harm. One possible explanation is the anxiety reduction model, suggesting that self-harm provides an immediate relief of stress and allows people to return to a calmer emotional state. Another possibility, the hostility model, posits that self-harm emanates from an individual's inability to outwardly express anger and hostility. Ross and Heath noted that there tends to be more empirical support for the hostility model, but relief of anxiety remains a factor in motivation for self-harm.

Ross and Heath's (2003) study was a bit restrictive in that it only considered two theories, both which started with the assumption that the self-harm is used to relieve tension. Klonsky (2007) tested seven possible motivations for self-harm among prisoners in England and Wales. The first was affect-regulation, where self-injury is used to address acute negative affect or affective arousal by attempting to regain control over one's emotions. Individuals who self-harm for this reason do so likely as a product of either learned ineffective coping skills or a biological disposition to emotional instability. Second, antidissociation is the use of pain to shock the system out of a dissociative episode. Third, antisuicide involves using self-harm to avoid a suicide attempt. Fourth, the interpersonal boundaries perspective suggests that injury is used to assert one's own identity distinct from others. The fifth is interpersonal influence, when self-harm is used to manipulate people who are in the self-harmer's environment. Examples of this include using harm to avoid abandonment or in the hopes of being taken seriously. Sixth is self-punishment, which is the hostility model discussed by Ross and Heath (2003) where people express their anger on themselves. Finally, the seventh is sensation-seeking in which people generate excitement from the self-injury.

After a review of 18 published studies, Klonsky found the most evidence that self-harm is used to address acute negative affect. These seven categories are not mutually exclusive, however, and people inside and outside of correctional facilities might harm to simultaneously accomplish multiple goals.

The Experience Avoidance Model (EAM) is similar to the anxiety reduction model discussed by Ross and Heath (2003) and the affect regulation explanation mentioned by Klonsky (2007). According to EAM, self-harm in the absence of suicidal intent is a form of negative reinforcement to stop, or at least reduce, undesirable emotional arousal. Where EAM differs from the other aforementioned theories is the suggestion that people use self-harm as a form of escape rather than to regain control. In other words, according to EAM, people use self-harm as an avoidance mechanism, and when they experience relief, that negatively reinforces the behavior and encourages repeat use of self-harm (Chapman et al., 2006). Researchers studying Australian females outside of the correctional setting who were diagnosed with borderline personality disorder (BPD) found that EAM was helpful in explaining the motivations of individuals engaging in NSSI (Hulbert & Thomas, 2010).

Kirchner, Forns, and Mohino (2008) were interested in the relationship between reliance on certain coping strategies and the use of self-harm among young prisoners in Spain. They identified eight coping strategies. Four of those are considered "approach coping" and include logical analysis, positive reappraisal, seeking guidance and support, and problem solving. The other four are considered "avoidance coping" and include cognitive avoidance, acceptance-resignation, seeking alternative rewards, and emotional discharge. Self-harmers tended to favor avoidance strategies while refraining from using approach strategies often. Inmates who used avoidance coping more than average but also frequently used approach coping had a lower risk of self-harm, suggesting that use of approach coping can mitigate the harm of avoidance coping, at least in this sample of incarcerated individuals.

Ireland (2005) studied bullying among young inmates and noted the role of interpersonal influence in motivation for NSSI. Ireland suggested that NSSI might be used to force the correctional staff to approve a change of the inmates' living conditions. The self-injury gets the attention of staff and may prompt closer supervision or even a transfer to a different part of the facility. Bullied inmates might seek this level of attention to get away from bullies. Ireland suggested that the self-injury could be used as a way for inmates to communicate their distress to staff without having to "rat" on anyone.

Just as inmates who are being bullied might use self-harm to get greater staff attention and possibly a transfer out of the housing area, there is always the possibility of inmates using self-harm or suicidal gestures to achieve a change in their current circumstances. Malingering is a real possibility, and it can be incredibly frustrating for staff members. Correctional staff members are naturally skeptical of inmates, as they are working with people who were arrested for stealing from and conning others. Staff members do not want to be fooled by inmates, and the institutions do not want to waste resources on people who do not need them. For those reasons, staff members have concerns about being deceived by inmates who are not truly having an emotional crisis. While this is understandable, there is a tremendous risk associated with ignoring or failing to act when inmates harm themselves or make suicidal gestures.

Who Commits NSSI

In the community, approximately 6% of adults commit acts of intentional NSSI (Klonsky, 2007). Nock and Kessler (2006) analyzed data from the National Comorbidity Survey and found that, while 4.6% of people in the community attempted suicide, 1.9% indicated that they did not actually intend to die. Muehlenkamp (2005) estimated that anywhere from 400 per 100,000 to 1,400 per 100,000 people self-harm per year in the community. Applebaum and colleagues (2011) reported that state and federal department of corrections medical directors estimated that 0.03% to 8.9% of prisoners engaged in some sort of deliberate self-injury in the previous year. Eighty-five percent of medical directors reported that self-injury took place in their facilities at least once a week, while half responded that these behaviors took place several times a week. In England and Wales, Hawton and colleagues (2014) found that 5% to 6% of male inmates harmed themselves each year from 2004 through 2009, but this behavior was much more common among incarcerated women (20%–24%). There were 139,195 recorded incidents of self-harm committed by 26,510 prisoners in England and Wales during that five-year period. The New York City jail system created a database and has been recording all incidences of suicidal and NSSI since 2007. In 2007, the rate of self-injury per 100,000 inmates was 33 but rose to 45.6 in 2011[1] (Fatos et al., 2015). In the database, the staff makes no distinction between those who had suicidal intent and those who did not, so the New York City Jail figures include attempted suicides as well as self-harm that was not intended to be fatal. In cases where staff members are unsure of the inmates' true intentions, they err on the side of caution and place inmates on suicide watch.

Gender and Age

NSSI tends to be more common among females in custody (Hawton et al., 2014; Ministry of Justice, 2018; Moore et al., 2015). When studying this behavior among prisoners in England and Wales, Hawton and colleagues (2014) found that the highest number of incidents occurred in local female prisons holding people on remand, followed by local facilities holding males on remand. Since facilities holding inmates on remand have high turnover rates, the high incidence of self-harm here is likely due, at least partially, to the high turnover rates of the facilities. Hawton and colleagues' research indicated that females at most risk for self-harm were under 20 years old, white, sentenced to life, or were on remand. In a multivariate analysis, the two variables that remained predictors of female self-harm were having a life sentence and having a history of at least five self-harm incidents in one year. Poor institutional adjustment has also been found to be a predictor of self-harm among female inmates (Wichmann et al., 2002). The Ministry of Justice (2018) reported that the rate of self-harm among female inmates is nearly six times that of male inmates. Additionally, females who do self-harm in prisons in England and Wales tend to be involved in twice as many incidents as male inmates.

Among both males and females, younger individuals tend to be more likely to self-harm in a way that is not intended to be fatal. Moore and colleagues (2015) researched young offenders in Australia. One-third of the females reported having self-harmed in their lifetimes, with 28% doing so in the past year, compared to 14% of lifetime occurrences for males, with 8% in the past year. Deliberto and Nock (2008) studied female adolescents in the community and found that the juveniles who self-harmed were more likely to have family histories of alcoholism, drug abuse, and violence. The researchers speculated that the self-harmers might be either biologically predisposed to impulsive behavior, or that they were raised in an environment where they learned poor impulse control. The juveniles who self-harmed were also more likely to be lesbian or bisexual than juveniles who refrained from harming themselves. Female Canadian juveniles were also found to be nearly three times more likely than male juveniles to self-harm while in detention (Casiano et al., 2016)

Other Predictors

One common finding in studies of people who self-harm is a history of physical or sexual abuse (Borrill et al., 2003; Lane, 2009; Matsumoto et al., 2005; Power et al., 2016). Histories of substance abuse were also cited in several studies of people committing NSSI (Borrill et al., 2003; Brown, Comtois, & Linehan, 2002; Hawton et al., 2014; Klonsky, 2007), although that finding was not universal across studies (Victor & Klonsky, 2014).

Depression and hopelessness are usually more common among those who attempt suicide, but there is also some evidence of a relationship between major depression and NSSI (Butler et al., 2018; Klonsky, 2007). A number of studies have found BPD to be related to NSSI (Hulbert & Thomas, 2010; Klonsky, 2007; Lane, 2009; Verdolini et al., 2017). Butler and colleagues (2018) interviewed inmates in Australia and found an association between likelihood of self-harm and depression, anxiety, substance use disorder, personality disorder, and schizophrenia. In a meta-analysis, Klonsky (2007) also found a relationship between NSSI and anxiety disorders, posttraumatic stress disorder (PTSD), schizophrenia, and several personality disorders.

In custody, suicide, attempted suicide, and NSSI have been associated with difficult institutional adjustment, and this includes inmates in the general population as well as those in restrictive housing (Lane, 2009; Wichmann et al., 2002). Dear, Slattery, and Hillian (2001) found that self-harmers in custody were less likely to use problem solving skills or other positive cognitive or behavioral strategies to deal with recent stressors. Incarcerated juveniles in Canada who self-harmed while incarcerated had records of negative institutional behavior (Casiano et al., 2016)

Where and When NSSI Occurs

As with suicides and attempted suicides, segregation is a setting where a disproportionate amount of self-harm occurs. In a survey of medical directors from state and federal departments of corrections in the United States, 76% of respondents identified segregation and other lockdown units as being the areas with the highest incidence of NSSI (Applebaum et al., 2011). When NSSI did take place in the general population, it was most likely to occur in maximum-security areas. These results are in line with suicide and attempted suicide research. These types of areas tend to provide inmates with more opportunity to injure themselves, as they are more likely to be locked in cells where corrections officers are unable to see them at all times. Additionally, segregated, locked-down, or maximum-security areas hold inmates who are either there due to poor adjustment and behavior or, in the case of maximum security, who are serving long sentences. Both types of inmates tend to be at a greater risk for fatal and nonfatal types of self-harm. These high security settings may also contribute to inmates' feelings of despair.

As with completed and attempted suicide, privacy and reduced supervision do seem to foster opportunities for self-harm. Acts of self-harm may not always require as much time and privacy as suicides and suicide attempts, though, as cutting or scratching takes less preparation than fashioning a ligature. Additionally, there might be a desire on the part of the self-harmers for people to see the act in progress or immediate aftermath of it, depending on the motivation for NSSI. Records for inmates housed in the South Carolina prison system indicate that 42% of self-harming incidents were discovered in the inmate's cell, 11% occurred in a crisis intervention housing area, and 23% were either in quasi-private or public locations, such as the shower, hallways, or the yard. Researchers were unable to ascertain from the prison records the location of 14% of the incidents. Self-harm was most likely to occur between the hours of 6pm and 10pm. One explanation for the temporal pattern could be reduced supervision due to lower staffing levels at this time. Another potential explanation, however, is that the harm could be a response to the idleness during this time, as most daily activities are finished, and inmates are being prepared to be locked in their cells for the night (Doty et al., 2012).

The previous sections of this chapter have provided evidence that pretrial facilities are likely to house more inmates who self-injure. This finding is similar to what has been reported for suicide and attempted suicides. Jails and facilities that house large concentrations of pretrial inmates have the challenge of higher turnover rates than prisons housing sentenced inmates. Not only are the jail staff members responsible for more inmates each year, but it becomes more difficult for them to get to know the inmates well enough that they can detect behavioral and emotional cues signaling distress. Pretrial institutions must also work with people who are withdrawing from drugs and alcohol.

Methods of Self-Harm and Their Lethality

Acts of self-harm in correctional facilities differ from suicides in that the methods that inmates use more closely approximate less lethal suicide attempts. Hawton and colleagues (2014) found that males who self-harmed in English and Welsh prisons most often used cutting or scratching (65%), followed by poisoning, overdoses, or swallowing objects (9% combined). Hanging and self-strangulation made up only 12% of self-harm incidents. Females used cutting or scratching in 51% of self-harm incidents, followed by self-strangulation in 31% of incidents. During this same time, 83% of suicides in these facilities were carried out via hanging or self-strangulation. Hawton and colleagues found that, of these self-harming incidents, 1% were highly lethal, and that people who self-harmed multiple times commonly used multiple methods. There does seem to be some variation in methods of self-harm from study to study. Heney (1990), for example, studied women in one Canadian federal prison and found that 92% of the cases of self-injury involved cutting.

To what extent is method of self-harm and dangerousness of the actions related to individuals' intent? One might assume that there would be a positive correlation between lethality of an act and suicidal intent, with suicidal individuals seeking methods that are more likely to result in death than people who are self-harming for other reasons. Dear, Thomson, and Hills (2000) studied incidents of self-harm among Australian inmates using the suicide intent scale (SIS) to measure their suicidal intent within three days following the incident. This study utilized nurses to rate the medical seriousness of the incidents. One-quarter of self-harming inmates revealed motivations that were deemed manipulative, and 43% appeared to be an effort to achieve psychological relief rather than death. Over three-fourths (78%) of the self-harming inmates were assessed as having at least a moderate degree of suicidal intent. Dear and colleagues concluded that even acts with manipulative motives were committed with at least moderate suicidal intent. Only 8% of manipulative self-harm incidents in this study were labeled both low in lethality and low in suicidal intent.

Contrary to the findings of Dear and colleagues (2000), Lohner and Konrad (2006) did find a relationship between type of self-injury and inmates' intent. Similar to Dear et al., Lohner and Konrad interviewed inmates within three days of an act of self-harm. They found that those with higher suicidal intent were more likely to choose hanging, which is highly lethal. Inmates who self-harmed with suicidal intent in this study had higher levels of hopelessness and depression than those who had low intent. People who self-harmed but seemed to have low suicidal intent were more likely to have a diagnosis of BPD and be highly impulsive. Haw et al. (2003) also found evidence of a positive relationship between the potential lethality of self-harm and suicidal intent. Hawton and colleagues (2014) found that, for male prisoners in England and Wales, a previous incident of moderate- to high-lethality was a predictor of future suicide in custody, but for females, lethality of self-harm was not associated with future chances of suicide. For females, it was the frequency of self-harm in custody that was predictive of future suicide attempts, with females having at least five self-harm incidents per year being more at-risk for suicide in custody. Again, readers should consider the results of these studies with caution, since results are based on inmates' interview responses after the self-harm has already been completed.

Clustering of NSSI and Suicidal Behavior

One possible consequence of intentional self-harm among individuals in corrections facilities is contagion, or clustering, of such acts. The Centers for Disease Control (1988 [cited in Niedwiedz, Haw, Hawton, & Platt, 2014]) define a suicide cluster as a "group of suicides or suicide attempts, or both, that occur closer together in time and space than would normally be expected in a given community" (p. 571). Niedzwiedz and associates conducted a systematic analysis of 82 articles published between 1960 and 2013 that researched clustering of suicidal and self-harming behavior. Of those, only four were conducted in the corrections setting. Two of those studies found evidence of suicidal clusters, while two did not. The studies that reported clustering estimated it to be associated with 5.8% to 45% of suicides. Hawton and colleagues (2014) reported a 15% clustering effect of self-harm among inmates in England and Wales. Heney (1990) studied self-injury among Canadian female inmates and asked both inmates and staff members their thoughts about "outbreaks" of self-injury. Seventeen percent of inmates stated that acts of self-harm by other inmates increase their own chances of committing self-injury. When staff members were interviewed, 10% cited the belief that outbreaks of self-injury were a product of copycat acts, and an additional 7.5% cited solidarity as their perceived motivation for inmate self-injury. Incarcerated juveniles in Manitoba, Canada, were more likely to engage in self-harm while in custody if they knew of another person's suicidal behavior (Casiano et al., 2016). Hales, Edmonson, Davison, Maughan, and Taylor (2015) compared incarcerated male juveniles who witnessed someone else's suicidal behavior in the previous six months with a matched comparison group. The males exposed to that trauma had higher levels of current mental health symptoms, including anxiety, depression, and hopelessness, and were more likely to express suicidal ideation. It is possible, however, that these findings, as well as that of Casiano and colleagues, are a product of like-minded individuals associating with each other. Researchers were unable to establish a time order to show whether the mental health symptoms appeared before or after being exposed to someone else's self-harm, so the symptoms experienced by the inmates exposed to trauma might have been present prior to the incident.

Repeated Acts of NSSI

NSSI can become a coping mechanism that some individuals use repeatedly during times of distress. Since incarceration can be particularly difficult, it is not uncommon to find small groups of people who frequently resort to NSSI to cope with their current problems. In England and Wales, Hawton et al. (2014) reported that males who self-harmed did so an average of twice a year, while females did so an average of eight times per year. Few inmates were involved in a disproportionate number of incidents, with two male inmates and 102 adult and juvenile female inmates each committing over 100 self-harm incidents in a year. During the 1996/1997 reporting period, four incarcerated people were involved in 23 incidents, and 3 were involved in

20 incidents in Australia (Victoria Department of Justice Correctional Services Task Force, 1998). The New York City jail system reported that repeat self-injurers were responsible for 28% of self-injury patients in their medical system (Sellings et al., 2014).

ADDRESSING ATTEMPTED SUICIDE AND INTENTIONAL SELF-HARM IN CUSTODY

Muehlenkamp (2005) identified nine ways that self-injurious behavior can differ from suicide, and the first is intent. As was noted earlier, there are numerous reasons why someone would engage in self-harm, and not all involve the goal of extinguishing life. Second is the potential lethality of the act. As I have already discussed, there is some research indicating that lethality of methods used for self-harm differ by levels of suicidal intent, but that is not the case in all instances. Also, the lethality-intent relationship only provides a window into motive if every potential self-harmer understands the dangers of each action. Additionally, inmates would have to appreciate that it might be difficult to get help in time while being confined to a cell. Third is chronicity, as acts of nonfatal self-harm tend to occur many more times than suicide attempts. Fourth, NSSI incidents tend to involve a variety of methods, more so than suicide attempts. The fifth differentiation is cognitions, where suicidal individuals would think about dying or relief in the form of death as opposed to self-injurers who would likely be seeking some sort of relief without giving up on life. Sixth, at least in the community, are reactions to the two types of behavior differ. Suicidal behavior is more likely to generate reactions of care and compassion from people, whereas self-injury without suicidal intent may generate feelings of disgust and anger. In the corrections setting, this may differ in that, depending on the individual, even suicidal inmates may receive limited sympathy and support. Seventh, in the aftermath of the incident, Muehlenkamp suggests that suicide brings no relief from distress (although this is debatable, since death results in the end of everything for that individual, including distress) while self-injury can bring about a sense of calm or relief. Eighth, the demographics of those who commit both acts tend to differ, with older males being more likely to commit suicide in the community while male and female adolescents are more involved in self-harm. Ninth, prevalence for such behavior differs. Muehlenkamp estimates that the prevalence of NSSI is 4 to 14 times that of suicide attempts.

Research has supported the distinctions that Muehlenkamp (2005) makes between attempted suicide and NSSI. Earlier in this chapter, I presented a meta-analysis by Klonsky (2007) that provided evidence of people committing NSSI for reasons other than suicide. While studying women in the community, Brown et al. (2002) discovered that females who self-harmed and subsequently said that they expected to die as a result were motivated to ease the burden they believed they placed on others. Women who were not planning to die revealed that they harmed as an expression of anger, a way to self-punish, or as an effort to restore their ability to feel emotions. Studies of offenders in custody have also uncovered different motives depending on the intent of the act. Snow (2002) studied suicide attempts and NSSI among prisoners. Those with intent to die were more likely to be motivated by hopelessness, grief, homesickness, concerns about sentence length, and relationship problems. Inmates engaging in NSSI were instead attempting to relieve negative feelings, such as anger or stress. After studying attempted suicide and self-harm in custody, Lohner and Konrad (2006) concluded that "deliberate self-harm and suicide attempts should be considered separate entities" (p. 381) and argued against seeing self-harm on a suicidal behavior continuum. To do so, they argued, would result in the loss of important information for treatment and diagnosis.

Those who argue that we should view NSSI on a suicidal continuum cite evidence that NSSI is one of the strongest predictors of suicide attempts, both inside and outside of correctional facilities. Klonsky et al. (2013) gathered data from four nonincarcerated groups: adolescent psychiatric inpatients, high school students, college undergraduates, and a random sample of adults. For all four samples, the strongest predictor of suicide attempts was suicidal ideation, followed by NSSI. Depression, anxiety, impulsivity, and BPD were also associated with suicide attempts, but once all factors were considered together in a multivariate statistical model, only suicidal ideation and NSSI remained predictors of attempted suicide. Victor and Klonsky's (2014) later meta-analysis of suicide and self-harm in the community supported these findings. They found a relationship between NSSI and suicide attempts. The only variable that was more important in predicting suicide attempts was suicidal ideation.

Research in correctional facilities has also found evidence that NSSI is often associated with suicide attempts and suicides. Hawton and colleagues (2014) studied men and women who were incarcerated in England and Wales and found that those who had previously self-harmed while incarcerated had a suicide rate of 334 per 100,000 for males and 149 per 100,000 for females. In comparison, prisoners who lacked a history of self-harm while incarcerated had much lower suicide rates of 79 for males and 98 for females. In another study, females who committed near-fatal suicide attempts in British prisons were more likely to have a history of self-harm than a comparison group of inmates who had not attempted suicide (Marzano et al., 2010). Additional researchers also found relationships between NSSI and attempted and completed suicide in incarcerated populations (Humber et al., 2013; Matsumoto et al., 2005; Penn et al., 2003; Serin et al., 2002). While Moore and colleagues (2015) found that 50% of young offenders in custody who committed any type of self-harm did not also attempt suicide, 35% did engage in both NSSI and behavior that was intended to be lethal.

All this work suggests that, while inmates might engage in NSSI for reasons other than being suicidal, a substantial percentage of people who engage in self-harm do later go on to commit suicide. Correctional facility staff members may attempt to determine who is suicidal versus who is using self-harm for other reasons, but (1) this is a very difficult distinction to make, and (2) even those not intending to die require a level of protection similar or equal to those who have expressed suicidal intent. The personal and financial costs of failure to do so are too high in the correctional setting.

By committing NSSI, incarcerated men and women are demonstrating that they are having difficulty coping with problems. At best, they are not suicidal and are using a maladaptive and very dangerous way to deal with crises. At worst, while they may not have been suicidal during their past instances of self-injury, they might be now. Earlier, I noted Joiner's (2005) discussion of acquired capability for self-harm. Even in instances where people who engage in NSSI lack a history of past suicide attempts, these individuals have already crossed an important threshold that will make a suicide attempt much more feasible should they become suicidal. They have already demonstrated to themselves that they are able to overcome one's natural instincts to avoid physical harm.

With this in mind, NSSI should be treated in a manner similar to suicide attempts in the corrections setting for two reasons. First, the consequences of a mistake made during self-harm are potentially higher in the corrections setting. Regardless of motive, accidents can happen during NSSI. For example, one way that inmates have been known to self-harm is to ingest foreign objects. This could lead to unintentional choking. If a person is locked in a cell and choking, it might be very difficult to get help. If there is a roommate, perhaps that person will be able to intervene or get staff members to open the cell door and help in time. Otherwise, this action, even if it was meant to be manipulative or for stress-relief, will turn fatal. Feigned hangings can accidentally turn fatal very quickly. All it would take is for a person who is simulating a hanging to slip and lose his or her footing, and the person will lose consciousness within seconds. Someone who still has contact with the ground but is attempting to asphyxiate might lose consciousness earlier than he or she anticipated and, with no one else around, could easily die.

Second, due to prisoners' lack of access to what might be a preferred method of self-harm, individuals will have to make a choice between fore-going self-harm or resorting to a more lethal method even though death is not necessarily their intent (World Health Organization, 2007). Before stat-ing that they believed attempted suicide and deliberate self-harm should be considered separate entities, Lohner and Konrad (2006) acknowledged "at this point, it should be mentioned that every self-injurious behavior presents a serious act from the medical-psychiatric and psychological viewpoint, i.e. from the aspect of care and the viewpoint of the penal institution" (p. 378). The National Commission on Correctional Heath Care (NCCHC) Standard MH-G-04 (2015) defines "acutely suicidal" inmates as "those who engage in self-injurious behavior or threaten suicide with a specific plan" (p. 110), so the NCCHC considers self-injurious behavior to be a strong predictor of suicide. The NCCHC recommends the same supervision protocol for both self-harmers and inmates attempting suicide, regardless of their motivation.

I am not suggesting that we ignore the inmates' goal of self-harm. Lohner and Konrad (2006) are correct in that it would result in the loss of valuable information that can be used to develop a treatment plan for the inmates. My concern here is about becoming dismissive of NSSI because it is not labeled a suicide attempt. This can, and has, led to inmate deaths. Histories of NSSI cannot be allowed to cloud the judgment of penal staff. There is a risk that staff will fail to recognize the potential lethality of the inmates' actions and not appreciate that the goals of different incidents of self-harm can be very differ-ent. While the goal during a previous incident was stress relief, the goal now might be death. Staff should never assume that they know inmates' motives and should always seek assistance from qualified medical mental health pro-fessionals. The NCCHC's (2015) accreditation standards specifically note that the role of custody staff is to support the implementation of clinical decisions.

Malingering

A common concern among correctional staff is the 12- to 16-hour advantage that inmates have over them. Inmates, who are incarcerated 24 hours a day, have every moment of the day to think of ways to work on things, whether taking a normally harmless item and converting it into a weapon, planning an escape, or just finding ways to make one's time as easy as possible. Staff members, however, do their best to think about work during the 8- to 12-hour shift but then turn their attention to other aspects of their lives during their off hours. Inmates quickly become aware of staff responses to various behaviors, including acts of self-harm. Inmates can and do take advantage of suicide and at-risk inmate protocols, such as rules mandating housing transfers.

Correctional staff members may often wonder which inmates are attempting suicide for the purposes of manipulation. Early in my career, I was visiting a segregation unit for male juveniles. Since the segregation units tend to have higher levels of suicide and self-harm than other areas, I asked the officers about suicide screening and precautions. One of them responded that the inmates who are truly serious about dying will be quiet about their intentions and then succeed in killing themselves. According to this officer, the juveniles in his care who talk about suicide and make gestures or even an unsuccessful attempt must not be serious about wanting to die. While it is understandable that seasoned officers might become cynical, this type of attitude might prompt officers to ignore talk about suicide, suicidal gestures, or some types of nonfatal self-harm. This officer is not alone in his cynicism. Marzano, Adler, and Ciclitira (2015) interviewed 15 corrections officers, 13, nurses, and 2 doctors in a male prison. A common theme in the interviews was frustration over having to waste time on "attention seekers" who self-harm. Corrections agencies have a legal obligation to assist and treat people who are in crisis, as failure to do so carries legal penalties and can result in inmate deaths.

There is no way to be absolutely certain about the motives of an individual each time he or she self-harms, and this is true even for repeated self-harmers and those who have a history of being manipulative. Fagan and colleagues (2010) gave an example of a 17-year-old incarcerated male who made a suicidal gesture. The staff became convinced that he was manipulating the system, and they placed him back in his cell without any assessments or treatment. He committed suicide within a few days. Fagan and colleagues cautioned staff members against thinking of all the reasons why someone might not be suicidal, particularly in situations when they are dealing with someone with a history of self-injury. While it is certainly tempting for frustrated or burnt-out custodial staff to try to determine who is "genuine" and who is just trying to game the system, such profiling is unlikely to be productive (Cummings & Thompson, 2009). In the previously discussed research by Dear and colleagues (2000), only 8% of manipulative self-harm incidents were found to be characterized both by low lethality and a lack of suicidal intent. In other words, even manipulative actions can be dangerous. Manipulative suicide attempters should, therefore, receive a comprehensive assessment and be the focus of suicide prevention measures.

One concern about responding to NSSI is that, if done to seek attention, the custody and treatment staff's response might reward the behavior. Determining whether an act is manipulative should not be the responsibility of the officers, and these situations should always be reported to qualified mental health personnel who are better equipped to evaluate people. Cummings and Thompson (2009) recommended that mental health counselors working in the facilities help train officers about risk factors for suicide.

CONCLUSION

Suicidal ideation, attempted suicide, and NSSI are so common in the corrections setting that they are likely to be encountered by every career corrections staff member. This chapter provided an overview of characteristics of inmates who might be especially vulnerable. There are particular locations, such as facilities holding pretrial inmates and maximum security or segregation units, that have higher levels of all self-harm, regardless of motive. There is some overlap between the inmates involved in suicide attempts and NSSI, so even instances of NSSI that appear to be minor should not be dismissed, as they could be warning signs of additional harm. That additional future harm could be a genuine suicide attempt, or it could be an inmate's effort to "up the ante" to achieve the goal of manipulating staff. Regardless of motive, the lack of conventional materials for self-harm, such as sharp objects, means that inmates may resort to something more dangerous, such as a feigned hanging or swallowing objects, and the incident could accidentally turn fatal. Self-harm, whether intended to be fatal or not, is a maladaptive coping strategy that needs to be properly addressed for the safety of the individuals using it, the well-being of the inmates and staff around them, and the overall functioning of the institution.

NOTE

1. Sellings et al. (2014) used a rate per 10,000, but I adjusted it to be in line with the rates per 100,000 that are used throughout the book.

Chapter Five

Screening and Assessment

While some individuals will express suicidal ideas at a crime scene, during transport, or while incarcerated without any prompting, others will not so readily disclose such personal thoughts. For example, research on incarcerated populations has revealed that male inmates are less likely to disclose and seek assistance for suicidal thoughts than they are for more general personal problems (Deane, Skogstad, & Williams, 1999; Skogstad, Deane, & Spicer, 2005). Since many individuals are unlikely to proactively disclose such information, screening presents an opportunity for corrections personnel to directly ask inmates about indicators of suicidality and learn about each individual's mental health and substance abuse history. The American Psychiatric Association (2000) defines mental health screening as "mental health information and observations gathered for every newly admitted detainee during the intake procedures as part of the normal reception and classification process by using standard forms and following standard procedures" (p. 32).

Screening is intended not to predict suicides but to assess the suicidal tendencies of individuals in custody and to estimate the probability of a suicide occurring (Daigle, Labelle, & Cote, 2006; Pompili et al., 2009). Packman et al. (2004) compared clinicians assessing suicide risks to cardiologists assessing heart attack risk, stating "While a cardiologist cannot predict which patients will have a heart attack or when such an incident would occur, he or she can, based upon certain characteristics of a patient (e.g., obesity, dietary and exercise habits, cholesterol level, etc.), determine the individual's level of risk" (p. 675). As has been discussed in the previous chapters, there are characteristics of individuals, such as current coping abilities and mental health symptoms, psychiatric history, and history of self-harm, that place some people at higher risk than others for suicide.

Suicide screenings have been the subject of numerous debates concerning who should conduct them, what should be asked, how extensive they should be, and their efficacy in the actual prevention of suicides. While there will be people who go on to commit suicide regardless of the comprehensiveness of the screening tool and the staff's adherence to proper protocol, proper screening as part of a multifaceted suicide prevention program can save lives. Thorough screening can be useful in identifying at-risk inmates, and the development of a strong protocol for staff communication can ensure that all appropriate parties are aware of risks.

HOW COMMON IS SUICIDE SCREENING?

The requirement of medical care for inmates was outlined in *Estelle v. Gamble* (1976). The U.S. Supreme Court ruled that the denial of reasonable medical care for inmates' serious medical needs is a violation of the Eighth Amendment of the Constitution. The *Estelle* ruling left open a number of questions, however, including whether inmates' right to medical care includes mental health treatment. The court settled that question in *Bowring v. Godwin* (1977) by ruling that there should be no difference between requirements to treat physical and mental illnesses. As of this writing, the federal courts have not ruled that inmates have a specific right to proper implementation of suicide prevention protocols or even that the departments must have written suicide screening or prevention plans (Chui, 2018). They have, however, mandated broader mental health screening for correctional facilities. The Supreme Court weighed in on the issue of screening inmates for mental illness in *Ruiz v. Estelle* (1980). The *Ruiz* decision, while ruling on the constitutionality of the Texas Department of Corrections' prison health care program, presented six components of a minimally adequate mental health treatment program for correctional facilities. One component was a systematic program for screening and evaluating inmates for the purpose of identifying those who require mental health treatment. The Court later applied the *Ruiz* standards to other states, including Idaho. In 1984, the Court ruled that the Idaho State Board of Corrections was implementing a substandard mental health treatment program and ordered the state to develop a systematic program to assess inmates for mental health needs (*Balla v. Idaho State Board of Corrections*, 1984).

Professional associations, such as the National Commission on Correctional Health Care and the American Psychiatric Association, include standards for medical and mental health screening in their guidelines (American Psychiatric Association, 2000, 2016; McMullan, 2011). Screening is part of the American Correctional Association's and National Commission on Correctional Health Care's accreditation standards for correctional facilities

(ACA, 2002, 2010; NCCHC, 2015). Details of these associations' standards will be discussed throughout this chapter.

Suicide screening has become a much more common practice in all types of correctional facilities, including police lockups, over the past forty years. The National Center for Health Statistics and the Bureau of Justice Statistics surveyed state prison systems and reported that all 45 responding systems administered some type of mental health and suicide screening during admission (Karishma, Simon, DeFrances, & Maruschak, 2016). The development and implementation of screening programs did not occur evenly across local correctional jurisdictions, with smaller facilities often being slower to introduce screening. Borum and Rand (2000) surveyed all 67 county jails in Florida in the late 1990s and found that the use of screening varied by jail size, with only 13% of the small jails conducting comprehensive assessments. Additionally, only 25% of the small jails had access to a psychiatrist, and that was only on an "as-needed" basis. Tartaro and Ruddell (2006) conducted a national survey of small jails and found that 83% of the facilities used some sort of suicide screening form, and 54% of the jails provided suicide prevention training to its officers each year. Many small jails were not able to offer as many services as the larger institutions due to funding and resource limitations. Applegate and Sitren (2008) reported differences between rural and urban jails in their ability to offer mental health services, with larger, urban jails having more resources for mental health services compared to the smaller, rural jurisdictions.

Screening can be especially difficult when offenders are under the influence of drugs or alcohol. In their review of deaths in police custody, Hannan and associates (2010) reported that 51% of the 247 people who died in British police custody over a ten-year period had not been screened at the time of death. The most common reason for the lack of screening was detainees' levels of intoxication. Anyone who is unable to be screened due to substance use needs to be watched carefully and placed in a safe setting until screening can be completed. The ACA's (2010) Core Jail Standards call for detoxification to occur under medical supervision that complies with the jurisdiction's laws. ACA notes that facilities should establish written standards that identify the criteria used to determine when an inmate's medical condition due to detox requires a transfer to an outside facility.

RISK FACTORS

Screening procedures attempt to measure inmates on several risk factors. Risk factors for suicide and self-harm are "the characteristics and circumstances associated with an individual which indicate a greater potential or likelihood of suicidal behavior" (Newcomen, 2014a, p. 7). As noted in Chapter 2, risk factors are commonly thought of in terms of static or dynamic factors. Static factors, also known as fixed factors, are not changeable and include things such as psychiatric and self-harm history, personality, offending history, and demographic characteristics. Dynamic factors involve situational and personal characteristics, such as coping abilities and current mental health symptoms that better describe individuals' present circumstances (McMullan, 2011; World Health Organization, 2007). Both sets of factors are relevant to risk assessment, but given the fluctuating nature of the dynamic factors, it is important to continuously screen inmates to record any changes throughout incarceration. Repeated screenings and careful observation can aid staff members in detecting signs of the onset of a suicidal crisis (McMullan, 2011).

There are a multitude of risk factors for suicide. Joiner, Walker, Rudd, and Jobes (1999) identified seven domains of risk factors. The first and most important domain is previous suicidal behavior, including thoughts of suicide, single attempts, and multiple attempts, with type of behavior and number of previous suicide attempts being the most important. A history of multiple attempts combined with any of the other six domains would qualify that individual for placement in at least a moderate risk group. The second domain involves current suicidal symptoms and whether the individual has a plan for an attempt or has had less well-defined thoughts about self-harm. Third, what recent triggers have occurred in the individual's life? Fourth, has the person been diagnosed with a fourth edition Diagnostic and Statistical Manual of Mental Disorders (DSM-IV) Axis I or II disorder, and is the person feeling hopeless? The fifth domain includes additional factors that are associated with higher risk of suicide, such as abuse history, change in living arrangements, change in residence, and family problems. The sixth domain is level of impulsivity. The seventh domain includes the presence or absence of protective factors, such as social support, coping skills, and self-control. Joiner and colleagues proposed the use of a five-item continuum of suicidality to assess risk level, ranging from nonexistent to extreme.

The ACA (2002) mandates that screening procedures for accredited facilities include collection of information about several risk factors, including present suicidal ideation, history of suicidal behavior, currently prescribed psychotropic medication, current mental health complaints, current treatment for a mental health problem, history of substance abuse, and history of psychiatric treatment. Additionally, the ACA requires that screeners observe the inmate's behavior and appearance and note any noticeable symptoms of depression, anxiety, psychosis, and/or aggression. Screeners should also make note of information pertaining to any past abuse or trauma.

Warning Signs and Triggers

Inmates' emotions will fluctuate throughout their incarceration, and there are specific things that corrections and medical staff can look for to guide supervision and treatment plans. Rudd and associates (2006) discussed the importance of looking for "warning signs" that imply a near-term risk. The authors defined a warning sign as "the earliest detectable sign that indicates heightened risk for suicide in the near-term (i.e., within minutes, hours, or days). A warning sign refers to some feature of the developing outcome of interest (suicide) rather than to a distinct construct (e.g., risk factor) that predicts or may be causally related to suicide" (Rudd et al., 2006, p. 258). It is important for all correctional staff members to be able to recognize the warning signs that could indicate that a suicide attempt is a possibility within the next few hours or days. Correctional staff, rather than medical personnel, are the people who have day-to-day contact with inmates and would, therefore, be in the best position to observe these signs. Some subtle signs that may precede self-harm are evidence of hopelessness, rage, reckless activity, withdrawal from friends, anxiety, change in sleeping patterns, and dramatic mood changes (Rudd et al., 2006). Giving away one's belongings is another potential warning sign. The NCCHC's (2015) accreditation standards call for all officers in contact with inmates to receive, at minimum, annual suicide prevention training. Officers working in the intake areas of the institution should receive even more training.

Newcomen (2014a, 2014b) encouraged correctional personnel to look for "triggers," which are events that are highly specific to each individual but may serve to increase a person's risk for self-harm or suicide. Some examples of triggers are the potentially dangerous situations that were discussed in Chapter 3, such as anticipation of a court appearance, the period following a court appearance with a negative outcome, announcement of new charges, key anniversaries, straining of relationships, placement in segregation, bereavement, transfer to a different facility, interpersonal problems with other inmates, and immigration issues. Newcomen (2014b) recommended that triggers should be listed prominently on the inmates' records. Additional screening around these times is recommended.

Pompili et al.'s (2009) work on suicide risk factors was derived from experience with psychiatric inpatients and includes four domains. The four domains are: environmental factors (type of housing, supervision levels), psychosocial factors, distal factors (level of family support, history of suicidal behavior, and mental health history), and proximal factors (current feelings of hopelessness or feelings of being bullied, suicidal intent or plan, loss of coping options and narrowed prospects for the future). Corrections staff, especially officers working directly with inmates, should be trained to recognize proximal factors and understand the institution's policies for communicating their observations and concerns to the appropriate personnel.

SCREENING IN THE COMMUNITY AND CHALLENGES FOR CORRECTIONAL ENVIRONMENTS

Much work has been done to develop instruments that will identify risk factors of suicide among nonincarcerated individuals. Wingate, Joiner, Walker, Rudd, and Jobes (2004) noted that organizations such as the American Association of Suicidology, the American Foundation for Suicide Prevention, and the American Psychological Association list over 75 warning signs or risk factors for suicide. Wingate and colleagues polled over 100 audiences at continuing education seminars on suicide and depression and asked the audience members to tell them the single most important suicide assessment question. The respondents generally gave one of two responses: (1) "Do you have suicidal ideas?" or (2) "Do you have a suicide plan?" Wingate and colleagues then developed two sets of variables relating to these questions. For the "suicidal desire and ideation" factor, the authors identified absence of reasons for living, a wish to die, a wish to not live, a passive suicide attempt (reckless behavior), frequency of suicidal ideation, lack of deterrents to an attempt, and talk of death or suicide. For the "resolved plans and preparation" factor, they identified courage to make the attempt, competence to make the attempt, availability of means and opportunity for the attempt, specificity of the plan, preparations for the attempt, duration of suicidal ideation, and intensity of suicidal ideation. While it will be difficult for corrections personnel to detect some of these indicators, these should be included in the training curriculum for every staff member. Line staff who understand that these may be signs of an impending suicide can be trained to alert their supervisor and the mental health team.

While many factors associated with suicide in the community are applicable to the correctional population, there are some differences that have implications for screening practices. Screening tools developed with community populations in mind might lack validity when used in the incarceration setting. In other words, once applied to a different population, such as incarcerated individuals, the tools may not measure what they were designed to measure. One example of this is measuring high-risk behaviors as a potential warning sign of suicide. For inmates, such activity would not necessarily be a potential warning sign for suicide so much as it would be part of the high-risk lifestyles that tend to come with criminal behavior and drug or alcohol addiction.

Perry, Marandos, Coulton, and Johnson (2010) warned about the transferability of suicide risk scales that were developed originally for the psychiatric population in the community. For example, the Beck Depression Inventory—II (BDI-II) (Beck, Steer, & Brown, 1996) is a well-regarded instrument, but use of some of the items with an incarcerated population would generate problems with validity. The BDI-II includes the statements "I feel particularly guilty" and "I feel I am being punished." These items were generated with the intention of measuring symptoms of depression, but when they are posed to criminal offenders, responses could actually reflect inmates' feelings of guilt about crimes that, by the nature of their incarceration, they are actually being punished for at that time.

Smith et al. (2013) discovered similar potential drawbacks to using an instrument to assess acquired capability for suicide with inmates. The Acquired Capability for Suicide Scale (ACSS) has been used with community samples to differentiate suicide attempters from non-attempters. When tested on inmates, however, the ACSS was not able to make such a distinction. One possible explanation was that inmates are likely to interpret some items differently compared to members of the community. For example, the statements "I am not at all afraid to die" and "people describe me as fearless" might be interpreted by some inmates, particularly males, as measures of their toughness, a trait highly valued in the correctional setting.

Validity issues are not the only potential drawback to using screening items designed for nonincarcerated individuals. Teplin and Swartz (1989) identified three challenges to using community-based psychometric indices in correctional facilities. First, the length of some of the instruments is too long. Correctional facilities vary in their mission and resources. Prisons, particularly admission and diagnostic facilities, may have the time and personnel to conduct full mental health assessments on some or all inmates, but jails, and especially police lockups, do not have the time or the staff for lengthy sessions. As a result, widely used instruments, such as the Minnesota Multiphasic Personality Inventory (MMPI) or the Millon Personality Inventory, are not practical for many correctional facilities given their required one- to two-hour administration period. Second, some screening tools must be administered by mental health professionals. While mental health screening conducted by mental health professionals is the ideal situation and is recommended (Georgiou, Souza, Holder, Stone, & Davies, 2015), it is rarely feasible given time and staffing constraints. As was noted earlier, smaller jails tend to have difficulty budgeting for and employing mental health staff (Borum & Rand, 2000). Third, Teplin and Swartz note that some community-designed screening tools require participants to be able to read English at a certain grade level. This can be problematic in the corrections setting, as there may be non-English-speaking inmates and low levels of English literacy. The MMPI-2 and the Millon Clinical Multiaxial Inventory (MCMI-III) require at least an eighth-grade reading level, so it would be inappropriate for half of the incarcerated population (Kroner, Mills, Grazia, & Talbert, 2011).

Teplin and Swartz (1989) presented the Referral Decision Scale (RDS) as a screening tool option for correctional staff, since it only takes 10 minutes to administer, and it is simple enough that facilities could rely on trained correctional personnel, rather than clinicians, to administer it. The RDS was not designed to diagnose inmates but rather allow staff to identify those who need a mental health referral due to the possible presence of a serious mental illness. The RDS has three subscales for schizophrenia, bi-polar disorder, and major depression. Researchers have found mixed results when attempting to validate this instrument (Slate, Buffington-Vollum, & Johnson, 2013). As with some previously mentioned tools, the RDS also had some validity issues due to the unusual nature of incarceration. For example, the scale includes items meant to measure the potential for schizo-phrenia that ask inmates if they feel they are being spied on, followed, or being plotted against. While answering affirmatively to these items would likely indicate paranoia for most people, it is possible that many inmates were being watched as police investigated them, and they continue to be watched and followed in custody. An affirmative answer to this question by an inmate may have a completely different meaning than an affirma-tive answer from someone in the community. Additionally, when the RDS includes questions about feeling guilty, offenders might feel that way on account of their crimes. The RDS also attempts to gain information about possible mental illnesses by asking about the presence of racing thoughts and lethargy, but offenders might be experiencing those due to substance abuse. One additional criticism of RDS is that the tool tends to focus on chronic symptoms of mental illness rather than current symptoms (Veysey, Steadman, Morrissey, Johnsen, & Beckstead, 1998).

Finding appropriate survey items is not the only challenge unique to the correctional setting. In the community, there is much more of an opportu-nity to find a private location to handle screenings. Booking areas in jails and police stations can be noisy and lack privacy (Hayes, 2003). The author has personally witnessed a situation where the screening process was being conducted in an area of a jail that was visible and within hearing distance of other inmates. This ability for others to see and hear the inmates answer questions about their mental health can result in inmates responding to screenings in socially desirable ways rather than being truthful (Kroner et al., 2011).

IMPLEMENTING A SUICIDE SCREENING PROGRAM IN CUSTODY

It is clear that there are numerous obstacles to establishing a sound suicide screening process in prisons and jails. What follows are suggestions that can improve efficiency and effectiveness.

Triage

An alternative to conducting full assessments of every inmate and involving clinical staff in that work is to take a triage approach. The American Psychiatric Association (2016) recommends the use of a triage model, beginning with an essential mental health screening for all inmates upon arrival to the facility. This involves a structured inquiry of current and past suicidal ideation, prior psychiatric hospitalizations, and current and past medications. I would also recommend asking about history of NSSI and suicide attempts as well as taking note of any visible scars that are indicative of self-harm. These screenings can be handled by a trained booking officer. If the results of the screening do not present areas of concern, then a more comprehensive mental health screening can be conducted by a mental health professional sometime within the first two weeks of incarceration. If, however, the initial screening produces red flags, that individual should be referred for a brief mental health assessment with a mental health professional within 72 hours of referral (ACA, 2002; NCCHC, 2015). The brief mental health assessment should take place in an office with sound privacy, if possible (APA, 2016). If the initial screening indicates an area of great concern, the staff should skip the brief mental health assessment and go right to a comprehensive mental health evaluation. The APA (2000) defines a comprehensive mental health evaluation as a "face-to-face interview of the patient and a review of all reasonably available health care records and collateral information. It concludes with a diagnostic formulation and, at least, an initial treatment plan" (p. 36). The comprehensive assessment involves a psychiatrist or another properly licensed or credentialed mental health professional. The staff member conducting the evaluation should review all screening data and any other health or behavioral information that has been added to the inmate's file since, observe the inmate, review the inmate's mental health history, and formulate a treatment and management plan. If, at this point, the inmate's psychiatric needs exceed the treatment and supervision resources of the institution, arrangements should be made for a transfer to a psychiatric facility (ACA, 2002).

Triage programs are likely to reduce, but not eliminate, the demand for clinicians in the correctional setting. Correctional facilities still need the assistance of clinical staff to work with inmates who are in crisis as well as those with mental illness and addiction issues. For smaller facilities that have difficulty finding the budget to employ staff, one option is telephonic triage. Such a service provides access to qualified mental health professionals 24 hours a day, every day of the year (Hayes, 2004a).

All inmates do need to receive a full mental health assessment early in their initial incarceration period as well as after transfers. This point about transfers is very important. Screening has become an increasingly accepted part of initial entry into a prison or jail but, given the dynamic nature of some of the most important risk factors, inmates should be screened and assessed repeatedly throughout incarceration. The ACA (2002) requires that all accredited institutions conduct screenings following intersystem transfers. By the ACA standards, not only is screening required, but a mental health assessment conducted by a qualified mental health professional needs to be completed within 14 days of transfer, unless the inmate has had such an assessment in the past 90 days. In that case, the assessment is only conducted if the designated mental health authority deems it necessary.

Establishing Trust

In any assessment procedure, it is important for the interviewer to establish a good relationship with the client. As was noted earlier, inmates have reasons to be dishonest when being asked about vulnerability. Shea (2002) provided seven justifications for an inmate to be evasive or not forthcoming: (1) feels ashamed for being so weak to think about suicide; (2) believes that suicide is immoral or a sin; (3) considers the topic of suicide to be taboo; (4) does not want interviewer to think that he/she is crazy; (5) worries about being locked up if truthful; (6) client truly wants to die, so it is best not to warn anyone who could interfere; and (7) client is convinced that no one can help.

Inmates have a legitimate reason to be concerned about showing weakness, particularly in male, higher security facilities where they are expected to exhibit toughness. While one may think that Shea's (2002) fifth concern of being locked up would be irrelevant, given that inmates are already "locked up," inmates who are severely mentally ill or in crisis do have reason to be concerned in some facilities. They might be placed in a humiliating outfit, such as a paper gown or a tear-proof smock (nicknamed "The Turtle Suit" in some jails) or put in a segregated area where their access to programs and recreation time are restricted. Such a move and change in status can damage inmates' reputations, since they are exhibiting signs of weakness. Prior to a lawsuit in the 1990s, inmates in the Los Angeles

County Jail who revealed to staff that they were suicidal or mentally ill were given a special yellow jumpsuit to wear and were targeted for exploitation (Butterfield, 1998). When questioned about their willingness to report suicidal ideation to correctional mental health staff in a New York state prison, 42% of the general population inmates and 31% assigned to an intermediate care program for individuals with mental illness responded that they would be unlikely to disclose that information (Way, Kaufman, Knowl, & Chlebowski, 2013).

It is important for correctional staff to respond to inmates' suicidality in a way that does not discourage inmates from disclosing mental health information. Deane et al. (1999) studied the question of inmates' willingness to disclose suicidal ideation to staff in New Zealand and reported some discouraging findings. Inmates were significantly more likely to seek help for personal problems than for suicidal thoughts. Skogstad and associates (2005) followed up on this work by attempting to identify barriers to help-seeking among inmates. Inmates doubted that staff members would adhere to confidentiality and worried that disclosures would then be used against them to justify denial of early release and an increase to their security rating. They were also skeptical that mental health staff would be available if they experienced a crisis during nonbusiness hours. In addition to concerns about the availability and trustworthiness of the staff, inmates also remarked that they believed that truly suicidal inmates would just kill themselves rather than discussing it, and that those inmates who do want to talk are attention seekers who lack strength. Inmates did acknowledge that talking about their problems would likely be helpful, but they had to weigh that relief against damaging their reputations among the staff and fellow inmates.

While inmates might be reluctant to seek help and be open with screeners and other institutional staff, family members might be willing and able to help provide valuable insight about the inmates' mental health histories. While it is ideal to establish positive working relationships with all inmates' families, these relationships are even more important when staff members are attempting to screen and treat adolescents. Young adults can present special problems for staff, since they are more likely than adults to have difficulty verbalizing their thoughts and feelings. In these cases, staff may be able to contact family members who are familiar with the incarcerated individual's psychiatric history and recent emotions and behaviors. Regardless of whether the detainee is a juvenile or adult, it is possible that family members will be aware of recent suicidal ideation, histories of suicide attempts, and history of medication compliance and will be willing to discuss these matters with either custody or mental health staff.

Multicultural Competency

Correctional facilities often hold diverse groups of people, particularly marginalized members of society. This is an important fact to keep in mind when considering the creation or adoption of screening instruments. All correctional staff should receive cultural competency training to assist them in better understanding the backgrounds of their clients. For example, the Victoria Department of Justice Correctional Services Task Force (1998) recommends providing Aboriginal inmates contact with trained Aboriginal and Torres Strait Islander staff within 24 hours of reception. The American Correctional Association (2002) mandates that all accredited facilities have suicide prevention and intervention plans that acknowledge the impact of demographic and cultural parameters on suicidal behavior.

Some regions of the United States have a high representation of Native Americans in correctional facilities. Native Americans are at a disproportionate risk for suicide in the community (Garroutte, Goldberg, Beals, Herrell, & Manson, 2003) and in correctional institutions (National Institute of Justice, 2004). Native Americans tend to be less open to correctional staff when being screened for mental health and substance abuse problems. This is particularly troublesome given the high frequency of alcoholism in this population. Multicultural competency training may help staff understand that some Native American cultures consider mental illness to be something that only affects whites and regard screening as prying into private matters. Some Native American cultures consider it appropriate to avoid discussing negative topics, such as mental health troubles, for fear that such conversations will allow spirits to enter their lives and bring about problems. There are ways to ask questions in a manner that will be considered less threatening to such groups. If possible, civilians, rather than officers, should conduct the screening in as private a setting as possible. A rewording of some questions may also be helpful. Instead of asking specifically about negative actions, such as suicide, some Native Americans might be more willing to disclose problems if they are asked questions in a less direct manner, such as "are you feeling all right" rather than asking them if they are thinking of suicide (National Institute of Justice, 2004).

Researchers in New Zealand have found similar reluctance among Maori inmates when studying their willingness to seek assistance for psychological issues in prison (Deane et al., 1999). Jail and prison staff should be mindful of the diverse cultures of their inmates and take steps to increase trust and cooperation among indigenous groups. Later in this chapter, I will discuss the importance of validating screening tools to ensure that they are appropriate for the population of each institution. This is especially important to consider when screening racial and ethnic minorities. Administering instruments that are inappropriate for use with the population likely to be frequenting a specific facility can be detrimental to screening efforts.

Staff Buy-In and Communication

One way that management can communicate the importance of screening for suicide is to make suicide prevention training a component of initial and follow-up training for all staff who have contact with inmates. The National Commission on Correctional Health Care's (2015) accreditation standards include suicide prevention training for all officers who work with inmates. This training must include, at minimum, lessons on recognizing the signs and symptoms of mental illness, intellectual disabilities, and substance abuse; learning how to communicate with individuals who are mentally ill; suicide prevention and intervention procedures; and proper referral procedures for inmates who are having a mental health problem. This training needs to be repeated annually for facilities to be eligible for accreditation.

There is a risk of mental health screening turning into merely an exercise in paperwork. Staff may screen inmates, because it is part of the checklist of things that must be done as part of the admissions process, but the screening is only half of the process. The next step is to use that information to make supervision and treatment decisions. Facilities can adopt good screening tools, but they will be of little use if the staff fails to implement a screening plan properly. I was once in a jail intake area where a corrections officer was speeding through a suicide screening with an inmate. The instrument contained a question designed to determine whether the person being screened was looking forward to anything in the future, as this has been found to be an important warning sign for suicide. When the officer asked "are you looking forward to the future," the inmate explained that he didn't understand the question. The officer rephrased it as "are you looking forward to getting out of here?" Of course, the inmate replied "well, yeah," and the officer quickly got through the rest of the form. The officer's reinterpretation of that question in his rush to finish the task resulted in the loss of valuable information. In this case, the officer needed to either be retrained or be assigned to other duties. Periodic monitoring of inmate screening can help identify staff who are either experiencing burnout or who do not have an appropriate skill set for the task. Staff should also participate in periodic in-service training to sharpen their skills. Once staff members are properly trained, supervisors must work with the rest of the institution to ensure that the results of those screenings are informing housing, supervision, and treatment decisions.

Screening is also just one part of the process of monitoring inmates for suicidality. Staff will be exposed to information outside of the formal screening, and this information could be vital to the health of the inmates. It is incumbent on everyone in the criminal justice system who has contact with the defendant or inmate to share any information that could constitute a warning sign of any type of self-harm. There has been litigation in the United States following suicides in custody that could have been prevented if transporting officers shared information about what transpired at the crime scene or in transport with correctional personnel.[1] While it may seem unethical to medical and mental health staff who are new to the corrections field that they are expected to share information with custody personnel, officers responsible for monitoring inmates in the living areas must know if inmates are at risk of self-harm (APA, 2016).

All mental health screening programs should include specific information outlining precisely which staff members are responsible for each set of responsibilities. In a review of self-inflicted deaths in United Kingdom prisons, Newcomen (2014a) found that prison officers and health care staff sometimes attributed responsibilities to each other, and there was little outlined procedure for how clinicians should integrate any information regarding risk of self-harm into their clinical assessments. There needs to be clear allocation of responsibilities for someone to compile all relevant information in order for there to be a holistic consideration of risk. Newcomen (2016) also recommended that all prisoners arrive with a Person Escort Record that includes information on known risks and vulnerabilities as well as information about any significant events that occurred in court, during the transport, or at the previous facility. After studying deaths in police custody in the United Kingdom, the Independent Police Complaints Commission (Hannan et al., 2010) recommended that, at the end of each shift, officers communicate information regarding at-risk inmates to the next shift verbally and in front of the closed-circuit television (CCTV), and the incoming shift should acknowledge, in writing, that they have been fully briefed.

Some suicidal people may have rescue fantasies in which they hope that friends, acquaintances, or even strangers will rescue them from self-destruction. Inmates may joke about killing themselves, write suicide notes that they leave to be found, communicate their wish to live and be saved, or behave in a noticeably depressed manner. These cues should be taken seriously by staff and other inmates. It is useful to post a daily list of inmates considered to be suicidal risks so that all the correctional staff are informed, but this list cannot be anywhere that is visible to inmates. The risk of other inmates finding out about suicidal ideation has been found to be a drawback to inmates seeking help (Skogstad et al., 2005).

Communication should also extend to the family members of the inmates. As noted earlier, family members may have valuable information about relatives' mental health history, including previous suicide attempts and hospitalizations. Family who maintain communication with inmates while they are incarcerated might also notice changes in inmates' mood, speech, writing, and behavior in visits, phone calls, and letters. Family should be encouraged to notify corrections officials if they become concerned about the incarcerated individual's mental state (World Health Organization, 2007), and there should be procedures for the communication of that information within the facility.

One more source of information that should not be overlooked is other inmates. In Chapter 6, I will discuss using trusted inmate volunteers to assist in suicide prevention measures as a supplement to staff efforts. Inmates who are not even an active part of a suicide prevention program, however, can still be valuable sources of information. Corrections officers can simply ask inmates that they know well "how is your roommate doing?" While some inmates will not disclose anything to officers, others will if they become concerned about their friends who may be at risk.

DOES SCREENING PREVENT SUICIDE?

Screening and appropriate response to the results can help to prevent correctional suicides. Patterson and Hughes (2008) studied suicides in California prisons and determined that 63% were either foreseeable or preventable. The researchers defined foreseeable as "cases in which already known and reasonably available information indicates the presence of a substantial or high risk of suicide that requires clinical, custody, or administrative interventions to prevent self-harm" (pp. 679–680) and preventable as "situations where if some additional information had been gathered or been undertaken, usually as required in existing policies and procedures, the likelihood of a completed suicide might have been substantially reduced" (p. 680). In the nearly two-thirds of suicide incidents that Patterson and Hughes examined, information regarding a now-deceased inmate's suicide risk was known, reasonably available, or could have been gathered, in most cases, by following existing policies. Screening can fail to prevent suicides if the information is not used as part of a comprehensive and properly implemented treatment plan.

Gallagher and Dobrin (2005) surveyed every juvenile residential facility in the United States in 2000 (N = 3690). About 60% of these facilities screened all youths, and another quarter screened only some youths. Facilities that screened all youth were less likely to have had a serious suicide attempt, as were those facilities that screened within the first 24 hours after admission. It is possible, however, that institutions with screening procedures also had more comprehensive suicide awareness and prevention programs in general.

In a very early study of the effectiveness of suicide screening, Hopes and Shaull (1986) explained how one jurisdiction was able to screen inmates for suicide risk and use this information to guide housing and supervision decisions. Upon studying the most recent suicides and attempts in their jail, staff members found some patterns. Specifically, they noted that the deceased tended to have a history of substance abuse, experienced suicidal ideation and hopelessness, and had a history of more than five prior suicide attempts. By sensitizing the correctional staff to this information and putting it to use, the number of inmates placed on suicide watch was cut from 15 per month to 7.5 per month, and the number of suicide attempts was cut from 2.5 per month to 0.3 per month. Therefore, identifying some predictors of future suicidal behavior using standard psychological/psychiatric screening reduced the suicide watches and reduced the incidence of suicidal behavior. An important lesson here is that the staff used the results of the screening to inform their supervision work, and this allowed them to get the most value out of the work put into the screening.

TYPES OF SCREENING AND ASSESSMENT

The focus of the screening will likely vary a great deal depending on the goals of the institution, the expected length of the inmate's stay, and the resources and available staff at each facility. Classification centers for federal or state prison systems, for example, may use a long assessment instrument, administered by a clinician, with the intention of identifying long-term treatment goals. Booking officers in jail, however, would likely be interested in a very short and simple assessment to determine whether inmates are at immediate risk.

There are several suicide screening instruments that have been developed and used with incarcerated populations. They vary a great deal in length, complexity, and ease of administration. Some assessments rely on self-reports from inmates, while others require a corrections staff member or even a clinician to provide opinions about the inmates' mental state. I will describe a few of these tools here. This is by no means an exhaustive list of the screening instruments that are currently available, but it will give readers who are looking for a particular type of screening tool some options. Before that, I need to explain how to produce evidence that the screening is appropriate for a given population.

A good screening tool is sensitive and specific. Sensitivity refers to the proportion screened with an illness who are correctly identified by the screen as having that illness. Screenings that lack sensitivity are problematic due to their high number of false-negatives. Specificity means that individuals who are not at risk for suicide will be classified as low/no risk. Low specificity results in high numbers of false-positives (Veysey et al., 1998). Inmates who are false-positives will be given resources and possible housing assignments that are unnecessary. False-negatives are a larger concern in that they require assistance but are not identified as needing it. Readers must understand that, while findings of high sensitivity and specificity for screening tools in one setting is certainly a positive development, this does not mean that the tool will be appropriate for a different incarcerated population elsewhere.

Examples of Brief Screening Instruments for Use in Correctional Settings

The Brief Jail Mental Health Screen (BJMHS) (Table 5.1) was derived from the previously discussed RDS. This is a free tool that can be administered by trained correctional officers in three to five minutes. Veysey and colleagues (1998) reworded some of the items on the RDS and changed the time frame from lifetime occurrence to current conditions (see below). The adjustment of time frame from lifetime occurrence to a focus on current symptoms is an effort to identify those who are in acute crisis. The first six items ask inmates

Table 5.1.   Brief Jail Mental Health Screen

	No	Yes	Comments
1. Do you *currently* believe that someone can control your mind by putting thoughts into your head or taking thoughts out of your head?			
2. Do you *currently* feel that other people know your thoughts and can read your mind?			
3. Have you *currently* lost or gained as much as two pounds a week for several weeks without even trying?			
4. Have you or your family or friends noticed that you are *currently* more active than you usually are?			
5. Do you *currently* feel like you have to talk or move more slowly than you usually do?			
6. Have there *currently* been a few weeks when you felt like you were useless or sinful?			
7. Are you *currently* taking any medication prescribed for you by a physician for any emotional or mental health problems?			
8. Have you *ever* been in a hospital for emotional or mental health problems?			

Source: Policy Research Associates (2005). *Brief Jail Mental Health Screen.* Delmar, NY: Policy Research Associates. Retrieved from http://www.prainc.com.
Note: Inmates should be referred for further mental health evaluation with a YES on item 7 or 8 OR a YES on at least two other items. Screeners can also refer for any other reason.

about mental health symptoms within the past six months. Any affirmative answer is followed up by a question asking about whether the respondent is currently experiencing that symptom. The final two questions are about lifetime hospitalization for mental health or emotional problems and whether the person is currently prescribed medication for mental health or emotional problems (Steadman, Scott, Osher, Agnese, & Robbins, 2005). An affirmative answer to two of any of the symptom questions or an endorsement of either of the hospitalization or medication questions requires a referral for a more extensive mental health evaluation (Policy Research Associates, 2005).

Steadman and colleagues (2005) tested the validity of the BJMHS by comparing its results to the Suicide Prevention Screening Guidelines (SPSG) and Structured Clinical Interviews for DSM-IV (SCID). Upon screening 10,330 detainees with the BJMHS, 11% of the inmates were referred for more extensive mental health assessment. The clinical interviews were used for comparison purposes, and 74% of men who did both the BJMHS and the SCID were classified the same way, as were 62% of women. The BJMHS had a false-negative rate of 15% for men but 35% for women. In a later study, Steadman, Robbins, Islam, and Osher (2007) added four additional items to the BJMHS but did not find that these items improved validity over the original instrument.

While the results of the BJMHS are promising, this does not mean that this instrument, or any other, can necessarily be used with inmates of different cultures. For example, Evans, Brinded, Simpson, Frampton, and Mulder (2010) tested the BJMHS and another short instrument, the English Mental Health Screen (EMHS), in a correctional facility in New Zealand. Whereas the BJMHS tends to result in a 10% referral of inmates in American facilities, 23% of New Zealand's prisoners were referred for further evaluation. The EMHS had much higher false-positive and false-negative rates with New Zealand prisoners and a slightly higher referral rate compared to when it was used with British prisoners.

The Correctional Services of Canada performs a very basic, quick screening of its federal inmates and then uses the results to determine who requires further evaluation by a clinician (Wichmann, Serin, & Motiuk, 2000). The Suicide Risk Assessment Scale (SRAS, also called Suicide Probability Scale [SPS] in some publications) requires intake officers to respond to nine statements ("yes" or "no") concerning their perceptions of an inmate. Affirmative responses to any question prompt a referral to a clinician. The SRAS consists of the following statements:

1. The offender may be suicidal.
2. The offender has made a previous suicide attempt.

3. The offender has undergone recent psychological/psychiatric intervention.
4. The offender has experienced recent loss of a relative/spouse.
5. The offender is presently experiencing major problems (i.e., legal).
6. The offender is currently under the influence of alcohol/drugs.
7. The offender shows signs of depression.
8. The offender has expressed suicidal ideation.
9. The offender has a suicide plan. (Wichmann et al., 2000, p. 10)

Wichmann and colleagues (2000) compared the files of 731 Canadian inmates who had attempted suicide to a random selection of 731 inmates who had not attempted suicide. They tested the SRAS and found that the checklist did discriminate between the two groups. The three strongest predictors of suicide attempts were disciplinary problems, contraband incidents, and previous adult convictions. The instrument had a false-positive rate of 14% and false-negative rate of 20%.

Daigle and colleagues (2006) tested SRAS and the SPS. The Suicide Probability Scale was developed by Cull and Gill (1998) and is a self-report instrument that takes about 20 minutes and includes 36 items. SPS respondents are placed into four categories: subclinical, mild, moderate, and severe. Unlike the BJMHS and the SRAS, the SPS needs to be administered by someone with a background in psychology. Daigle and colleagues found both instruments to be equally effective.

Perry and Olason (2009) tested the Suicide Concerns for Offenders in Prison Environment (SCOPE) (Table 5.2). SCOPE is a 27-item, self-administered, paper-and-pencil test that was generated by studying risk factors among British inmates. Inmates are asked to respond to statements on a six-point Likert-type scale. Fifteen items measure optimism and self-worth, while 12 items focus on the presence of a social network and problem-solving abilities. The researchers tested the validity of the instrument by comparing SCOPE to results of the Beck Hopelessness Scale among a sample of inmates. The researchers found SCOPE had moderate reliability, was correlated with the Beck Hopelessness Scale, and was able to discriminate between those who were at risk for suicide and those with no known history of self-harm.

Earthrowl and McCully (2002) field-tested two brief screening tools to identify female inmates who might have a psychiatric disturbance and who might be at risk for self-harm. They used the RDS (Teplin & Swartz, 1989) for identification of possible psychiatric disturbance that requires more in-depth assessment, and the Suicide Checklist (SCL). The SCL is short, with 11 items measuring symptoms of depression and suicide ideation and six questions measuring history of suicidal behavior, problem behaviors, and psychiatric issues. Trained corrections staff may administer the survey, and they have to indicate that each item is either not in evidence (0), somewhat

Table 5.2. Suicide Concerns of Offenders in Prison Environment (SCOPE)

Name:

Are you on remand: Yes   No

Sex: Male   Female

Age:

PLEASE READ THE FOLLOWING STATEMENTS AND CIRCLE THE RESPONSE ON THE RIGHT TO INDICATE IF YOU AGREE OR DISAGREE

PLEASE CIRCLE YOUR RESPONSE

	Strongly Agree	Mildly Agree	Agree	Disagree	Mildly Disagree	Strongly Disagree
1. I will not feel lonely in my room on my own.	1	2	3	4	5	6
2. If I had a job I would not commit crime.	1	2	3	4	5	6
3. If I were feeling suicidal I would speak to someone.	1	2	3	4	5	6
4. I will speak to an officer when I have a problem.	1	2	3	4	5	6
5. If I were on remand I would not feel stressed out.	1	2	3	4	5	6
6. I do not think about harming myself.	1	2	3	4	5	6
7. I do not feel suicidal when I receive bad news.	1	2	3	4	5	6
8. I feel fine about coming into this establishment.	1	2	3	4	5	6
9. If I had been arrested I would try and get in contact with my family.	1	2	3	4	5	6
10. If I had been arrested I would say I was sorry.	1	2	3	4	5	6
11. If I am nervous I do not lose my appetite.	1	2	3	4	5	6
12. If I stole money for drugs I would feel like I had let myself down.	1	2	3	4	5	6
13. I do not feel fed up.	1	2	3	4	5	6

14. I think that everyone likes me.	1	2	3	4	5	6
15. The day before I am due in court I do not think about the future.	1	2	3	4	5	6
16. I enjoy everything.	1	2	3	4	5	6
17. I do not feel helpless.	1	2	3	4	5	6
18. If I worry about things I sleep OK.	1	2	3	4	5	6
19. If I were depressed I would talk to someone.	1	2	3	4	5	6
20. My family supports me.	1	2	3	4	5	6
21. I do not think about how I can end my life.	1	2	3	4	5	6
22. If I had a fight with a prisoner I would ask to see the governor.	1	2	3	4	5	6
23. I can think straight when I am depressed.	1	2	3	4	5	6
24. I feel like there is hope in my life.	1	2	3	4	5	6
25. If I were depressed I would not think about harming myself.	1	2	3	4	5	6
26. If I had a supportive family I would not kill myself.	1	2	3	4	5	6
27. I always turn up in court.	1	2	3	4	5	6

Source: Perry, A. E. & Olason, D. T. (2009). A new psychometric instrument assessing vulnerability to risk of suicide and self-harm behaviour in offenders. *International Journal of Offender Therapy & Comparative Criminology*, 53(4), 385–400.

in evidence (1), or very much in evidence (2), for a total score ranging from 0 to 22. The SCL identified 44% of the sample as possibly high risk. Raising the cut-off score from four to six reduced this percentage to 30%. Earthrowl and McCully concluded that the two instruments together provided a useful screening process. In particular, *none* of the female inmates judged to be *not* at risk for suicide by the screening instruments harmed themselves in prison. The instruments were quick to administer, tolerated by the majority of the inmates, and sufficiently specific and sensitive for use. The instruments should be tested on larger groups of inmates, though, to confirm that the combination is an effective screening tool.

Perry et al. (2010) conducted a systematic analysis of screening tools developed specifically for use with incarcerated populations. They examined some of the previously described instruments, including SCOPE, SPS, SCL, and the SRAS. After studying the screening efficacy by calculating the positive and negative predictive values of each instrument, the researchers found the SCOPE and SRAS to have the best levels of sensitivity and specificity. The researchers did caution, however, that all of the instruments were tested with different populations, in different settings, so the results need to be considered with this in mind. Gould, McGeorge, and Slade (2018) worked to update the systematic analysis literature on suicide screening tools for offenders by analyzing the results of eight studies. As with Perry et al., Gould and colleagues reminded readers that conducting systematic analyses of screening tools used in the incarceration setting is difficult with small sample sizes and the forms being tested on different populations. Gould et al. reported that the previously discussed SRAS appeared to be the easiest to implement and showed promise for prediction of completed suicides.

Since there is evidence that thwarted belongingness and perceived burdensomeness are associated with suicidal ideation both in the community and among inmates (Mandracchia & Smith, 2015; Van Orden, Cukrowicz, Witte, & Joiner, 2012), it might be useful to assess inmates on these two constructs. Mandracchia and Smith (2015) tested the Interpersonal Needs Questionnaire (INQ) on a sample of inmates in Mississippi. The INQ is a 15-item self-report survey that measures perceived belongingness and burdensomeness (Van Orden et al., 2012). Mandracchia and Smith found that both feelings of thwarted belongingness and burdensomeness were related to inmates' suicidal ideation.

Longer Instruments

The primary focus of this chapter is short screening tools that could either be administered by a corrections staff member or self-administered. Facilities that have the ability to utilize mental health or nursing staff members for screening have more options, as there are tools that can only be administered by qualified professionals. Long-term prisons and reception/diagnostic units may have the time to use longer instruments. One example of such a tool is the Personality Assessment Inventory (PAI). It is a long test—344 questions—but it could be useful for long-term treatment purposes, since the instrument also measures violence potential. The PAI is appropriate for the corrections setting in that it is written at a fourth-grade reading level. This instrument was tested on 334 male inmates at an inpatient psychiatric facility in the Institutional Division of the Texas Department of Criminal Justice, and it was found to be moderately correlated with the number of suicidal gestures performed by this sample (Wang et al., 1997).

Selecting a Screening Instrument

How should correctional facilities choose screening instruments? Kroner et al. (2011) suggest TODATE, which stands for *T*ype of client, nature of the *O*utcomes, *D*ecision assistance, guidance for *A*ction, *T*heory, and *E*ffort required. I previously discussed one issue that does complicate screening practices, and that is finding screenings that are normed to the types of clients being screened. As is evident from some of the research discussed in this chapter, a tool that is high in both specificity and sensitivity when used with a population of British males, for example, may not be appropriate for male prisoners in New Zealand or female inmates. Corrections agencies might want to screen and/or assess inmates for a number of reasons, only one of which is suicidal intent. It should be obvious that the tool selected for suicide screening would need to include questions about mental health, previous suicide attempts, and current suicidal ideation in order for it to be useful for the purposes discussed in this book. Of course, screenings are of no use unless staff can use them to make decisions. As has been discussed in this chapter, the validity of the instrument is key. The screen should also help to guide staff in their decision-making for what the next step should be with any given inmate. For example, facilities using tools that measure constructs such as hopelessness or perceived burdensomeness would indicate whether staff should address those specific problems with the individuals who test positive on the screening. Finally, effort is important, particularly in busy and poorly staffed institutions. Instruments that are easier to use may be perceived as less burdensome to staff and are more likely to help supervisors achieve staff buy-in.

EXAMPLE OF A SCREENING
PROGRAM—THE UNITED KINGDOM

The British government introduced the F2052SH form to the Prison Service between 1992 and 1994 (Newcomen, 2014b). The form could be "opened" not only by mental health staff but by court, escort, or prison staff if they witnessed, heard of, or otherwise learned of an inmate's risk to oneself. This was the first step in the process of assessing and observing inmates (Borrill, 2002). Following the completion of this form, facility staff were supposed to work out a treatment plan and adhere to that plan. After a few years, the Home Office (1999) criticized the program, noting that "Writing on the form is not what sees someone through a crisis" (p. 44) and expressed concern about the extent to which positive screens led to treatment. Shaw and associates (2003) also studied the use of the F2052SH forms and associated treatment program and were critical of the lack of communication between mental health agencies and custody personnel.

The Assessment, Care in Custody, and Teamwork (ACCT) care planning system was piloted in five facilities in 2005 and introduced to prisons nationwide from 2005 to 2007 as a replacement to the F2052SH. As with the F2052SH, an ACCT plan can be opened by any staff member who considers an individual to be at risk. Once the form is completed, a trained assessor interviews the inmates and develops a care and management plan (CARE-MAP). All staff members who interact with the inmates are required to read the CAREMAP and record any new information that they might have. Case managers are responsible for monitoring the plans and seeing that they are completed (Shaw & Turnbull, 2009). The Prisons and Probation Ombudsman (Newcomen, 2014b) estimates that approximately 2% of the British prison population is on an ACCT plan.

The ACCT plan is intended to be a multidisciplinary process to address risk and respond to the underlying causes of distress. To be truly multidisciplinary, facilities must work to include staff members outside of the medical unit, including line corrections officers. These officers are especially important given their daily proximity to inmates. It is important to have these officers at the CAREMAP meetings. Additionally, law enforcement and court staff are encouraged to complete person escort records to inform the custody staff of any exchanges or incidents that occurred while inmates are in court or in transit. Treatment staff are also encouraged to engage the inmate in the goal-setting process and provide support to inmates as they work to achieve those goals (Shaw & Turnbull, 2009).

While the ACCT plan has important components of screening, such as encouraging communication among all criminal justice personnel and procedures to create a treatment plan based on the screening results, a 2014 review of 60 self-inflicted deaths in custody revealed problems with implementation. Researchers conducted a retrospective analysis of inmate files thirty days after reception into five local prisons in England and Wales. Three percent (59) of the files had positive screenings for current thoughts of self-harm, yet 29% of these inmates were given no further mental health intervention in the month after the screening. Twenty-nine percent did not have an ACCT document opened, despite protocol dictating that they should. Seventeen percent of the 2,166 inmate files included documentation of histories of self-harm, but 57% of these inmates received no further mental health treatment following the screening (Hayes, Senior, Fahy, & Shaw, 2014). This report and the earlier work by the Home Office (1999) illustrate the importance of periodically evaluating the implementation of screening procedures and the subsequent actions of staff to ensure that there are appropriate responses to screening.

MALINGERING

One more issue that is somewhat unique to the correctional setting is the potential for malingering. As was noted in Chapter 4, some correctional staff members are concerned with distinguishing genuine suicidal behavior in inmates from manipulative behavior. Correia (2000) argued that a simple self-report instrument to measure depression is susceptible to malingering. He noted that a cursory interview should be used to identify those inmates pretending to be suicidal in order to get attention or to amuse themselves. If there is no evidence of a genuine psychiatric illness or withdrawal from substance abuse, then malingering should be assumed. If an inmate responded affirmatively to whether he/she is having suicidal thoughts, Correia felt that the presence of clear risk factors (such as, a DSM Axis I disorder, a clear triggering stressor, or withdrawal from alcohol and drugs) was necessary to determine whether suicide risk was present. Correia argued that even suicide attempts should not always be viewed as "true" suicide attempts but sometimes as "suicidal gestures." He was also concerned with distinguishing self-mutilation from suicidal behavior. This approach seems counterproductive. It is likely that such a skeptical position, without any clear guidelines for making these distinctions, will lead to potential suicides being missed during screening. This, in turn, will lead to trauma to the surviving inmates and staff as well as lawsuits against the individual staff and the government entity responsible for the institution. Correctional staff should never try to make these judgments. All potential instances of inmate distress must be reported to the mental health staff, and even they should use caution before dismissing inmates. Inmates may try to "up the ante" and make a suicidal gesture. As I discussed in the previous chapters, there is the danger that gestures can accidentally become fatal.

In other treatment settings, such as psychiatric clinics and crisis counseling centers, it is always possible that clients may be malingering and "faking" suicidal risk when, in fact, there is little or no risk. However, there is a danger of assuming, without thorough investigation, that a client is malingering. There is a good analogy here with a medical illness such as cancer. With cancer, it is better to assume that the patient may have cancer and to investigate further than to assume that the problem is not serious. The latter approach may lead to missing cancer in the patient who may, therefore, die as a result. A similar risk occurs when a possibly suicidal individual is dismissed as a case of malingering or as "not serious." Additionally, I noted in the previous chapter that deliberate self-harm, regardless of the motive, is a predictor of future suicide attempts.

Finally, I have had conversations with corrections officers in facilities that respond to suicidal ideation in a way that humiliates inmates, partially in an effort to weed out suspected malingerers. The problem with this approach is that it may deter those who are truly suicidal and are knowledgeable about the consequences of disclosing this information. It is part of the burden of dealing with potentially suicidal individuals that the staff may be manipulated and deceived. More extensive investigation by qualified mental health professionals will detect the malingering, if present, and then the inmate may be reclassified as a minimal risk for suicide.

CONCLUSION

Screening should be considered an essential component of any suicide prevention policy. It allows staff members to hear directly from the source about current suicidal ideas, recent suicide attempts, and mental health history. Staff also have the opportunity to learn from their observations of inmates' demeanor during the screening process. While there are inmates who will not be forthcoming about their current psychological status, it seems illogical to forego the opportunity to ask.

Screening can be seen as burdensome to staff, particularly in facilities with high turnover rates, as higher levels of churn result in more screenings. A triage approach to screening can help staff handle this in the most efficient manner possible while still providing inmates with the attention and protection that they need. Administrators should periodically confirm that staff members are always acting on screens that result in red flags. Initial screenings that produce red flags must result in more comprehensive evaluations conducted by qualified mental health staff, and inmates must be kept safe in the time between the initial screening and the longer assessment.

It is not possible to review all the available screening and assessment tools in this chapter. I provided a few for consideration, but it is important to remember that an instrument that was valid and reliable when tested with one population may not be as useful with other populations. Finding and implementing an appropriate screening tool may not assist corrections personnel in identifying every individual who is suicidal, but evidence from previous research suggests that these tools can help staff better identify at-risk inmates compared to when staff rely on clinical judgment. Correctional administrators' ability to document the existence of a solid screening program can help protect against civil litigation in the event of a suicide.

NOTE

1. See *Jacobs v. West Feliciana Sheriff's Department*, 2000; *Turney v. Waterbury, 2004; Wever v. Lincoln County*, 2004.

Chapter Six

Working with Suicidal Inmates

The earlier chapters of this book described the hardships of incarceration and the potential coping deficits and psychiatric problems found among the inmate population. Inmates' distress could be a product of mental illness, drug or alcohol addiction, problems with family and friends on the outside, legal concerns, interpersonal problems inside the facility, and/or overall frustration and dissatisfaction with the current state of their lives. When the despair rises to the level that inmates are contemplating harm or are actually harming themselves, there are two broad types of prevention measures that can be utilized: strategies to address inmate motivation to self-harm and strategies to address inmate opportunities to do so. The focus of this chapter will be the former, addressing inmate motivation for self-harm, while Chapter 7 will provide a greater focus on limiting inmates' opportunities for such behavior.

Suicide and other acts of self-injury produce tremendous harm to the individual who is acting out the behavior, but such incidents can also wound other inmates and staff members who may become traumatized by seeing someone else in so much mental and physical pain. Self-harm may also trigger people who are struggling with their own stress or loss. This chapter will discuss why the corrections environment is a particularly difficult setting in which to provide treatment. I will review some treatment programs that are currently being used, and I will go over the steps involved in crisis intervention. Additionally, there will be a discussion of dealing with suicide attempts in progress and a description of mortality reviews, which are analyses of the circumstances leading up to the inmate's death. Mortality reviews are essential, as they allow for comprehensive research on what transpired and an exploration of whether changes should be made to existing policies and procedures.

OBSTACLES TO PROVIDING
TREATMENT IN THE CORRECTIONAL SETTING

It is worth repeating something from Chapter 1: Prisons and jails were never meant to be mental health facilities. Unfortunately, prisons and jails have become our de facto mental health centers. In most cases, these institutions do not have the budget, the staff, or the type of environment that is conducive to assisting people who are distressed. Regardless, correctional institutions now have to find ways to keep inmates safe and provide mental health services. This is a daunting task, as there are several aspects of the correctional setting that hinder the availability and operation of effective interventions.

The Nature of the Inmate Population and Culture

The first obstacle faced by corrections staff is the number of incarcerated people in need of medical, psychiatric, and drug treatment. Chapter 2 highlighted the overrepresentation of mentally ill and drug/alcohol addicted individuals in the corrections setting. The incarceration environment would be difficult even for people who have established positive coping skills, so it should be expected that those with an inadequate ability to cope in a prosocial manner would experience problems that occasionally lead to crisis.

The presence of co-occurring disorders makes treatment of individuals even more difficult. Researchers estimate that at least half of people with an identified psychiatric disorder also have a co-occurring substance abuse disorder (Franczak & Dye, 2001). Historically, psychiatric and substance abuse problems have been considered to be separate domains, with different staff members and treatment programs available for each. This model is problematic, as inmates with a primary diagnosis of mental illness are, at times, barred from substance abuse programs and vice versa, as the programs are not equipped to address dual diagnoses.

The large number of incarcerated people in need of some type of intervention is challenging in itself, but the culture of correctional institutions presents an additional obstacle. Prison and jail culture can be detrimental to help seeking, particularly among males. As discussed in Chapter 5, male inmates might be reluctant to seek help not only from custodial staff but also from mental health personnel who are affiliated with the institution. Inmates expressed concern that psychologists employed by the facilities would break confidentiality and that disclosure of suicidal ideation would result in undesirable housing, a reclassification of security level, and possible delay getting paroled (Deane et al., 1999; Skogstad et al., 2005).

Inmates, particularly males, must also consider the impact of help seeking on their reputations among other inmates. Sykes (1958) discussed the inmate code that outlines appropriate behavior for inmates. The code requires inmates to do their "own time," not to trust anyone, and to avoid any appearance of weakness (Rotter & Steinbacher, 2001). The act of requesting help from staff because of suicidal feelings could damage inmates' reputations and expose them as weak. In the Skogstad and colleagues (2005) study, male inmates largely held the belief that those serious about suicide would quietly do it rather than talk about it, and only a "wuss" would seek staff assistance. This concern for one's status among peers can have a chilling effect on inmates' willingness to seek help.

Staffing Challenges

The primary missions of prisons and jails have always been custody and security, and correctional budgets reflect that. Smaller jails are more likely to have problems finding the funding to pay for staff, equipment, and space to offer as many programs and services, including on-site health services, as larger jails (Applegate & Sitren, 2008). Even in the prison systems, with their more robust budgets and staff, finding and retaining health professionals remains difficult. Gondles, Maurer, and Bell (2017) surveyed health professionals from all 50 state departments of corrections, the country's five largest jail systems, and the Federal Bureau of Prisons. Survey participants identified medical and mental health professionals as the toughest correctional employees to recruit. Ninety percent of responding representatives from these agencies reported having overall employee retention problems, but they specifically identified medical and mental health staff members as the most difficult to retain in the corrections setting. The reasons that respondents provided for this were the noncompetitive salaries offered in corrections settings, the undesirable work environment, and the geographic location of prisons. When faced with the choice of taking and holding a position in a corrections facility or another setting, many health care professionals are tempted to work elsewhere. The result is, even if corrections agencies can budget for adequate numbers of medical and mental health staff, they may not be able to recruit or retain them.

The staff members who are present in the correctional facilities find that working with incarcerated suicidal individuals is very difficult. Brown (2016) interviewed master's-level counselors who worked with suicidal inmates. When asked about their work, counselors expressed frustration that they lacked the time to provide any therapeutic services to people who were not in immediate danger. One counselor noted that he was unable to do parts of his job because he is "so bogged down with crises." The result is that inmates who might be helped before they reach a crisis stage are not seen, and then once they are in crisis, they receive some care but only for a little while. When surveying medical directors for state departments of corrections, Applebaum and colleagues (2011) found that 47% considered incidents of self-injury to be moderately disruptive to the institution, and 18% regarded these as extremely disruptive to the functioning of the facility. Dealing with inmates who are suicidal involves a tremendous amount of work among staff members from multiple departments within the facilities. Providing the necessary care, especially to people who are not deemed to be in imminent danger, is difficult as departments deal with budget, staffing, and training issues. Such staffing and treatment challenges add complications to an already difficult job and may prevent the facility from providing much meaningful treatment.

Security Needs versus Treatment Needs

The nature of incarceration limits some of the options that treatment staff have as they work with inmates. There are stress-reduction techniques that mental health staff would ordinarily suggest to individuals that are unavailable to inmates. For example, people in the community who are self-injuring in reaction to stress, frustration, or sadness, would likely be encouraged to engage in activities to relieve stress. These activities might involve taking a bath, doing something outdoors, such as gardening or engaging in a favorite sport, or just walking outside (DeHart, Smith, & Kaminski, 2009). While inmates generally have access to the outdoors, that access is limited, particularly in higher security institutions. Access to whatever limited activities are available is halted during lockdowns, which can be particularly stressful times. Additionally, an outdoor activity, such as going for a walk, can be stress-inducing in high security institutions where the threat of assault on the yard is commonly present. Inmates who are placed in segregation may be limited to one hour of "recreation" in a small concrete or fenced pen.

This brings up another challenge of the incarceration setting, which is the fact that security needs often trump treatment needs. The bars, gates, walls, and wires surrounding jails and prisons are there to serve one of the primary priorities of correctional administrations—to keep people inside. Security is paramount, and the higher the level of security of each institution or unit, the larger a priority security will be relative to treatment. In my work as a program evaluator for corrections agencies and treatment providers, I have personally seen the impact that security concerns can have on the functioning of various programs. For example, juveniles who were supposed to be participating in a program that I was evaluating repeatedly missed class due to being "locked up" as punishment for rule infractions. Program facilitators teaching the juveniles about becoming good fathers were prohibited from bringing food into the institution when they wanted to model prosocial family meal time.

Another barrier to treatment in custody is the staff practice of trying to differentiate self-injurious behaviors as either "mad" or "bad." Correctional staff often try to discern whether the self-injury or inmate's statement was an attempt at manipulation or truly in the domain of a mental health issue. Fagan et al. (2010) caution against such characterizations, since they tend to foster the belief that all acts are either/or and need to be placed into one of the two categories. This inhibits much-needed collaboration between the custodial and mental health staff to address the behaviors and is counterproductive given that self-harming behavior can have multiple, simultaneous goals, some which might be manipulative while others are truly due to distress. Historically, custodial and mental health staff have approached self-injury differently. Custodial staff observe inmates to see if they violated any directives, and, if they did, they assign what they deem to be appropriate punishments for rule violations. Mental health staff are generally inclined to resort to therapies and techniques that are used in hospitals and residential settings. The National Commission on Correctional Health Care's (NCCHC) standards for Mental Health Services in Correctional Facilities requires that custody refrain from interfering with implementation of mental health decisions (NCCHC, 2015). Compliance with NCCHC standards, however, is not mandatory, as accreditation is optional.

Negative reactions to self-harm and suicide attempts are not exclusive to custodial staff. Health care professionals in the corrections setting may also display resentment toward self-harming inmates. Marzano, Ciclitira, and Adler (2011) interviewed self-harming male prisoners in England who reported that the prison health care staff accused them of attention seeking and even offered to show them how to "do it [self-harm] properly." In a later study that involved interviewing officers and health care staff instead of inmates, Marzano et al. (2015) found that staff members expressed resentment of self-harming inmates. One possible reason for these findings is that the health care staff were not trained specifically on psychological or mental health issues. This highlights why it is vital to conduct periodic training of all staff, but especially those who are expected to interact with self-harming inmates.

One of the consequences of staff members' lack of insight into mental illness and their attempts to label people and behavior as either "mad" or "bad" is that staff may use punitive measures to address stated suicidal ideation and acts of self-harm rather than seeing the inmates' behavior as a problem requiring mental health intervention. Inmates who report suicidal ideation or thoughts of self-harm, and even those who actually self-harm, may be subjected to discipline for their self-harm. For example, Applebaum et al. (2011) found that 63% of state departments of corrections treat self-injurious behavior as a rule infraction. Doty and colleagues (2012) conducted a content analysis of inmate medical records with mentions of self-harm from the South Carolina Department of Corrections. Seventy-five percent of those cases included a staff statement of "inmate will be charged accordingly" or "inmate will be charged with mutilation" in the files. When Heney (1990) interviewed incarcerated women in Canada who self-harmed while in prison, several women mentioned the use of segregation without even being asked about it. Of those who mentioned it, 97% expressed frustration that segregation was used as a response to self-injury. One woman stated "You are all treated the same [taken to segregation] whether you hurt someone else or hurt yourself" (Heney, 1990, Section 2, p. 2). The placement of self-injury in the category of a disciplinary problem or a problem that requires a solution similar to what would be used for disciplinary cases is likely to be counterproductive. Inmates who know of such consequences may avoid seeking help. Furthermore, segregation is unlikely to improve inmates' conditions, as will be addressed further in Chapter 7. The American Psychiatric Association (2016) recommends that prison and jail administrations work to eliminate such disincentives to inmates who would otherwise seek help.

Not only might there be resistance to therapeutic approaches from cynical or burnt-out staff, but there also might be political pressure on elected officials, such as sheriffs, to avoid any actions that could be considered "coddling" of correctional populations. The principle of least eligibility is the idea that offenders should never be eligible for services that the poorest members of free society are lacking (C. Johnson, 2002), and there can be political incentives to apply this principle to jurisdictions. For example, some facilities have established co-pays for inmates seeking medical care. The American Psychiatric Association (2016) recommends that facilities refrain from doing so, as requiring co-pays could serve as a deterrent to getting much needed help prior to a suicide attempt.

STAFF PREPAREDNESS
FOR WORKING WITH SUICIDAL INDIVIDUALS

Correctional facilities clearly need to offer some level of mental health services to inmates, since every institution will house people in crisis at some point. Options include on-site outpatient treatment, on-site inpatient treatment, crisis intervention/stabilization in an infirmary, or transfer to a psychiatric hospital (American Psychiatric Association, 2016). The NCCHC's (2015) accreditation standards call for, at minimum, the availability of the following *outpatient* mental health services in correctional facilities: procedures to identify and then properly refer inmates with mental health needs, crisis intervention services, medication management when appropriate, individual and/or group counseling when appropriate, and psychosocial/psycho-educational programs. All activities associated with mental health treatment must be documented. It might be in the best interests of state prison systems and large jails to explore the possibility of setting up partial-care or inpatient wings if the department is faced with high demand for intensive psychiatric treatment. One advantage to having on-site inpatient options is that the correctional system will have its own group of mental health staff who are familiar with working within the constraints of a correctional system. On the other hand, providing mental health units inside of prisons and jails might make it all too convenient for society to consider the correctional setting to be the appropriate location to house people who are mentally ill. Severson (2004) argued that

Too frequently these units fall into the trap which spelled the downfall of hospital systems, that is, they become institutional warehouses for those with mental health challenges. If used as a permanent place to house persons with mental illnesses, these units may exist in conflict with the objectives of our newest disability laws: inclusion, reasonable accommodation, and access to programs and places generally available to the "public" (Severson, 2004, p. 14).

Providing any mental health services in a correctional setting comes with its own set of challenges. As previously noted, inmates may be distrustful of the mental health staff, as they suspect that the employees will show more fidelity to the institution than to the inmates' need for confidentiality (Deane et al., 1999; Skogstad et al., 2005). Inmates in New Zealand indicated that they would prefer to speak to a mental health professional from outside of the prison, given their reluctance to trust anyone associated with the corrections regime (Skogstad et al., 2005). The American Psychiatric Association (2016) acknowledges the potential dual loyalty, or dual agency, that correctional mental health staff may feel and recommends that any mental health interviews or information that will be used in an adversarial context, such as a parole or disciplinary hearing, be handled by a staff member outside of the inmate's treatment team. The APA also recommends that the mental health staff clearly articulate any limits they will put on confidentiality prior to the start of treatment. For example, staff who learn that inmates are planning to hurt themselves or others or plan to escape will have to share this information with security personnel.

All staff who interact with inmates should undergo initial mental health and suicide prevention training at the start of employment and then refresher training throughout their careers. The American Psychiatric Association (2000) recommends "cross training" between the security and clinical staff. Mental health professionals would benefit from learning about the institutional culture and the potential for manipulation. Security staff would benefit from learning about what the mental health staff has to offer, the rules of confidentiality, and the importance of cultural awareness when working with inmates in crisis. As was noted in Chapter 5, facilities seeking NCCHC accreditation are required to provide suicide prevention training to all officers who come into contact with inmates, and officers in the screening and mental health parts of the institutions must receive extra training (NCCHC, 2015). Training might help to reduce bad practices, such as trying to neatly categorize behavior into either "mad" or "bad" categories and hopefully cut down on officer and staff resentment of inmates whose mental illnesses are interfering with their ability to follow orders.

Multicultural Competency

In previous chapters, I noted the importance of multicultural sensitivity in screening procedures. Such sensitivity remains important to any treatment services developed for inmates. It was evident in Chapter 2 that indigenous groups are overrepresented in custody and at an increased risk for suicide relative to other inmates in multiple countries. Treatment programs should not be developed with a "one-size-fits-all" approach. For example, the Canadian Centre on Substance Abuse (2006) noted that Canada needs health care and counseling services appropriate for Aboriginal women that include a female-centered approach. In the United States, jails and prisons that house Native Americans need to not only adjust their screening approaches but also be culturally sensitive when considering treatment, as Native Americans might be more reluctant than others to engage in talking about mental health problems (National Institute of Justice, 2004). Maori inmates in New Zealand tend to also be reluctant to seek and accept psychological assistance (Deane et al., 1999). The NCCNC (2015) and ACA (2002) include standards that require staff to consider cultural issues when working with at-risk inmates.

Staff should also be cognizant of the impact of trauma on inmates and how inmates' previous experiences might shape their current approaches to treatment. The American Psychiatric Association (2016) recommends that staff receive training about gender differences in responses to trauma, as women are more likely to exhibit anxiety-related symptoms while males may become aggressive.

TYPES OF TREATMENT PROGRAMS

It is not possible to review every corrections-based therapeutic program that targets suicidality and self-injury. The goal here is to provide an overview of some noteworthy types of programs. Some of the following are programs to deal with specific types of inmates during particular times. Of course, prisons and jails that hold higher proportions of long-term inmates will have more flexibility in the types of programs that they can offer. Jails with high turnover rates are likely to be restricted to reliance on crisis intervention, medication management, education programs, and short-term therapeutic options (APA, 2016). The reader should remember that a key part of any comprehensive suicide prevention program is screening and evaluation, as was discussed in Chapter 5.

Crisis Intervention

Crisis intervention involves a series of steps mental health and social work staff members can take to establish a relationship with inmates and see them through crises that might lead to self-harm or suicide in the absence of intervention. Correctional staff tasked with working with inmates needing mental health services should be trained in the following crisis intervention techniques:

1. *Make an initial evaluation regarding the severity of the crisis situation.* One of the first questions that crisis workers should ask themselves is, "How much time do I have before I must make a decision regarding this inmate"? This question is necessary to reduce the anxiety of working with people in crisis, for most cases are not life-or-death. Through this question, the crisis is placed into the perspective of time, reduces the anxiety of the crisis worker, and facilitates a better atmosphere with which to deal with the inmate.

2. *Develop a relationship with the inmate in crisis.* The crisis worker's initial step is to establish a relationship with the inmate in crisis, and this is where person-centered therapy, as developed by Carl Rogers, is appropriate. Person-centered therapy encourages the clients to take the lead in finding solutions to their problems while the therapist provides guidance and encouragement (Lester, 1991). Trust is an essential element of this relationship and will be characterized by the free flow of information from the inmate to the crisis worker. The relationship requires communicating a feeling of interest and concern and a nonjudgmental attitude on the part of the crisis worker. A relationship is best established through listening to

and reflecting on the emotional components of the individual's story. By doing this, the inmates in crisis will feel that the crisis worker is a person who cares and is concerned about them. This process is called "tuning in" to the feelings of the person in crisis or "active listening."

3. *Help the inmates identify the specific problems they have.* Inmates in crisis are usually confused and disorganized and have difficulty defining their problems. Care must be taken to explore their total field of interaction before focusing in on an individual problem, as inmates in crisis are often confused, and their desire to work toward an immediate solution to a problem may lead the helper astray. When the problem is specified and placed into perspective, the inmates will often feel relieved. With suicidal individuals, it is important at this point to evaluate the potential for suicide. If the potential is high, immediate hospitalization may be needed, but this may sometimes be averted through Step 4.

4. *Assess and mobilize the inmates' strength and resources.* Inmates who are in crisis often feel like they have no resources on which to draw and no friends to give them assistance. In their confusion and disorganization, they often overlook people who are willing to help them. By examining the crisis situation and identifying the individuals in the inmates' life space who may be able to help, the crisis worker often locates resources that the inmates have forgotten, resources that can be crucial to recovery. At the same time, the crisis worker explores with the client means by which these resources can be mobilized and used as a support network for the inmate during the time of crisis. In general, the inmates should be encouraged to do this as much as possible for themselves. However, the crisis worker must be willing to accept the responsibility to assist the inmates in this activity, especially during the initial stages when confusion and disorganization may be great. Unfortunately, this step will be especially difficult with inmates, since they are locked away from just about all of their known resources. Additionally, inmates may be incarcerated for crimes that they committed against their families, so it may be difficult to call on relatives for help.

5. *Develop an action plan.* A crisis is a call for action and for decision. It is important to include the inmates in crisis in making their action plan so that they develop a commitment to this plan, sense its appropriateness in terms of them and their environment, and make it succeed. Such an action plan, or treatment plan, should state short-term and long-term goals and methods through which those goals will be pursued (NCCHC, 2015).

Roberts and Bender (2006) described a seven-stage crisis intervention model that they find appropriate when working with juvenile offenders: (1)

Plan and conduct a crisis assessment; (2) Establish rapport and a good relationship with the client; (3) Identify the dimensions of the presenting problems; (4) Explore feelings and emotions (using active listening); (5) Generate and explore alternative courses of action; (6) Develop an action plan; and (7) Formulate a follow-up plan and agreement with the client.

Crisis intervention and initial symptom management play a critical role in the early stages of cognitive therapy for suicidal individuals (Rudd, Joiner, & Rajab, 2001), and the role that crisis intervention can play in jails and prisons has been recognized by researchers and clinicians (Cox, McCarty, Landsberg, & Paravati, 1988). Crisis intervention is especially suitable for inmates with problems such as drug addiction (Yeager & Gregoire, 2005) and HIV (Lewis & Harrison, 2005), which are common problems among inmates.

Cognitive-Behavioral Interventions

Cognitive behavioral therapy (CBT) is a widely used, evidence-based intervention that has been successful in treating drug and alcohol addiction and criminal behavior among community and correctional populations (Latessa, Listwan, & Koetzle, 2014). CBT addresses faulty thinking patterns among individuals, with the belief that it is one's thinking that leads to the inability to abide by society's rules or cope with problems in prosocial ways. CBT has the potential to address suicidal behavior, since the thought-stopping techniques used in CBT could be applied to people who are suicidal (Rudd et al., 2001). Training in thought-stopping teaches individuals to interrupt negative thought patterns, hopefully before they embark on any destructive behaviors.

CBT has been used in the community to assist juveniles in finding more effective means of coping with a variety of problems. The 12- to 16-week program teaches safety-planning techniques to initially keep clients safe until the next session. After that, the juveniles gradually learn both internal and external strategies, with the former being tools that the person could implement individually while the latter involves support systems and, if all else fails, emergency medical personnel. The program ends with juveniles using guided imagery techniques to test their newly acquired coping abilities. Stanley and colleagues (2009) surveyed juveniles in the community who were enrolled in a CBT program within 90 days of a suicide attempt and found that 100% of the clients believed it to be helpful.

Of course, any program that is to be implemented in the correctional setting might need to be modified due to security priorities and the forced separation from family and friends. The program that Stanley and colleagues (2009) evaluated, for example, emphasized familial cooperation in treatment. While the ideal scenario is to involve families in juvenile treatment programs, this might not be feasible with inmates whose relationships with family are so damaged that the family is no longer interested in having contact. It also may be difficult to have family involved in treatment given various institutional policies regarding inmates' contact with people in the community. While modifications may be necessary, CBT programs can, and have, run in prisons and jails.

Rohde, Jorgensen, Seeley, and Mace (2004) tested a cognitive-behavioral program aimed at improving the coping skills of incarcerated juvenile delinquents and compared them with similar youths who were not in the program. The youths in the program improved on most measures, including self-esteem, social adjustment, and coping skills, but they did not show a decrease in current suicidal ideation. Pratt et al. (2015) evaluated a pilot randomized control trial of a CBT program for incarcerated individuals in the United Kingdom. The program specifically targeted suicidal behavior among male prisoners. Inmates identified as in need of treatment were randomly assigned to either the CBT program or the treatment-as-usual (TAU) group. The TAU group got the usual attention and treatment given to any inmates who were in the Assessment, Care in Custody, and Teamwork (ACCT) care planning system used in the United Kingdom that was discussed in Chapter 5. Inmates in the CBT program experienced a 50% decrease in self-harm incidents, while the TAU group had little change. Both groups showed improvement in reduced suicidal ideation, hopelessness, depression, anxiety, and self-esteem issues. The CBT group had better outcomes with clinically significant improvement, with 56% in CBT achieving clinically significant improvement compared to just 23% in the TAU group.

Behavioral Management Plans and Dialectical Behavioral Therapy

Behavioral management plans are inspired by social learning theory and use positive and negative reinforcers to encourage good behavior and deter undesirable actions. These techniques have been used in response to repetitive self-harming behaviors (Barboza & Wilson, 2011). The Massachusetts Department of Corrections uses such a program in phases with the hope of bringing about behavioral changes, such as increasing the time between self-injurious episodes, using positive new skills to deal with problems, and verbally communicating needs. Inmates can be put in a specific behavioral management unit or can be treated in their regular housing units, depending on the severity of the current behavior. Inmates who are repeatedly committing acts of serious self-harm may need to be moved and put in a very structured unit with several restrictions. As behavior improves, inmates will be given rewards (positive reinforcement) and/or removed from restrictions (negative reinforcement). Andrade, Wilson, Franko, Deitsch, and Barboza (2014) do caution that harmful behavior might increase temporarily under such programs, as inmates work to test limits if they are used to being rewarded for self-injury. That tends to pass, however, and inmates' behavior will go through ups and downs prior to stabilizing and sustaining change. Andrade et al. evaluated a program in Massachusetts and found encouraging results. Trips to outside hospitals decreased by 75%, on-site emergency medical care declined by 33%, and incidence of self-injury decreased by 50%. They did use a very small sample size (N = 13), so more evaluations are necessary.

Dialectical behavior therapy (DBT) is based on cognitive behavior therapy and is used to improve inmates' problem-solving skills. DBT was formulated by Linehan (1993) to work with women who have borderline personality disorder (BPD). It is an intensive program that typically lasts for a minimum of one year and requires two psychotherapists for each client. The goal of DBT is to introduce clients to meditational techniques to help them focus on the present and relax.

DBT has become a popular treatment program for individuals in the community and in the corrections system who are diagnosed with BPD. BPD is characterized by poor tolerance of distress, problems in regulating emotions and behaviors, and poor interpersonal skills. Individuals with BPD are often violent both toward themselves and toward other people and objects. They have a high incidence of self-harm and suicidal behavior (Eccleston & Sorbello, 2002).

The Correctional Service of Canada has used DBT in federal prisons, specifically for female offenders with mental health needs. Their program involves individual psychotherapy, skills training, and telephone consultations. The program has several goals, including (1) improving behavioral capabilities, (2) improving motivation to change, (3) promoting the application of newly acquired skills to other environments, and (4) creating an environment supportive of the individual and treatment program. Program designers believe that work on emotional regulation and distress tolerance skills will assist inmates with adapting to dealing with difficult situations (McDonagh, Taylor, & Blanchette, 2002).

Eccleston and Sorbello (2002) modified Linehan's (1993) DBT program to make it suitable for inmates, renaming the modules, reordering them, and adjusting them to the reality of the prison environment. They implemented the RUSH program (Real Understanding of Self-Help) in an Australian prison. The program consisted of 20 sessions, 2 hours each, delivered twice a week for 10 weeks. As is common in correctional facilities, security matters often took priority over therapy. Lockdowns and fights interfered with program implementation. It was difficult to find an available room for group sessions, and they often had to use the laundry room as a meeting space.

Modifications were also necessary to make the program more suitable for inmates. One important adjustment was the simplification of the handouts, as prison and jail inmates often have low educational achievement. The sessions met only twice a week, and the individual counseling was as-needed rather than weekly. The program also had to address issues that are not common among community members, such as loyalty to criminal peers, use of violence as a coping tactic, and drug use. Participants often tried to divert the meetings to discussions of these problems. They also had difficulty understanding the concepts of DBT, showed hostility and belligerence which disrupted group cohesion, and challenged boundary issues (inmates wanted the counselors to share the same level of personal information as the clients) (Eccleston & Sorbello, 2002).

Evaluation of the program was hindered by transfers and drop-outs. However, improvements in some areas, such as depression, anxiety, and stress level were noted in some, but not all, units. Results show that the inmates reported that the program was innovative and stimulating, group cohesion was established and solidified, most of the inmates were motivated and committed, and there was evidence that their interpersonal skills improved. The program was too limited and the follow-up too brief for Eccleston and Sorbello (2002) to evaluate the program's impact on suicidal behavior.

Her Majesty's Prison Service in England and Wales implemented a pilot program utilizing DBT in three women's prisons. Thirty women participated across the three prisons, and as is typical for DBT programs, there was a 33% voluntary dropout rate. For those who did complete the program, they experienced reductions in self-harm and reduced lethality of self-harming incidents. The program completers also had decreased impulsivity and dissociative experiences and increased self-esteem (Nee & Farman, 2005). Overall, DBT and similar programs that focus on behavior management appear to be effective programs that can be implemented in community as well as incarceration settings (Knoll, 2010).

Intermediate Care and Alternative Housing

Intermediate care units (ICUs) or programs are being implemented in some prisons to address the needs of inmates with psychiatric disorders. These day programs are similar to partial-care options that are available in the community. To qualify for inclusion, inmates must have (1) a serious diagnosable psychiatric disorder, (2) significant psychiatric history measured by prior hospitalizations and recent mental health treatment, and (3) difficulty coping in the general prison population due to the psychiatric disorder (Condelli, Bradigan, & Holanchock, 1997). ICUs typically accept 60 inmates in a unit separate from the general population and have three to five mental health correctional staff members. The programs utilize milieu therapy, skills training, crisis intervention, and vocational and academic instruction.

The New York City jail system is using a program called "Beyond the Bridge." This program provides inpatient psychiatric treatment to inmates, including individual therapy, group sessions, access to social workers, psychiatrists, and psychologists, and discharge planning. The staff members treat inmates using CBT, motivational enhancement therapy, and motivational interviewing. Staff focus on helping inmates develop coping and problem-solving skills in this six-week program. An evaluation of the program revealed that it did help to reduce the amount of time participating inmates spent on suicide watch (Glowa-Kollisch et al., 2014).

The New York State Department of Correctional Services has 13 residential ICUs with correctional staff who have self-selected into those units. The treatment teams are prison-based but strive to be interdisciplinary, with corrections and mental health staff working in close collaboration. Toch (2016) describes the New York ICUs as a type of informal residential therapeutic community. These units serve as "enriched, low-pressure enclaves for prisoners who would otherwise have difficulty dealing with the challenges of prison life" (Toch, 2016, p. 654). Condelli et al. (1997) evaluated the effectiveness of an intermediate care program in the New York State Corrections System. They studied 209 inmates who had been in the program for at least six months and compared their progress to the prior six months that they spent in prison. Inmate suicide attempts decreased by 63%, the provision of emergency medications declined by 43%, and the officers requested 65% fewer mental health observations.

The North Carolina Department of Corrections has an ICU as part of its four-tier plan for working with inmates suffering from mental illness. The Social Skills Day Training Program at the Brown Creek Correctional Institution in North Carolina houses that program and accepts the following types of inmates referred by intake staff: those requiring a "step up" in care from the strictly outpatient treatment offered in the general population and those needing a "step down" who are working to transition from an inpatient setting to the general population. The program offers inmates classes throughout the day, but during times when they are not in class, they are able to participate in the recreation and programming offered to all general population inmates. Inmates who succeed in intermediate care may move into the general population and then receive medication and treatment on an outpatient basis in the prisons (MacKain & Messer, 2004).

Some inmates experience crises and need to be stabilized for a short period of time in special housing. Once the crisis has passed, they may be medically cleared to be moved back to the general population. Other inmates may have moved beyond the immediate crisis but may still require inpatient treatment. Correctional agencies can either contract with an off-site psychiatric hospital to take inmates who are in need of inpatient treatment, or they can provide such services within one of their own facilities. MacKain and Messer (2004) noted that relying on facilities outside of the prison system for treatment increases transportation and processing costs, is difficult for both inmates and their families, increases the staff workload, and frustrates the staff. For jails, it will likely be impractical to offer these services on-site, but for state and federal prison systems, it might be preferable to have inpatient options within some institutions. Smaller county jails may also enter into contracts to share an inpatient unit at one facility, similar to how some counties work together to share a regional jail. These units can reduce what MacKain and Messer call the "revolving door" of hospital admission, otherwise known as "riding the bus" back and forth to psychiatric hospitals (Slate et al., 2013).

The North Carolina Department of Corrections does have a medical facility with single cells for the specific purpose of stabilizing inmates who are in crisis. Once they are stable, they are moved to a residential setting where they will continue to receive inpatient care. If inmates do well and are cleared for transfer, they can then step down to North Carolina's aforementioned ICU (MacKain & Messer, 2004).

The Colorado Department of Corrections built the San Carlos Correctional Facility to house inmates with severe mental illness who are suffering from co-occurring disorders. These inmates tend to require additional support and slower-paced programs than inmates who only have substance abuse problems. As inmates start to improve, the facility staff offer a transitional program to prepare them to move back into the general prison population (Stahl & West, 2001).

As part of a class action settlement, the New Jersey Department of Corrections agreed to increase its spending on behavioral health programs for inmates (Wolff, Bjerklie, & Maschi, 2005). Prior to the *D.M. v. Terhune* (1999) case, the department had no internal housing options for inmates suffering from mental illness who had an impaired ability to exist peacefully in general population units. While transfer to a psychiatric hospital was an option, it was an expensive alternative that the department rarely used. Instead, they tended to rely on disciplinary measures, particularly administrative segregation, to handle inmates who became disruptive due to symptoms of mental illness. As part of the settlement, the department was ordered to develop a comprehensive set of housing options for inmates (Wolff et al., 2005). Inmates with mental illness must receive a mental health assessment within 72 hours of admission to a facility. Mental health and classification staff have the option of sending inmates who are in acute crisis to a stabilization unit. These stabilization units provide the highest level of care available in New Jersey prisons, where staff focuses on crisis intervention and management during an inmate's stay. Residential treatment units, which are long-term care units for inmates whose mental illness makes it too difficult for them to remain in the general population, are a second housing option. Lastly, transitional care units are available and provide a step-down program for inmates who are preparing to reintegrate into general population from the stabilization or residential care units. All three types of units provide inpatient-level mental health treatment (Settlement agreement for *D.M. v. Terhune*, 1999).

Fagan et al. (2010) proposed that, since transfer to a different housing setting is often one motivation for NSSI in custody, jail and prison staff should work to keep inmates in their same unit following the undesired behavior. The justification for this is to remove the reward of getting the transfer. Fagan and colleagues did acknowledge that this could be dangerous, and it is necessary to find a balance between safety and reward removal. They suggested that the institutions could use a transfer or visit to an infirmary or outside hospital as a condition of demonstrated appropriate behavior for a period of time. This suggestion seems very risky, however, so I do not recommend it. Besides the risk, it seems counterproductive and financially unlikely to expect correctional institutions to transfer someone to an infirmary or an outside hospital, not in response to harmful behavior, but as a reward after the person demonstrates being able to resist self-harm.

Working with Clients with Co-Occurring Disorders

Throughout this chapter, I have noted that inmates with co-occurring disorders present heightened challenges for medical and mental health staff. They tend to be more difficult to treat, as there are two problems that need to be addressed simultaneously, but most mental health and drug treatment programs are designed to handle only either mental illness or substance abuse, but not both. Co-occurring disorders are also underdiagnosed. The American Psychiatric Association (2016) recommends that, once corrections staff find evidence of one type of disorder, they should immediately screen for the presence of another. For treatment, one common approach is to address the disorders in a sequential fashion: mental health treatment then substance abuse treatment or vice versa. That is problematic, since both medical issues complement each other. Another approach is to do two parallel treatment programs simultaneously, but this is often difficult to coordinate. The best option to treat comorbidity is to use an integrated treatment program that simultaneously addresses both problems with one group of clinicians whenever possible (American Psychiatric Association, 2016; Franczak & Dye, 2001). Regardless of which type of approach is available to the inmates in the correctional facilities and the community, substance abuse and mental illness both need to be addressed to increase the chances that clients will be able to live productive lives.

Utilizing No-Harm Contracts and Safety Plans

Therapists in private practice and mental health staff in correctional facilities have attempted to use no-harm contracts to secure commitments from inmates to refrain from self-harm for an identified period of time. These agreements involve a written promise from the inmate or client to refrain from suicide or other types of self-harm, usually until the next treatment session. No-harm contracts are controversial, as they are considered to be of little use in preventing suicide or legally protecting therapists. Hayes (2010) found that 14% of correctional suicides occurred after inmates agreed not to attempt suicide or self-harm in other ways. Critics worry that, once clients sign the contract, clinicians might be apt to ignore warning signs for suicide due to overconfidence in the efficacy of the contract (Lewis, 2007). Additionally, these contracts are likely to be much less meaningful to inmates if they have yet to establish a therapeutic bond with the counselor who is asking them to make that promise. Contracts are also likely to be meaningless when used with inmates who are suffering from a mental impairment that would interfere with their ability to commit to any type of behavioral agreement (Knoll, 2010).

An alternative to no-harm contracts may be a safety plan. Safety plans are developed through collaboration between the client and therapist who work to identify available coping strategies and sources of support (Weinrath, Wayte, & Arboleda-Florez, 2012). This collaboration between client and therapist may help to build a therapeutic alliance and provide inmates a set plan for what to do at a time when they may be so overwhelmed that they are unable to problem-solve (Lewis, 2007).

INMATES AS RESOURCES FOR SUICIDE PREVENTION

When working with suicidal inmates, there is the need to ensure that they have the proper levels of supervision at all times, and then there is the challenge of working to improve how they feel. Fellow inmates may be useful to corrections agencies as they develop suicide prevention plans.

One widely used model for enlisting inmates to assist other inmates with suicide prevention is the Samaritans program. The Samaritans group is a worldwide suicide prevention organization with an established telephone crisis counseling service and walk-in clinics for suicidal individuals in many nations. In recent years, several Samaritan centers have worked with inmates in prisons to set up crisis intervention programs for suicidal inmates. The Samaritans work in several prisons in Canada and England and Wales. The correctional facilities are not required to have a Samaritans (SAMS) branch, but many do have this or some other type of peer support programs (Newcomen, 2014a).

Schlosar and Carlson (1997) described a Samaritans program in a Canadian federal medium-security penitentiary. The inmate volunteers were trained by the local Samaritan branch, and a community liaison coordinated between the inmate volunteers and the prison administration. The volunteers were trained in active listening, nonverbal communications, facts regarding the nature of mental illness, and the concept of befriending. The administration agreed to permit confidentiality during crisis counseling. An inmate volunteer talked to all new admissions to the prison to inform them of the service, and the inmate counselors wore identifiable T-shirts or sweatshirts (black with a white eagle head crest). Schlosar and Carlson noted that the existence of the program had changed the atmosphere of the prison, because the program established the norm of showing compassion and kindness to fellow inmates. This helped to generate a sense of community, not only among the volunteers themselves, but to the prison population as a whole. The inmate volunteers were on call 24/7, and they had access to the Samaritan branch in the community 24/7 for advice and debriefing.

The U.S. Federal Bureau of Prisons runs an inmate buddy system. Inmate participants are trained about suicidal behavior, empathetic listening, and communication skills. In 1992, inmates completed 72% of the 75,363 hours of suicide watch that was necessary in the federal system (White & Schimmel, 1995).

Barker et al. (2014) recommended inmate buddy programs based on the results of their systematic review of correctional suicide prevention tactics. The mere presence of the buddy can reduce inmates' sense of isolation, but the buddy work must be supplemented by the frequent presence and observation of trained staff members. The World Health Organization (2007) also recommends using inmate companions but only as a supplement to staff presence and other treatment and prevention techniques.

The Samaritans program, and others like it, may help to address inmates' reluctance to trust mental health staff members who work for the institution or contract with the corrections department (Snow, 2002; World Health Organization, 2007). The program may also benefit the inmate listeners, as they gain a sense of purpose (Snow, 2002) and experience personal growth (Dhaliwal & Harrower, 2009). Langley (1991) noted that inmates make ideal aides, since they are tuned in to the prison grapevine and hear about the events in the lives of other inmates that might precipitate a suicidal crisis, such as bad news from a lawyer or a "Dear John" letter from a girlfriend. Inmate aides make referrals to the mental health staff and vice versa depending on the needs of the inmate in crisis. They are available to sit with inmates in crisis during the night when necessary. In order to avoid attracting inmates who seek personal gain from volunteering, volunteers should not receive extra privileges for their work, save perhaps an extra recreation period in which they are expected to work as aides, and they should not receive time off from their sentence.

Devilly, Sorbello, Eccleston, and Ward (2005) reviewed three peer counseling programs in prisons in Australia, Canada, and England. They were all Samaritan-based, and all provided inmate counselors on a 24/7 basis. The counselors were permitted to spend the night in the cell with the inmate in crisis. They found that the general prison population supported the existence of these programs, and clients of the programs reported feeling better (less depressed and isolated) after receiving help. In addition, the peer counselors had an increased sense of self-worth and self-confidence.

Junker, Beeler, and Bates (2005) reported on a program in an American federal prison that provided inmate volunteers, trained in active listening skills, to be with suicidal inmates, thereby providing direct and constant observation. Although Junker and colleagues did not examine the impact of the program on suicidal behavior per se, they noted that the average length of the suicide watches declined from 109 hours to 64 hours, which suggests that the inmate volunteers helped to ameliorate the suicidal crises.

One possible danger in using inmates for such a sensitive task is that they might behave in an unethical manner. In an effort to prevent this problem, volunteers are not accepted into the SAMS in the Pen program if they had a recent history of violence, intimidation, drug use or drug trafficking, numerous minor infractions, or a few major infractions while incarcerated. Additional reasons for disqualification were unmanaged mental illness and a diagnosis of antisocial personality disorder (Hall & Gabor, 2004). Snow (2002) cautions that the use of inmate listeners would not be appropriate in juvenile facilities, as juveniles may lack the maturity to handle the work and to maintain confidentiality. Instead, juvenile facilities can attempt to work with outside volunteer groups.

Suicide prevention programs that rely on volunteers who are inmates raise many more potential problems than similar volunteer programs in the community. Potential breaches of ethics (professional conduct, especially involving confidentiality), boundary issues (such as the lack of knowledge of the peer counselors), and abuse of the system need to be considered and prevented. Hall and Gabor (2004) found some corrections officers to be concerned about the true reasons for requests to see Samaritans, as they suspected that requests from inmates in segregation had more to do with social visits than inmate crises. Additionally, correctional staff must be very careful in screening and training inmates. Inmates who are not appropriate for this position could cause serious harm, such as declining to summon a corrections officer in the event of a suicide attempt. One of the advantages of having inmate listeners with inmates in crisis is that the presence of the listeners allows for constant supervision, and with that constant supervision comes the possibility of letting the inmates in crisis keep their personal belongings. This can help inmates tremendously, as they aren't necessarily being moved out of general population, and they have personal items that they can use to distract themselves. The drawback, though, is that these items can be used for a suicide attempt (World Health Organization, 2007).

MEDICATION MANAGEMENT
AS PART OF SUICIDE PREVENTION

Thus far, this chapter has focused on using social and psychological interventions to help inmates cope with incarceration and other stressors in their lives. Since I am a social scientist rather than a psychiatrist or a pharmacist, it would be inappropriate for me to make recommendations regarding types of medication to use. Some inmates have never used legally prescribed medication, while others have with little success. Some, however, have experienced periods of medically assisted stabilization. Correctional staff should consult with inmates to learn about their medication history. Family members can also be important resources, as are treatment personnel in the community who may have worked with these individuals. Such discussions may remove a lot of the guesswork, save weeks to months of time that would be otherwise spent experimenting with different types of medication, and spare the inmate periods of suffering without the appropriate medication.

Unfortunately, even if correctional medical staff are able to identify medication that has worked for inmates in the past, there is no guarantee that the inmates will be able to receive that medication. In an effort to save money, some correctional medical contracts have preferred drug list clauses that require inmates to spend weeks on cheaper medication before the staff can administer the medication that has been successful in the past. If inmates have already tried that cheaper medication and have found it to be unsuccessful, they may still have to try it again while incarcerated due to fail first policies (Slate et al., 2013).

MULTIFACTORED SUICIDE PREVENTION
PROGRAMS AND STRONG INSTITUTIONAL CULTURE

I have discussed some effective individual programs and tactics that can be used to assist prisoners in crisis. While these individual programs have the potential to be helpful, they should be components of a comprehensive, multi-factored suicide prevention program. Barker and colleagues (2014) conducted a systematic review of the institutional suicide prevention literature and concluded that multifactored prevention programs had the greatest potential for being successful. The more successful programs included good intake screening, enhanced staff training, observation to assess suicide risk, psychological treatment for suicidal inmates, limits on the use of isolation, safe housing, and increased social support. To maximize success, program implementation should begin upon inmate arrival and continue throughout incarceration. The National Commission on Correctional Health Care's (2015) accreditation standards call for facilities to have multifactored programs with staff training and inmate screening and evaluation, proper referral procedures, use of appropriate housing and monitoring, plans for intervention in the event of a suicide attempt, and a full review and debriefing if a suicide does occur.

The U.S. Pretrial Services Office in the Central District of California has developed a multifactored program to prevent suicide among pretrial individuals accused of sex offenses. Defendants are immediately referred for a psychological assessment after their initial court appearance. During this assessment, staff screen the defendants for depression, anxiety, and suicidal ideation. Those in need of assistance are put into support groups to focus on dealing with the impact of arrest, and they are also enrolled in CBT to address catastrophic thinking patterns (Byrne et al., 2009).

The ACCT program in England and Wales is intended to be a multifactored program. I note "intended" here, because I wrote in Chapter 5 that there have been implementation issues that have allowed some at-risk inmates to go without the necessary treatment. When implemented properly, inmates whose screenings indicate that they are at risk for self-harm are fully assessed. Staff then develop individual care programs that include mental health treatment and may also include family involvement when appropriate, peer-support activities, access to religious mentors, and access to recreational and in-cell activities (Newcomen, 2014b).

Slade and Forrester (2015) studied the implementation of the F2052SH/ACCT program in England and Wales as well as other key developments in suicide prevention in prisons. The authors tracked the evolution of suicide prevention plans in one London prison from the time when the institution lacked a comprehensive plan to prevent suicides (1978–1990), to the introduction and use of the F2052SH and ACCT forms (1991–2008), to the implementation of additional multifactored programming at the local level (2009–2011). The authors found significant reductions in suicide during the implementation of the national suicide prevention strategy and then again with the local innovations. Specific elements of the successful local policy were changes in the overall institutional culture, with a value placed on listening skills and compassion along with a belief that segregation should be used as infrequently as possible. Senior managers regularly communicated that suicide prevention was an institutional priority and that suicides were not inevitable. The facility held multiagency meetings with senior members of each department present to discuss management of high-risk individuals. Additionally, a senior level forensic psychologist served as a boundary-spanner to help link all of the various disciplines in the prison, so they could work toward the common goal of suicide prevention.

Just as a strong institutional culture that backs suicide prevention programs can help to facilitate the development of strong multifactored programming, a weak culture or one that does not prioritize safety in the institution can have the opposite effect. Thomas, Leaf, Kazmierczak, and Stone (2006) warned criminologists about the hazards of ignoring the role prison conditions play in the incidence of self-harming behaviors. In previous chapters, I discussed the link between in-prison victimization and suicides and self-harm. When considering the recent increase in suicide rates in prisons in the United Kingdom, Liebling and Ludlow (2016) noted that this uptick coincided with organizational changes, prison population growth, and an increase in unrest among prisoners. This is in marked contrast to the decrease in suicide rates in the United Kingdom following the implementation of the 2001 Safer Custody Strategy. The impact of the correctional environment and management practices of the facilities will be addressed in greater detail in Chapter 7.

RESPONDING TO SUICIDES

Responding to an Attempt in Progress

Prevention programs can go a long way toward reducing suicide attempts, but staff must always be prepared for the possibility that an inmate will self-harm or attempt to take his or her own life. Officers should be equipped with tools that can help them cut through materials used as a ligature. All officers should be certified in CPR and first aid, and the facilities should have external defibrillators available and accessible (ACA, 2010). Officers should be trained to enter the cell as soon as possible and, if there is any chance that the inmate is still alive, begin life-saving measures immediately. Staff should also immediately call 911 to expedite the arrival of emergency medical technicians. It may seem like common sense that officers should cut down a hanging person or work to cut a ligature in the event of postural asphyxiation. There have been instances when staff members have chosen to leave the scene intact for investigators rather than attempt to save the person's life (*Heflin v. Stewart County*, 1992). In another case, officers left the body hanging because they were afraid that the inmate staged the suicide attempt in order to lure officers into the cell and attack them (*Turney v. Waterbury*, 2004). In both cases, there were questions about whether the inmates would have survived had they been cut down immediately upon detection. It will likely be easier for medical personnel to check for vital signs once inmates are placed flat on the floor, so even if it appears that they are dead, it would be wise to err on the side of caution and check vital signs once the body is on the floor.

BEREAVEMENT COUNSELING
AND THE PSYCHOLOGICAL AUTOPSY

The aftermath of a suicide is likely to be traumatic for everyone involved. Those who survive a suicide often have great difficulty dealing with the emotions and thoughts aroused by the death. In the penal setting, there are fellow inmates and staff as well as family and friends who must cope with these feelings. The work that the corrections staff must do for the suicidal inmate does not end at the time of death. Bereavement counseling is necessary for those who knew the inmate, and the institution should also conduct a mortality review to try to prevent such an incident from occurring again.

The NCCHC (2015) recommends reviewing every death by suicide within 30 days of its occurrence. The work should include an administrative review, a clinical mortality review, and a psychological autopsy. The administrative review allows the staff to assess the actions surrounding the inmate's deaths, such as areas where the facility operations, policies, and procedures might be improved. The clinical mortality review considers the clinical care that the inmate received. The purpose here is to find areas of patient care or system policies and procedures that need improvement. Psychological autopsies are also sometimes referred to as postmortem or psychological reconstruction. This is a written reconstruction of the deceased's life. In the psychological autopsy, investigators attempt to study mental health factors that might have contributed to the suicide. According to the NCCHC, the clinical mortality review and the psychological autopsy should attempt to answer three questions:

(1) Could the facility improve the medical or mental health response; (2) Was an earlier intervention possible; and (3) Is it possible to improve patient care?

The British Home Office (1999) recommends assigning a staff member to serve as a personal link between the decedent's family and the correctional facility. This staff member should be able to provide the family with recommendations for bereavement counselors. It is also important to have good communication with the other inmates residing in the facility. They should be provided with as much information about the deceased and the suicide as possible (without violating confidentiality), and correctional institutions should allow the deceased's relatives to meet inmates who were friends with the deceased. Snow and McHugh (2002) suggest that the correctional staff should consider letting the family see where the suicide occurred and offer to hold a memorial service for the inmate at the facility.

The Victoria Department of Justice Correctional Services Task Force (1998) recommends a post-incident debriefing within a few days of the suicide with the goal of rectifying any immediate supervision or physical plant problems that facilitated the suicide. The debriefing should involve all lockup/jail/prison employees as well as representatives from any outside agencies that were involved with the inmate's custody and treatment. The full investigation will likely take months, but there are some things that could be done in the first few days after the incident that can prevent additional suicides. For example, if the inmate strangled himself with a phone cord that was in the lockup area, removal of that cord is a commonsense move that does not require months of interviews and analysis: it should be done immediately. Hayes (1994) recommends commencing with a Critical Incident Stress Debriefing (CISD) within 24 to 72 hours of the incident. There are two purposes of the CISD. The first is to get information about the circumstances surrounding the suicide. The second is to allow staff members to process their feelings about the incident. The full mortality review should include a thorough look at any of the facilities' procedures that are relevant to the suicide. This could include the training provided to all involved staff members, review of the medical and mental health services, discussion about whether the physical characteristics of the facility facilitated the attempt, screening and supervision procedures, and any other operational procedures that may have been pertinent to the incident (Hayes, 2005).

It is difficult to overemphasize the importance of learning as much as possible from an incident of self-harm in custody, especially suicides. In England and Wales, Her Majesty's Prison Service Safer Custody Group studied 172 self-inflicted deaths, 58% of which were determined to be suicide and 14% with open verdicts. The group determined that 15% of the inmate deaths were preventable. They cited the need for greater supervision in 46% of cases, need for better staff training in risk assessment for 26%, placement with another inmate in 26%, more staff for 23%, improved clinical management and inmate support for 22%, and enhanced communication between staff members in 21% (Shaw et al., 2004). Administrators have an ethical, and perhaps legal, obligation to ask themselves if there was anything that could have prevented the death and then adequately address those issues.

It is important to recognize that the staff members directly involved in the incident, as well as those who were not involved but knew the deceased, are likely to be deeply affected by the suicide. The American Psychiatric Association (2016) urges correctional administrations to be mindful of the staff members' need for assistance during this time. Peer-to-peer discussion groups may be helpful. An employee assistance program should also be made available to the staff members who may wish to seek counseling (APA, 2016).

CONCLUSION

While prisons and jails were never meant to be psychiatric facilities, the reality is that they have been assigned that function. Incarceration does present an opportunity to reach and help inmates who have not received adequate mental health services in the past or those who have experienced periods of medically and/or therapeutically assisted stability but have destabilized. There are, of course, also inmates who do not have a psychiatric history but may experience high levels of stress and depression simply due to the situation in which they find themselves. Fortunately, there are programs that correctional administrations can implement to reduce suicide and NSSI among inmates. Multifactored programs, beginning with well-implemented assessment and ending with reentry-planning and aftercare when available, are effective when executed correctly. CBT and dialectical behavior therapy have the potential to teach inmates effective coping strategies, while crisis intervention procedures are likely to help with more immediate problems. While well-trained inmates can certainly be an integral part of an overall suicide prevention program, they cannot be utilized as the institution's sole response to inmates in crisis.

Training is absolutely essential, as is a positive institutional culture. Facilities should have employees trained in crisis intervention on staff at all times. All staff should receive some level of initial training as well as yearly in-service follow-up. Correctional administrators should also keep abreast of what professional organizations have to offer. For example, the American Correctional Association has established the Correctional Behavioral Health Certification and Training (CBHCT) program to train correctional staff members. The program gives staff the opportunity to learn more about the signs and symptoms of mental illness and the role that it plays in the behavior of inmates with mental illness (Sloan & Efeti, 2017). This, and other programs, may be of great help for correctional agencies looking to professionalize their staff.

Chapter Seven

Facility Design and Suicide Prevention

The primary focus of Chapter 6 was counseling and treatment of inmates who are in crisis or are experiencing symptoms of mental illness. Such treatment has the potential to help people get through the crisis, learn about the symptoms associated with their psychiatric diagnosis, and discover and practice the use of safe and effective coping mechanisms. These are all very important services and can help to prevent suicides. In the previous chapter, I also discussed the importance of multifactored suicide prevention programs. Part of these programs should include strategies to restrict inmate access to ways to commit suicide while the staff helps inmates through the crisis period. Multifactored programs should also include plans to help establish a culture throughout the facility that prioritizes the safety of everyone and serves as primary suicide prevention. The focus of this chapter is suicide prevention with an emphasis on how the environment influences behavior. Specifically, I will draw on situational crime prevention research to provide some insight into individuals' decision-making processes and ways that correctional administrators and facility designers can reduce suicide attempts. The strategies can range from subtle adjustments to the environment that make suicide attempts more difficult to substantial changes to both the physical structure of the facility as well as management strategies. As we know from Chapter 3, suicides and suicide attempts are not distributed equally across all security levels, facility types, and housing settings. In this chapter, I will present research on ways to produce more positive living conditions that can reduce violence, stress, and suicides.

BRIEF REVIEW OF CHARACTERISTICS OF INMATE SUICIDES

There are some clear patterns that have emerged from the correctional suicide research discussed in Chapters 3 and 4. We know how and where the majority of correctional suicides happen: the typical inmate suicide involves hanging or asphyxiation while an inmate is alone. Suicides are also more likely to occur when inmates are in segregation. Of course, there are exceptions, and some inmates have died while housed in multiple-occupancy cells, by finding a place to jump, or by cutting themselves. Hanging and asphyxiation tend to be much more common, since inmates often have the tools for this at their disposal. For hanging or asphyxiation, all that is required is a bed sheet or an article of clothing and a tie-off point, which is usually a piece of furniture, window/door bars, or vents. Given this information, it is logical to assume that measures taken to reduce inmates' opportunities to make and attach ligatures will help to reduce the number of suicides and suicide attempts.

SITUATIONAL CRIME PREVENTION

Researchers and criminal justice professionals who utilize situational crime prevention (SCP) techniques to prevent crime aim to make "discrete managerial and environmental changes to reduce the opportunity for those crimes to occur" (Clarke, 1997, p. 2). SCP is rooted in the rational choice perspective of crime, which suggests that people engage in at least some rudimentary weighing of the advantages and disadvantages of committing any given act (Cornish & Clarke, 1985, 1987). The rational choice perspective was inspired by the classical school of criminology. Jeremy Bentham (1789 [1948]), one of the leading theorists of the classical school, believed that people, including offenders, consciously seek pleasure while avoiding pain. SCP techniques aim to increase the chances that criminal behavior will be detected and/or will be less rewarding than the potential benefits to be gained from the crime. If it is possible to create an imbalance of risks and rewards that favors the risks, SCP supporters believe that this strategy will deter potential offenders. SCP techniques can be applied to suicide by making a suicide attempt more difficult to initiate or complete and to remove desirable methods for suicide.

Clarke (1997) identified three characteristics of SCP tactics: (1) They are directed at highly specific forms of crime; (2) They involve the manipulation of the immediate environment; and (3) They make crime more difficult and risky or less rewarding and excusable to potential offenders. It is possible to apply SCP to custodial suicide, since it is a very specific act that tends to occur in known locations using particular items. One of the reasons why environmental techniques have the potential to be successful at preventing custodial suicides is because there is evidence that most people make choices about the types of risk that they are willing to take, even when choosing a way to die. Before I get to that, let's look at an example of how decision-making can influence offending. Why do people rob convenience stores when these establishments rarely have much money? Banks, on the other hand, are full of money. One reason why convenience stores are such popular targets is that what makes them convenient—24-hour access—also makes them available for crime at all hours, particularly during the evening when there are few witnesses. Convenience stores also have very little security, especially when compared to banks. The factors that impact this decision-making process are what Cornish and Clarke (1985) called "choice-structuring properties." Clarke and Cornish argued that there are elements of each act that may make them more or less attractive to individuals. In the case of choosing a location for a robbery, the lower risk of getting caught is what tends to make convenience store robberies more attractive to most potential offenders.

Clarke and Lester (1989) argued that a similar thought process occurs with suicides, as individuals seek certain methods for suicide attempts but avoid others. Earlier in this book, I noted that males in the community are more likely to use a gun in a suicide, whereas females tend to resort to cutting or medication overdoses. Researchers have speculated that women prefer to stay away from the very violent and disfiguring death associated with gunshots. Women also tend to select less lethal methods, perhaps because they might be more ambivalent about their desire for the suicide to be successful or that they want to have an "out" in the event that they do decide to live after the attempt is already in progress. If the desired method of suicide is unavailable, alternative methods may lack certain choice-structuring properties, thereby reducing the likelihood that individuals will switch to the available method (Clarke & Lester, 1989; Lester, 2009). Clarke and Lester (1989) concluded

> that availability of lethal agents does influence suicidal behavior suggests, however, that the act of taking one's life is in large measure also a product of situational factors. This is consistent with the crisis model of suicide intervention, which posits that the suicidal crisis is usually temporary, and intervention may be needed only to get the suicidal person through a bad night or couple of days (p. 98).

Table 7.1 includes a list of choice-structuring properties as they apply to methods of committing suicide.

Table 7.1. Choice Structuring Properties of Suicide

1. Availability	11. Discovery of body
2. Familiarity with the method	12. "Contamination" of nest
3. Technical skills needed	13. Scope for concealing/publicizing death
4. Planning necessary	14. Certainty of death
5. Likely pain	15. Time taken to die
6. "Courage" needed	16. Scope for second thoughts
7. Consequences of failure	17. Chances of intervention
8. Disfigurement after death	18. Symbolism
9. Danger/inconvenience to others	19. Masculine/feminine
10. Messiness/bloodiness	20. Dramatic impact

Source: Clarke, R.V. & Lester, D. (1989). *Suicide: Closing the exits.* New York: Springer-Verlag.

A common argument against efforts to restrict access to popular methods of suicide is the substitution hypothesis, meaning that if the preferred method is suddenly unavailable, a suicidal individual will simply switch to another method. Findings of suicide research, however, do not support the substitution hypothesis (Florentine & Crane, 2010; Lester, 2009; Sarchiapone et al., 2011). Researchers have provided examples of successful efforts to limit access to preferred methods of suicide in the community, such as detoxification of domestic gas, changes to catalytic converters to produce less carbon monoxide, reductions in firearms availability, changes to the chemical makeup of antidepressants, and installation of barriers at common jumping sites (Florentine & Crane, 2010; Sarchiapone et al., 2011). These changes have resulted in overall reductions of suicide in the community rather than an even displacement to other tactics. Florentine and Crane concluded that "If access to highly lethal methods of suicide is reduced, even where substitution occurs, the proportion of people who survive attempts will be increased" (p. 1628).

While people are in custody, many of the conventionally used methods of suicide are unavailable. As was discussed in Chapter 3, the restrictions of access to materials for most methods of suicide leave only one highly lethal option—hanging/asphyxiation. If that method is restricted and others are controlled by vigilant staff, inmates are left with no conventional options. What is left is repeatedly banging one's head against a hard surface, such as a wall or toilet seat. This is extremely painful, and it would take the inmate a long time to die. It is also difficult for a person to repeatedly overcome one's instincts for self-preservation and continue to hit the wall headfirst. Additionally, it is possible for the individual to lose consciousness, thereby ending the suicide attempt. Another method, which has been used occasionally in jails, is forcing oneself to choke on toilet paper. An inmate can stuff a wad of toilet paper into his or her mouth and then pour water on it. This causes the toilet paper to expand, and it also makes it difficult to remove the paper from the inmate's throat. Neither of these methods are popular, and they are rarely used. The consequence is that displacement of tactics would be unlikely should hanging/asphyxiation become unavailable. The increased costs of more pain, prolonged suffering, and increased likelihood of detection, all of which are associated with a method such as head-banging and gagging on toilet paper, are likely to be viewed by many who contemplate suicide as impractical.

Research suggests that suicidal crises can be fleeting. In a study of 26,000 college students, Drum, Brownson, Burton Denmark, and Smith (2009) found that 84% of people had a crisis that lasted a week or less, while 56% were suicidal for a day at most. In some early correctional suicide research, Felthous (1994) suggested that, for inmates who are not seriously mentally ill but who are facing a crisis due to either incarceration itself or a by-product of incarceration (separation from family, fear of victimization, etc.), correctional staff will need to keep them safe during their "window of vulnerability." Given the evidence that suicidal crises do not persist for long in most people, situational prevention might be effective in getting them through the immediate crisis. Inmates who have had persistent problems with mental illness and tend to be vulnerable on a more regular basis will require mental health treatment, but situational prevention techniques could reduce the opportunity for suicide attempts during the crisis periods.

Clarke (1997) identified four general categories of SCP techniques: increasing perceived effort, increasing perceived risks, reducing anticipated rewards, and removing excuses. Within each category, the techniques were further divided. Tartaro (1999) applied these 16 techniques to suicide prevention in a jail or lockup setting. I made some minor modifications to the list of those techniques (Table 7.2). These techniques vary in their effectiveness of preventing suicide. With that in mind, one might assume that the methods that eliminate the possibility of anyone being able to commit suicide would automatically be best, but that is not necessarily true. Strapping an inmate to a bunk and keeping the person restrained for days will certainly stop a suicide attempt for that period of time, but besides the likely unconstitutionality of this idea, it is inhumane and can be damaging to people in the long run. For that reason, I have identified techniques that are "negative" in that they may promote additional stress and negative feelings and those that are "positive" and have the potential to promote prosocial behavior and reduce stress. Some of the prevention techniques, such as improving officer sight-lines, cell redistribution for vulnerable inmates, screening, and use of an inmate buddy system are identified as positive prevention measures. I also added behavioral management and use of podular direct supervision to the "facilitating compliance" category. While some aspects of those models might not directly

Table 7.2. Situational Approaches to Suicide Prevention

Increasing Perceived Effort	Increasing Perceived Risks	Reducing Anticipated Rewards	Removing Excuses
Target hardening[b] Refined air grills Hidden door hinges Collapsible clothing hooks	*Entry/exit screening*[a] Screen for suicidality Screen for psychiatric history Screen for intoxication	*Target removal*[b] Remove tie-off points	*Rule setting* Clothing and room restrictions for noncompliance
Access control[a] Cell redistribution	*Formal surveillance*[a] Increased officer surveillance Mental health visits	*Identifying property* Not applicable	*Stimulating conscience*[b] Behavioral contract
Deflecting offenders[b] Use of restrictive housing	*Surveillance by employees*[a] Trained inmates CCTV	*Reducing temptation* Caution about failure	*Controlling disinhibitors* Supervise issuance of medication Removal of drugs/alcohol
Controlling facilitators[b] Remove belt, shoelaces, and suspenders	*Natural surveillance*[a] Podular direct supervision Improve sight lines Install larger door panels Plexiglass doors	*Denying benefits* Not applicable	*Facilitating compliance*[a] Podular direct supervision Inmate behavior management

Adapted from Tartaro, C. (1999). Reduction of suicides in jail and lockups through situation crime prevention. *Journal of Correctional Health Care, 6,* 235–263.
[a] Positive prevention techniques.
[b] Negative prevention techniques.

address suicide, they work to change the overall corrections environment. As will be explained later in this chapter, both systems offer inmates not only punishments, but rewards for good behavior. The incentive to behave helps to foster less violent and less stressful environments. Being housed in such an area can reduce fear and stress, thereby helping to prevent the onset of a suicidal crisis. Other commonly used techniques, such as target hardening (making the cells suicide-proof), deflecting offenders (use of isolation), and controlling facilitators (removing an inmate's belongings) are effective in that they can serve to reduce the opportunity for a successful suicide attempt, but they can be negative in that they can increase an inmate's sense of despair and motivation for self-harm. Behavioral contracts were also placed in the unhelpful category, for reasons discussed in Chapter 6.

Power's (1997) study of the strict suicidal observation (SSO) program in a Scottish prison provides support for the idea that some prevention techniques that reduce the opportunity for suicide may actually be harmful to inmates. Inmates on SSO were stripped of most items and placed in a bare single cell with a canvas gown and were checked by officers every fifteen minutes. Twenty-nine percent (n = 58) of prisoners surveyed in Power's study reported feeling humiliated and degraded when placed on SSO, primarily because of the canvas clothing they were forced to wear and the conditions of the cells. While 10% of the inmates did report that the isolation was beneficial in that they were permitted time for self-reflection and given protection from other inmates, 20% claimed that the rooms had a "negative emotional impact" on them. The inmates who considered this to be a negative experience reported that the conditions of confinement made them feel more depressed and gave them the impression that they were being punished. As was discussed in Chapters 4 and 5, a substantial proportion of inmates are reluctant to seek help from correctional staff for suicidal ideation for a variety of reasons, including fear of poor treatment. Programs that are interpreted as punitive in nature may deter inmates who need help from seeking it.

Wortley (2002) approached violence in prisons and jails with an environmental point of view, but he construed it quite broadly, focusing on any aspect of the environment that affects the behavior of individuals. In earlier work on SCP, Wortley (1998, 2001) warned that a strong reliance on opportunity reduction measures can be counterproductive and encourage the very behavior that the prevention technique is designed to prevent. Other scholars have made similar arguments. While studying the design of public housing projects, Newman (1972) noted that the extensive use of vandal-resistant fixtures throughout the facilities seemed to actually encourage vandalism instead of deter it. To apply this to suicide prevention, strict opportunity reduction measures that fail to take into consideration the potential negative emotional impact on suicidal inmates might prevent a suicide at that very moment but worsen the inmates' outlook and encourage a later suicide attempt. Wortley (2002) noted that situational tactics are not long-term solutions for suicidal individuals. In Wortley's (2002) words, "situational intervention is about creating safe situations rather than creating safe individuals" (p. 4). While situational tactics are very important and can serve to save lives, it is important to have mental health staff perform psychological evaluations to determine if inmates will need counseling and/or medication to prevent the onset of another crisis.

The next section of this chapter involves descriptions of environmental prevention techniques that can aid in reducing the chances of a suicide attempt. It is important to keep in mind, though, that while some techniques can be helpful over the short-term, they can be harmful if used for prolonged periods of time.

CELL DESIGN

The design of a prison or jail cell can impact an inmate's ability to attempt suicide. Factors, such as officers' ability to see inmates inside the cell and inmates' access to tie-off points, are important to consider; however, access to tie-off points are less of an issue when visibility is high. For example, tie-off points in double- or triple-bunked cells are less likely to be utilized provided that inmates have at least one roommate. Additionally, cells that have high visibility from the outside, such as observation cells that have floor-to-ceiling clear Plexiglass doors, are less likely to have suicide attempts take place in them. If an inmate is suicidal and is going to be housed alone, the safest situation would be to have no tie-off points available.

Prison and jail cells typically have numerous tie-off points that can be used to attach a ligature. Cell bars, shower fixtures, bed frames, door knobs, and air vents are examples of fixtures that have been used for suicides in cells, (Hayes, 2009; Humber et al., 2011; Shaw et al., 2004). Pompili and colleagues (2009) suggest having a few safer cells available for short-term use. Such cells lack exposed pipes, light fixtures, and bars and include modified air vents. Instead of bunks, the bed frame area should be a slab with no sharp corners. The cell should not have any door knobs or hinges, and any hooks should be the kind that will collapse if exposed to a significant amount of weight.

Jails should have some of these cells available, but the suicide-resistant cells should never be considered the totality of a satisfactory suicide prevention program, nor should they be used extensively or for long periods of time.

The availability of some suicide-resistant cells is likely necessary in facilities, particularly those that are unable to provide constant staff supervision of suicidal inmates. One way to attempt to mitigate the unpleasantness of being in these cells is to make them less institutional-looking. Such cells can be painted warm colors, the bed slab can be colored plastic rather than concrete, there can be music playing, and correctional staff can have the inmate placed with a cellmate who is a trained suicide prevention worker. Television screens, outside of the cells but still visible to the inmates, can provide some much-needed stimulation and possibly serve to turn inmates' attention to other topics (Bell, 1999).

INMATE CLOTHING

If an inmate is considered to be in immediate danger and, if constant face-to-face supervision is not possible, provision of special clothing will be necessary. Companies that cater to the needs of corrections agencies manufacture clothing that is difficult to use for a suicide attempt. Some corrections facilities use paper gowns, but there are also tear-proof/fire-proof smocks that are made of much heavier material. Such clothing is typically used in conjunction with a suicide-resistant cell. If placement into this type of cell and provision of special clothing is warranted, movement back to a different cell and a change of clothing should only occur after a qualified mental health professional conducts an assessment and agrees that it is safe to move the individual.

If constant supervision is available, depending on the psychological state of the inmate, it may be possible to forego the special clothing and the suicide-resistant cell. Some correctional staff, however, prefer to have access to a suicide prevention option that inmates will consider unpleasant and/or stigmatizing, thinking that this might deter malingering. I was called to a jail to provide advice on updating a suicide prevention policy a few years ago. This facility puts inmates who self-report suicidal ideation into a green tear- and fire-resistant smock, and then places them in a holding cell with a Plexiglass door and no furniture or toilet. The outfit fits inmates like an ill-fitting dress, which is likely to be especially humiliating for males. These cells are located in the booking area, so all incoming inmates can view the suicidal inmates in cells, wearing the smocks. I suggested that the current plan might be detrimental to the jail in that it could discourage those who are suicidal from seeking help. An officer immediately countered with the argument that the plan helped them weed out the truly suicidal from the malingerers, as the latter typically recant their statements about suicide within an hour or two of being placed in the special outfit. This is likely true, but it could also prevent those who need help from disclosing that to staff. While at the same facility a few years later, I heard treatment staff members talking about an inmate who mentioned that he was hearing voices. When the staff member encouraged the inmate to tell a corrections officer, he refused, saying that he did not want to be placed in the special outfit in the watch area. Out of concern for the inmate, the treatment staff member did go to the administration and report what she knew about his condition, but the inmate refused to do so himself out of fear of the repercussions.

To summarize, special clothing and housing in suicide-resistant cells should be reserved only for the acutely suicidal, and they should be kept in these conditions for the minimum amount of time necessary until other arrangements, such as transfer to a hospital wing or a mental health center, or movement into an area with constant supervision, can be made (Hayes, 2005). Transfers must be made only after consultation with qualified mental health professionals.

MONITORING

Monitoring can be the most powerful tool in preventing suicidal inmates from harming themselves. Inmates who are being watched constantly should not be able to succeed in attempting suicide, as staff should be able to get to the individual and disrupt the attempt before it becomes fatal. If done properly, constant monitoring may allow suicidal inmates to keep some of their belongings, such as books. Monitoring might also reduce reliance on suicide-resistant clothing and cells. Even if the removal of all belongings and placement in special clothing is warranted, the presence of another person may help the suicidal individual feel less alone. Monitoring can be handled in three ways: staff supervision, video surveillance, and inmate supervision.

Staff Supervision

Staff supervision refers to a staff member viewing an inmate with his or her own eyes without the aid of any video surveillance. This means that the staff member must be in somewhat close proximity to the at-risk inmate. The staff member does not have to be in the same room, as an officer can be situated on the other side of a Plexiglass barrier and observe one or two inmates housed in a cell or a few inmates in a dormitory setting.

The National Commission on Correctional Health Care's (2015) accreditation standards recommend different levels of monitoring depending on the inmate's current state. The NCCHC requires constant monitoring for the acutely suicidal, defined as "those who engage in self-injurious behavior or threaten suicide with a specific plan" (p. 110). These individuals require constant supervision, meaning that a person is constantly looking at the at-risk individuals without interruption. Inmates who are nonacutely suicidal, meaning that they have not expressed current suicidal ideation and/or have a recent prior history of "self-destructive behavior," should be monitored with unpredictable checks that occur no more than 15 minutes apart. The unpredictable aspect of these checks is important to either deter suicide attempts or interrupt ones in progress.

Video Surveillance

Video surveillance is common in prisons and jails. Surveillance equipment helps to enhance supervision, especially in hard-to-see areas. Cameras may deter both inmates who are planning an assault and officers who want to use excessive force. They should not, however, be used as the primary method of supervising suicidal inmates. Pompili and colleagues (2009) identified two potential problems with closed-circuit television (CCTV). First, cameras cannot always cover every corner of a room. Inmates observing the angle of the cameras may be able to surmise which areas are not being recorded and then attempt suicide in blind spots. The second problem is the potential for staff members responsible for monitoring the cameras to become distracted.

Most of us have walked past a security guard who was supposed to be monitoring cameras but was, instead, handling other work responsibilities or personal matters. Fortunately, in most of those situations, no harm was done. When CCTV is being used to monitor suicidal inmates, it only takes a few minutes of distraction for there to be a fatality. The *Sisk v. Manzanares* (2002) case illustrates why using CCTV for suicide prevention is so risky. Scotty Ray Sisk became suicidal while incarcerated at the Shawnee County (Kansas) Department of Corrections. Sisk wrote a suicide note that the corrections officers found. In response, the staff placed him on "hard lockdown," rather than assigning him to the rubber cell they regularly used for suicide prevention. Contrary to policy, Sisk was given a standard-issue blanket rather than the tear-away ones the jail used for suicidal inmates. Sisk's new cell was only partially visible with the naked eye, so officers were supposed to watch him on the video monitor and do 15-minute in-person wellness checks. The officers neglected to watch the video and do the checks, and the result was that Sisk was able to attach the blanket to a metal plate and commit suicide. In another case, a Rhode Island corrections officer was responsible for watching a monitor to supervise the suicidal inmates, but the same officer was also responsible for answering the phone and reviewing reports. An inmate was able to make a noose and hang himself without being discovered on this officer's shift (Hayes, 2003).

I have personally witnessed officers responsible for monitoring suicidal inmates ignoring the cameras that were being used as the sole means of supervision. I was in the medical wing of a county jail when the lieutenant escorting me stopped to talk to a few officers. When there was a lull in the conversation, one of the officers assigned to the desk where we were standing asked if I had any questions. I asked what type of supervision was offered for suicidal inmates, and the officer responded "constant." I expressed surprise, since I knew that the suicidal inmates were housed in a hallway around the corner from where we were standing, and it was not possible for any of us to see what they were doing in their cells. When I questioned if it was truly constant supervision, the officer said "Yes, constant. Here, let me show you." He walked around the desk, clicked a few keys on his computer, turned the monitor toward me and said "See, constant." I am uncertain whether any of those inmates would have been able to commit suicide, as they were in barren cells with only a paper gown and no blankets, but in the time that I was standing there, they were completely unmonitored for 10 to 15 minutes.

Electronic surveillance can also malfunction. Between the possibility of malfunctioning and the temptations associated with being pulled away from video observation duties, video surveillance of suicidal inmates should never be used as a substitute for monitoring. At best, it can be used as a supplement (Hayes, 2010; NCCHC, 2015; Pompili et al., 2009).

Use of Inmate Companions for Surveillance

Chapter 6 included a section devoted to the use of inmate companions, or buddies, as part of suicide prevention programs. Trained inmates who have established good reputations can supplement staff observation. The extent of inmates' responsibilities tends to vary from program to program, with some inmates being used only for monitoring, while others engage in active listening and act as a support for inmates who are having difficulty coping. These programs work to address multiple challenges faced by jail administrators. First, it is difficult to devote staff to monitor just one inmate, or even a few inmates. Jails and prisons are rarely short of inmates, however, and some inmates can be trustworthy and reliable. Second, the mere presence of a peer may help to reduce inmates' feelings of isolation. Third, the suicidal inmate might feel more comfortable interacting with a fellow inmate compared to a staff member.

Junker and associates (2005) presented research that supports the use of inmates to supplement supervision of suicidal individuals. The Bureau of Prisons Suicide Prevention Program trained staff at all levels about risk factors for suicides, behaviors that might precede a suicide attempt, and the procedures for communicating concerns about an inmate. As part of this program, the Inmate Observation Program paired suicidal inmates with inmate observers to provide constant supervision. Inmate volunteers were screened to confirm that they had clean institutional conduct records. Those who passed the screening stage participated in a four-hour training session and learned to observe, but not counsel, the inmates in crisis. The researchers found that the average stay on suicide watch decreased from 109 hours prior to implementation of the program to 64 hours when inmates were used to supplement monitoring. Junker and colleagues provided two possible explanations for this finding. The first possibility is that the inmate observation program reduced opportunities for potentially suicidal inmates to manipulate staff members. While inmates on suicide watch continued to interact with staff members, they primarily found themselves in closer contact with fellow inmates rather than staff, thus reducing the reward of increased staff attention. The second possible explanation was that the involvement of peers in this program might have provided much-needed extra support that helped inmates' moods improve, resulting in fewer hours spent on observation. Junker et al. reported that the program helped the Bureau of Prisons' Medical Referral Center save $30,000 in overtime pay in one year.

Of course, not all inmates can be trusted to do a good job. All of the inmate observation programs discussed in this book involved thorough screening of inmates prior to their participation. Pompili and colleagues (2009) caution that placement of suicidal inmates in just any double-bunked cell could be counterproductive. Some cellmates may remain quiet and fail to alert staff members of a suicide attempt in progress. Even when proper volunteer screening does take place, the use of inmate volunteers for suicide prevention should serve as supplement to, not a replacement of, staff involvement and observation (NCCHC, 2015).

The Role of Crowding in Inmate Suicides

Crowding places a strain on resources as medical departments, counseling services, and other offices become overwhelmed and are unable to provide services and see inmates in a timely manner. Crowding, on the other hand, makes it more difficult for inmates to find themselves alone, thereby possibly reducing the number of completed suicides. Researchers have studied the relationship between crowding and suicide, and most studies have found no association. Leese et al. (2006) studied self-inflicted deaths in prisons in England and Wales from 2000 through 2002 and found that, when considering other facility-level characteristics such as program availability, prison type, inmate visitation, and number of positive drug tests per facility, crowding was not related to the number of suicides. Van Ginneken et al. (2017) expanded on Leese et al.'s work and analyzed suicides in prisons in England and Wales from 2000 through 2014. They also did not find crowding to be a predictor of inmate suicides. Rabe (2012) obtained data on prison suicides in Russia, Turkey, Albania, Norway, Switzerland, and Croatia from 1997 through 2008. While overall inmate mortality was positively correlated with crowding levels, suicide was not. One study that did find a relationship between crowding and suicide analyzed prior suicide data from Germany from 2000 through 2011. Opitz-Welke et al. (2013) suggested that it was likely inmates' reduced access to programs and services due to crowding that impacted suicide rates. Sharkey's (2010) interviews of inmates who attempted suicide while in prison support Opitz-Welke and colleagues' theory about the link between lack of resources due to crowding and suicides. Nine of the 10 individuals that Sharkey interviewed cited crowding as a motivator for their suicide attempt and, of these individuals, two-thirds said that the staff members in the crowded facilities were too busy to talk with the at-risk inmates.

Additional Thoughts on Monitoring

In a national study of suicide in custody, Hayes (2010) found that 7.5% of inmates who committed suicide did so while they were on precautions to prevent that very act from happening. Humber and colleagues (2011) reported that 58% of correctional suicides in England and Wales had an open Assessment, Core in Custody, and Teamwork (ACCT) form, meaning that they were identified as being at risk. Hayes discussed how it is possible that inmates can succeed in committing suicide while seemingly part of a plan of action to ensure their safety. Of Hayes's five explanations for inmate suicides occurring despite precautions, four were related to problems with monitoring. Hayes attributed these suicides to (1) staff failing to observe inmates at the required intervals, (2) staff placing inmates on an inappropriate observation level given the inmates' risk levels, (3) use of an observation level out of line with national standards, and (4) use of unreliable CCTV monitoring. The only factor that Hayes identified that was not directly associated with monitoring was placement of inmates in a cell that contains fixtures usable for attaching a ligature. Even that issue could be ameliorated with more effective monitoring, as inmates under constant monitoring would be unlikely to have the opportunity to create and attach a ligature.

Although the percentage of suicides occurring in the first 24 to 72 hours of incarceration has declined over the past decade (Hayes, 2010), this period of time remains critical for inmate supervision. The British Home Office (1999) recommends that all new receptions to corrections facilities be held under close observation in a special reception area for the first 48 hours of incarceration. In addition to close observation by staff, the Home Office recommends that new inmates be housed in multiple-occupancy cells and that inmates trained in listening and looking for signs of suicide spend some time with the newcomers. Newcomen (2014a) suggested using listeners for inmates who require peer support. Listeners are adult prisoners trained by the Samaritans. As was discussed in the previous chapter, the Samaritans are a suicide prevention group that operates both inside and outside of correctional facilities. Listeners are adult inmates trained by the Samaritans who can act as peer supporters to incoming inmates. Since new inmates are likely to need extra help, Newcomen also suggested utilizing the Insider's Scheme. This is a group of trained inmates who offer assistance specifically to new inmates as they adjust to the shock of initial incarceration and work to navigate their new setting.

USE OF ISOLATION/RESTRICTIVE HOUSING FOR MENTALLY ILL AND/OR SUICIDAL INMATES

Isolation has historically been a commonly used tool to address suicidality in the corrections system, with the thought being that the suicidal person might be too dangerous to be around others. Isolation has also been used for inmates with mental illness who are difficult to manage. The term "padded cell" is known for being the place where people deemed "crazy" would be housed inside psychiatric hospitals. Of course, the idea behind placing a person alone in a padded cell is to remove any opportunity for self-harm or harm to others. Over the past few decades, advocates for prisoners and individuals with mental illness have warned of the drawbacks to using isolation, particularly in a barren environment with little to no stimulation. Isolation is still a tactic that is used in prisons and jails for a variety of reasons. While isolating inmates can address some security problems, such as violence against others and escapes, the information shared in Chapter 3 shows that it also increases the chances of suicide attempts.

For inmates who may not be suicidal but are experiencing symptoms of mental illness that make them a challenge to manage, isolation may be deemed necessary due to the possibility that they are a danger to others, but it should still be used as sparingly as possible and should be combined with several precautions. What follows is a discussion of different types of isolation and restrictive housing options used in corrections settings.

As discussed in Chapter 3, there is an important distinction between being housed alone and being put in isolation. Some inmates actually prefer being alone, as it provides safeguards against inmate assaults. Additionally, people who are more introverted are likely to feel much more comfortable in an area where they are not forced to interact with others (Toch, 1992b). Being housed alone is not necessarily isolation. Inmates may be placed in single cells in the general population and have full access to programs and recreation offered · in the facility. Isolation involves placement in a restrictive setting. There are, of course, instances where inmates will feign suicidal ideation or even commit infractions with the hope of being placed in a restrictive isolation setting (Pizarro & Narag, 2008). More often than not, though, isolation, segregation, or restrictive housing are considered to be undesirable and, for some, unbearable.

The National Commission on Correctional Health Care (2015) refers to segregated inmates as "those isolated from the general population and who receive services and activities apart from other inmates" (p. 87). As was noted in Chapter 3, the U.S. Department of Justice (2016) uses the term "restrictive housing" instead of isolation. Restrictive housing is a broader term and includes three criteria: (1) removal from the general population, (2) placement in a locked room or cell (alone or with another inmate), and (3) an inability to leave the cell for most of the day. This type of housing can be used for punitive purposes, with placement in this setting for a determinate period of time, for preventive reasons such as the inmate's protection against self or others, or for administrative segregation, meaning that the inmate is deemed a danger to the safety of others or to the security of the institution.

There has been increased interest in restrictive housing units in the past 20 years, with inmate protests, federal court filings, and policy statements from professional organizations bringing attention to the danger of overreliance on this type of housing. Researchers have found that inmates in some states were being housed in restrictive housing for years, with the average length of stay in administrative segregation of six years in Illinois, prior to the closure of their units in 2009. Inmates in Washington State averaged 11 months, and the average stay in Texas was nearly 4 years (Shames, Wilcox, & Subramanian, 2015). Inmates in Pelican Bay in California organized a hunger strike that lasted for eight weeks and involved hundreds of inmates to bring attention to how difficult it was to be removed from the security housing unit (SHU) once placed there (Reiter, 2016; Shames et al., 2015). Shames et al. (2015) reported that anywhere from one-third to one-half of people placed in segregated housing across the country are mentally ill. It is unclear, however, what percentage were mentally ill prior to the housing transfer and what percentage were diagnosed with mental illness during their time in segregation.

In the United States, the federal court system became more active in examining the living conditions in restrictive housing units in the 1990s.

The conditions at Pelican Bay were scrutinized in *Madrid v. Gomez* (1995). While the federal court did not find that segregation itself was a violation of the 8th Amendment, it did find that housing mentally ill inmates in this way constituted cruel and unusual punishment. Six years later, one of Wisconsin's prisons was the target of a federal suit, and again, the court emphasized the negative impact that this type of setting has on all inmates, but especially those suffering from mental illness (*Jones 'El. v. Berge*, 2001). The *Jones 'El* court noted that Dr. Terry Kupers, an expert on solitary confinement, discussed "segregated housing syndrome," which is a combination of several psychiatric diagnoses, such as dissociative disorder, schizophrenia, panic disorder, and delusional disorder.

> According to Kupers, isolated confinement intensifies symptoms for those prone to mental illness. The almost total isolation and inactivity deprives seriously mentally ill inmates of reality checks; they receive no feedback to keep their psychosis in check. Seriously mentally ill inmates in isolated conditions lose total control of their lives. They feel incapable of being an active agent in their lives; this feeling exacerbates depressive tendencies. Without interaction and without diurnal rhythms provided by light, seriously mentally ill inmates lose their sense of time and of the future, leading to great despair and hopelessness. This sense of doom is compounded when seriously mentally ill inmates are not capable of following the rules necessary to earn their way out of the most restrictive status (*Jones 'El v. Berge*, 2001, p. 1103).

Federal lawsuits were important factors in what appears to be a significant shift in the way the United States approaches isolation of prisoners. Wisconsin, California, Pennsylvania, New York, New Jersey, Mississippi, and a few other states have had their segregation policies reviewed in federal court, resulting in significant reforms. In Illinois, it was the executive branch of government that acted to reduce the use of solitary confinement, with the governor cutting off funding for prisons with administrative segregation units. As of 2015, the legislatures in 12 states were working on bills to pass reforms regarding isolation in their states (Reiter, 2016). The U.S. Department of Justice (2016) announced that it would start to limit the use of restrictive housing in the federal prison system. Federal inmates who are deemed suitable for restrictive housing are to remain there only as long as necessary to achieve the specific goal of the placement. The team assigned to review inmates' cases must include mental health professionals. Additionally, correctional staff must establish a clear plan for inmates to return to less restrictive conditions as soon as possible. Juveniles and inmates with serious mental illness are no longer permitted to be placed in restrictive housing, and inmates needing protective custody should be placed in a safe, yet less restrictive, setting.

Some professional organizations have recently passed resolutions regarding the potential danger of solitary confinement. The American Psychiatric Association announced their opposition to prolonged segregation of inmates with serious mental illnesses in 2012 (APA, 2016). In 2014, the American Medical Association's (AMA) House of Delegates released a statement asserting that solitary confinement is detrimental to adolescent health. They recommended ceasing the use of this practice, except for extraordinary circumstances where safety of the juvenile or others is at stake. The AMA also stated their opposition to the use of adolescent solitary confinement for disciplinary purposes (Moran, 2014). In 2016, the American Correctional Association (ACA) released a policy statement regarding the use of restrictive housing for adult inmates. The ACA recommended that facilities give "due consideration" to special needs offenders when determining appropriate housing settings and that restrictive housing should only be used if no other form of housing would achieve the required safety and stability. The ACA recommended that agencies refrain from using this type of housing for juveniles and for people with serious mental illness. The ACA also called for extra training for staff assigned to restricted settings to better prepare them to work with inmates struggling to deal with isolation (Boston Congress of Correction Policies and Resolution, 2016).

Pennsylvania created an alternative housing program for inmates suffering from serious mental illness who would have previously been placed in restrictive housing. They can now be housed in a diversionary treatment unit (DTU) or be subjected to involuntary inpatient mental health treatment. The DTU is a secure setting, but its residents are given at least 20 hours of out-of-cell activity per week. If inmates continue to demonstrate that they need to remain in a secure unit due to violent or otherwise maladaptive behavior, they can be placed in a secure residential treatment unit (SRTU). The SRTU is a longer-term unit that emphasizes mental health services. Inmates in both units receive an individualized recovery plan (DeAmicas, 2017).

If inmates must be placed in segregation, the NCCHC (2015) has recommendations to ameliorate the potential harm from such housing assignments. Mental health staff must review the inmate's mental health record to determine whether the inmate is appropriate for segregation. If the answer is yes, qualified mental health professionals should provide mental health services and respond to referrals in a timely manner. Inmates who are scheduled to be in more isolated settings, such as those without a roommate or with few out-of-cell activities, should have more frequent monitoring.

The American Psychiatric Association (2016) encourages corrections departments to use other forms of housing for people with serious mental illness, particularly if it appears that their symptoms are likely to worsen in isolation. If isolation is deemed necessary, inmates with serious mental illnesses should be given both unstructured and structured out-of-cell time (at least 20 hours a week) to reduce the possibility of worsening symptoms and to allot time for working on positive behavioral changes. The out-of-cell time can include clinical work with therapists, as the APA believes that it is inappropriate to provide mental health treatment in front of a cell.

The United States is not alone in examples of excessive use of restrictive housing for individuals with mental illness. In 2007, Ashley Smith committed suicide while incarcerated in a segregation cell in Canada. Smith had spent much of her juvenile years in juvenile court or in youth centers, largely due to misbehavior related to her attempts at self-harm. When she turned 18, she became part of the adult correctional system. Smith had been disciplined repeatedly for self-harming behavior, including cutting, head-banging, and self-strangulation. In the last weeks of her life, she spent all her time in segregation in a suicide-resistant gown, with barely any human interaction and no programming or activities. Hours before taking her own life, she spoke to a staff member about wanting to die. She committed suicide while in segregation. The Correctional Services of Canada launched an investigation of Smith's life in custody and concluded that this was "a preventable death" (Sapers, 2008). Specifically, the investigator wrote "There is reason to believe that Ms. Smith would be alive today if she had not remained on segregation status and if she had received appropriate care" (p. 28). Smith's death resulted in a recommendation for the Correctional Services to immediately review every case of long-term segregation where mental health problems contributed to the decision to place the inmate there (Sapers, 2008).

CREATING A BETTER CORRECTIONAL ENVIRONMENT

In Chapter 1, I discussed taking a public health approach to suicide prevention. Thus far, most of the book has focused on secondary and tertiary prevention strategies. Primary prevention strategies can help reduce the need for secondary and tertiary prevention work, as primary prevention helps to reduce the risk of suicides by improving the overall correctional environment. There are ways that correctional facilities can make both environmental and managerial changes that can impact the entire correctional population and foster the growth of a setting with high behavioral expectations. While this is a considerable task, it could improve the climate of the facility and reduce the need to rely on the aforementioned techniques of opportunity reduction to prevent suicide. In an analysis of civil cases pertaining to correctional suicide, DeGroote (2014) cautioned that "It seems that while many facilities have not gone far enough to *properly* treat suicidal prisoners, many others have gone too far to *improperly* isolate, restrain, and neglect suicidal prisoners" (p. 278). DeGroote argued that we need tort law to bring attention to instances where segregation is being used for excessive confinement of individuals with mental illness, as this may foster utilization of safer and more humane approaches.

The rest of this chapter will focus on reducing the need for isolation and restraint and creating a safer, less stressful atmosphere in facilities. While it is still possible that individual inmates will experience suicidal crises while incarcerated, the goal here is to cultivate an environment where most inmates will be able to serve their time in a setting with few threats to their safety. This will not only help inmates but assist staff and reduce the need for segregation and other types of restraint.

Niches and Sanctuaries for Inmates

Toch (1992b) studied the impact of the prison environment on the emotional well-being of inmates in prisons. He identified eight environmental concerns for inmates, and these included privacy, safety, structure, support, emotional feedback, social stimulation, activity, and freedom. Toch (1992b) and Hagel-Seymour (1982) noted that each inmate places a different priority on each of these concerns. For example, extroverted inmates would likely consider social stimulation and activity to be two of their most important needs, whereas privacy and safety would likely be more important to an introvert who is new to incarcerated life. As a result, different prison and jail settings will likely have differential impacts on various inmates. While an introverted newcomer to the prison would probably prefer to spend as much time as possible by himself (probably in a single cell), the extrovert would likely do well in a dormitory setting.

Some corrections researchers have discussed the importance of inmates finding a suitable niche to be able to do time in a safe and productive manner (Stohr, Jonson, & Cullen, 2014; Hagel-Seymour, 1982; Johnson, R., 2002). Hagel-Seymour defined niches as self-assessed optimal solutions to the problems and preferences of individual prisoners. These solutions may come in the form of housing, programs, and work assignments that provide inmates with what they need. For example, inmates who crave autonomy may be able to obtain a work assignment that involves little contact with staff members or occurs in a setting where staff and inmates interact with each other much more informally. Johnson (R. Johnson, 2002) argued that a suitable niche can help inmates stay safe and even promote mature coping. Mature coping involves building supportive relationships with others and dealing with one's own problems using the legitimate resources that are available. Mature coping involves working on one's problems as a prosocial adult. While a niche is unlikely to prompt all inmates to handle problems prosocially, it can help them do time safely and peacefully and allow them the opportunity to work on acquiring these skills or at least refrain from adopting any more maladaptive behaviors.

The unit management, direct supervision, and inmate behavioral management models work to address the subject of niches for inmates. Facilities that utilize unit management and behavioral management are better able to identify the needs of individual inmates. Direct supervision jails were originally designed to provide inmates with privacy in single cells when they needed it and socialization in the dayrooms whenever they preferred.

Unit Management

The U.S. Bureau of Prisons (BOP) started using unit management in 1975, and it has spread to state and local facilities within the United States and internationally. Facilities with this management style are divided into several functional units. According to Levinson (1999), a functional unit is a "small self-contained inmate living and staff office area, operating semi-autonomously within the confines of a larger institution" (p. 10). The goals of unit management are to establish a safe and humane environment that will minimize the detrimental effects of incarceration and to successfully deliver programs and services to inmates. The functional units allow for decentralized management, so that managers responsible for each individual unit can focus on the needs of the inmates in that smaller space rather than dealing with the needs of an entire institution full of inmates. This means that decisions about inmates can be made faster than they are in a centralized facility, and there tends to be more flexibility when working to meet inmates' treatment needs in unit management institutions. Staff members also benefit from dealing with a smaller group of inmates, as they are able to get to know the inmates and work closely with them. Levinson recommends that each unit have, at minimum, one unit manager, two case managers, two correctional counselors, and one secretary. The unit should also have education advisors, a recreation specialist, and a psychologist working on the unit at least part-time.

Wortley (2002) recommended using unit management to deal with prisoner misconduct and self-harm. He suggested that functional units can provide less depressing architecture, an emphasis on communality, easier supervision, and would reduce the risk of suicide, but he noted that there was little research to document its potential impact. Levinson (1999) found that inmates in a unit management facility seemed to fare better than inmates in a traditional incarceration setting in terms of inmate behavior. The evaluation did not, however, include information on inmate suicides or self-harm. The Victoria Department of Justice Correctional Services Task Force (1998) also recommended using unit management and reported a noticeable reduction of tension and conflict in the facilities that operate under such a structure.

The He Ara Hou Prison ("a new way" in Maori) is a unit management-style facility in New Zealand. The staff members have case management committees that monitor the progress of each inmate. The facility puts a strong emphasis on rehabilitation programs and positive relations between staff and inmates. The staff members have taken this so far as to operate on a first name basis with the inmates. Under this unit management style, the suicide rate in the prison fell 40% for 19- to 24-year-old inmates, while at the same time the suicide rate rose by 25% for the same age group in the nonincarcerated community. While this is a positive development, the prison did have some problems with inmates and staff becoming too close and having sex and using drugs together (Newbold & Eskridge, 1994). It is important to remember that the unit management structure will involve staff members working more frequently and for a longer duration with a set group of inmates, so the administration will have to ensure that proper boundaries between the two groups are maintained.

Direct Supervision

The Federal BOP contracted architects in the late 1960s and early 1970s to create a new type of jail, with the Metropolitan Correctional Centers in New York, Chicago, and San Diego being the first locations for the new model. The BOP took an approach for its short-term facilities that "If you can't rehabilitate, at least do no harm" (Nelson & Davis, 1995, p. 2). The BOP directed the architects to include four characteristics: individual rooms for inmates, living units that house fewer than fifty inmates, direct supervision of inmates by officers, and restricted movement within the facility (Gettinger, 1984). The architects came up with the podular direct supervision design, also known as new generation jails.

Podular direct supervision jails contain several semiautonomous pods that operate under the unit management approach. The facility design allows for better sight lines for the officers, since the cells are placed along the walls of a square or rectangular dayroom. The interior of the pods includes noninstitutional, commercial-grade fixtures and furnishing as opposed to the vandal-resistant, institutional furnishings found in traditional jails. This is supposed to provide an incentive to behave, since they can be moved to a less pleasant, more institutional part of the facility if they do not follow the rules. The noninstitutional furnishings and fixtures also serve to normalize the environment, as these pods have fewer echoes and unpleasant noises found in other jails. The environment with breakable items places inmates in a setting that is more like a college dormitory or an office waiting room, and this type of setting communicates more prosocial expectations (Newman, 1972; Wortley, 2002).

The officers in these units perform direct supervision, which is a dramatic departure from the traditional work of jail officers. Whereas supervision in other facilities tends to be reactive, officers in the direct supervision jails are expected to be proactive. Officers are located in the living areas with the inmates, not inside a control room or on the other side of the bars. They are expected to use their interpersonal communication skills to work with the inmates and defuse tension before it escalates. The presence of the officers and their proactive management style is supposed to discourage inmates from misbehaving while protecting the inmates who are looking to do their time peacefully (Tartaro, 2004).

The three BOP facilities that were the flagships for the podular direct supervision model experienced much less violence, property damage, and fewer suicides than other more traditionally designed jails (Wener, Frazier, & Farbstein, 1993). County jail administrators were initially skeptical, believing that the new design was effective only because federal inmates tended to be less violent and destructive than those housed in county and state institutions (Nelson & Davis, 1995). A few counties adopted the direct supervision design in the early 1980s, and many others have followed upon hearing of encouraging reductions in inmate infractions.

As the direct supervision model became popular, and hundreds of these jails opened across the country, findings were mixed with regard to the jails' effectiveness at preventing suicides. Jackson (1992) researched the Sonoma County Jail in California as the county moved from the old, traditional jail to the new podular direct supervision jail and found a decline in the number of attempted suicides. Senese (1997) also found a decline in suicides as the county being evaluated moved from a traditional facility to a new generation jail. Bayens, Williams, and Smykla (1997a, 1997b) reported similar results. Wener, Frazier, and Farbstein (1985) did find a slight increase in suicides and attempted suicides in a new-generation facility, but this was attributed to the lack of visual surveillance of inmates with mental illness. Tartaro (2003) did an analysis of over 600 jails and found that jail design was not associated with the number of suicides in the jails. Upon closer inspection, many of the facilities identifying as direct supervision jails did not actually adopt all the components of the design and management style that were thought to make the facilities effective (Tartaro, 2002). Tartaro and Levy (2008) surveyed 150 podular direct supervision facilities with the goal of determining which factors associated with these jails were related to the odds of a suicide taking place in the facilities. They found that jails lacking the noninstitutional furnishings and fixtures that are supposed to make the interior less stressful tended to be more likely to report having a suicide during the study period.

Much more research needs to be done on the effectiveness of unit management and direct supervision for preventing suicides and attempted suicides. While both practices seem promising, there is not yet enough evidence to firmly conclude that they are effective. A note of caution: Concepts such as unit management and direct supervision are attractive to corrections personnel who are looking to do something innovative. Some administrators and managers, however, are not willing to fully commit to the idea, and the result is the creation of a watered-down shell of a program that bears little resemblance to the original successful models. An example of this can be found with podular direct supervision jails. The early jails were successful, so many jail administrators and government personnel wanted to build these jails in their districts. They did not, however, want to spend the money for the training or adopt some of the politically risky aspects of the jail, such as the comfortable, normalized environments (Tartaro, 2002, 2006). Wener (2012) also noted a degree of "backsliding," as the original proponents of the direct supervision model retire and are replaced by new staff who are not "true believers." Evaluators of these programs need to be cognizant of the fact that the facilities and programs they are evaluating might not be true to the original design, and this needs to be noted by the researchers. Otherwise, the negative findings might encourage policymakers to deem programs or designs ineffective, when it is the partial implementation of that design that might explain the lack of effectiveness.

Researchers have offered some suggestions to maximize the chances that the direct supervision model will be successful in creating a calmer environment that has fewer suicides. It is important to adhere to the full model rather than picking and choosing cheaper or less politically controversial aspects of the design (Tartaro, 2006). Even small changes can have a big impact on the operations of the facility. For example, Wener (2012) discussed the tendency to place two officers in the pod with inmates. While this initially might sound like a good idea, as it would double officer presence and increase supervision, it may actually have the opposite effect. Multiple officers in one space are often tempted to reterritorialize an area, meaning that instead of roaming around the dayroom and interacting with inmates, officers find one small patch of the dayroom and stay there together. The result reduces the officers' presence in the pods, as they spend less time interacting with inmates (Wener, 2012).

Behavioral Management Units

Podular direct supervision facilities rely on a certain architectural design as part of its model. Many jurisdictions already have an existing prison or jail and do not have the ability to do a complete renovation or build a new structure. Communities that are considering doing such a renovation or new construction are encouraged to consider full implementation of the podular direct supervision design, but what about jurisdictions that cannot do that? One option is the inmate behavior management model.

Inmate behavior management is a six-part plan that can work with any type of jail design (Hutchinson, Keller, & Reid, 2009). Its goal is to help control inmate behavior and increase the efficiency of the facility (Hoke, 2013). The first step is to assess the risks and needs of each inmate. Just as with suicide screening, assessments of inmates' risks and treatment needs should be conducted repeatedly, as these factors are all subject to change. Information gathered from these assessments can then help to guide inmate housing and programming decisions. Second, inmates need to be assigned to appropriate housing settings. In addition to considering the level of security, the amount of supervision each inmate will require, and any legal requirements mandating the separation of certain categories of inmates, staff should also consider programs and services that might benefit the inmates and their ability to function with others. The assessment conducted in step 1 should help to inform decisions in step 2. Third, the jail staff should confirm that inmates' basic needs are being met. Basic needs are (1) physical needs such as food, shelter, medical services, hygiene products, etc.; (2) safety needs, meaning protection from other inmates and environmental hazards; and (3) social needs, including ability to contact family and friends and have positive interactions with inmates and staff (Hutchinson et al., 2009).

Once the first three steps of this plan are addressed, the next three steps in inmate behavior management focus much more on establishing a culture of accountability and safety within the facilities. Step 4 involves defining and conveying expectations for inmate behavior. Distribution of inmate handbooks and a discussion of such expectations during orientation to the facility are good first steps. There should be clear mechanisms for inmates to lodge complaints if they are to be expected to handle their frustrations in a nonviolent manner. Officers should require that inmates keep living areas clean and orderly, and the jails should have both punishments for bad behavior and incentives for good behavior (Hutchinson et al., 2009).

The fifth step is supervision of inmates. The ideal jail design for this is podular direct supervision, as officers can interact with inmates in the pods. Podular remote supervision and linear intermittent designs tend to keep inmates and officers physically separated by bars or Plexiglass for most of the day. Podular remote design facilities have square or rectangular dayrooms, with cells lining the walls, just as they are in podular direct supervision facilities. Rather than being in the dayroom with the inmates, podular remote supervision officers are typically stationed inside a control room with barriers separating them from inmates.

If the facilities are designed as podular remote supervision, the administration should require the officers to spend a certain amount of time inside the dayrooms, but this should not happen until officers receive communication skills training, which is essential if officers are to be expected to proactively address tension and misbehavior in the pods. The facilities can still station officers inside the enclosed control room, but an additional officer should be responsible for spending time inside the pods. More traditionally designed linear intermittent jails have long corridors where officers can walk while inmates are locked inside cells along those corridors. In these facilities, staff can set up duty stations close to inmate housing areas, while other staff members periodically walk through recreation and programming areas. When possible, the facility supervisors should consider making small adjustments to the physical design, such as removing the Plexiglass from officer work stations in remote supervision facilities (Hutchinson et al., 2009).

The sixth and final step is to keep inmates occupied with productive activities. All inmates who are able to work should do so. When inmates are not working, there should be positive structured and unstructured activities inside the housing unit and structured programs outside of the unit. Additionally, staff should work with each inmate to create an individualized behavioral management plan with specific and measurable goals as well as times for periodic assessment (Hutchinson et al., 2009).

Hoke (2013) evaluated the effectiveness of a behavioral management program in Northampton County, Pennsylvania. The administration implemented the program in two units—one housing area for males and one for females. Both units experienced a 70% to 80% decrease in misconduct reports in the 21 months following implementation of the new program compared to the 56 months prior to the program commencement date. While no studies to date have specifically explored the impact of behavior management programs on inmate suicides, their impact on jail disorder is encouraging. Reduction of disorder can make inmates feel safer and reduce stress. It is also a sign of strong facility management. Tartaro and Levy (2008) found that the number of inmate-inmate assaults in jails was also a strong predictor of the jails having at least one suicide in a year, so reductions in misbehavior can also impact the probability of suicides occurring.

As with the direct supervision model, the behavioral management program must be *completely* and *fully* implemented. Hutchinson and colleagues (2009) cautioned that it is essential to correctly implement steps 1 through 4 before jumping straight to addressing inmate supervision. It is important, for example, to properly assess inmates and to base housing assignments not only on security level and bed availability, but also on treatment needs.

CONCLUSION

There are a variety of approaches to suicide prevention. Since our surrounding environment can impact our feelings and actions, it is important to consider ways to use it to promote desirable behavior and discourage destructive actions. Of course, one way to prevent inmates from committing suicide would be to lock them in a barren cell with no belongings that can be used for hanging. Inmates would do their time with barely any stimulation, have no opportunity to address the problems that prompted them to be incarcerated, and have little to no human contact. The drawback, of course, would be that this is inhumane, and the research on segregation and solitary confinement has provided evidence that such living conditions are counterproductive to improving one's psychological state. Isolation of persons who are suicidal or mentally ill should be used as sparingly as possible. If there are alternatives, such as offering constant monitoring, it might be possible and far more desirable to house inmates in more "normal" settings.

Corrections experts have introduced design and management plans that help transform correctional environments from the traditional, institutional-looking settings to more conventional environments, similar to office waiting rooms or college dormitories. Contrary to what was expected, inmates did not seek to destroy these more pleasant areas. When faced with the choice of behaving and staying in the nicer areas or misbehaving and being sent to a lockdown unit, inmates of various security levels tended to behave (Farbstein & Wener, 1989; Nelson, 1983, 1988; Nelson & Davis, 1995; Senese, 1997; Wener et al., 1993). These jail settings not only look nicer but tend to be safer, as inmates are motivated to behave, and officers communicate high behavioral expectations. While incarceration will always be stressful due to the forced removal from home, continued separation from friends and family, and concerns about current or pending legal issues, increased feelings of safety and presence in a less stressful environment can help to hasten or prevent the onset of a crisis.

It is important to remember that all the proposed changes in this chapter, from the reduction in overreliance on segregation for inmates in crisis to adoption of the new generation strategy to implementation of behavioral management units, require strong leadership. These are likely to be most effective when the plans receive buy-in from all staff, and that has to start with the leaders. As was discussed earlier, the new generation jail design was met with much skepticism from jail officers who assumed that, while the change was feasible with low-risk federal inmates, county jail inmates would destroy the pods and assault each other and the officers stationed in the pods. Managers have to project a strong belief in what they are doing and be seen leading by example throughout the institutions. Leaders need to show enthusiasm for changes and demonstrate that they fully support all phases of operation.

Chapter Eight

Diversion and Transition Planning

One obvious way to prevent exposure to the negative aspects of incarceration is simply to keep people out of these institutions. This, of course, is a daunting task, especially in countries that have grown dependent on incarceration. The United States embarked on an unprecedented increase in the use of incarceration starting in the early 1980s, and it was not until 2010 that incarceration rates ceased climbing. Not only has it become customary for the criminal justice system to rely heavily on incarceration as a response to offending, but institutions are convenient places to house undesirables and people who are difficult for society to manage (Irwin, 1985; Rothman, 1971 [2002]). There appears to be a change occurring, though, as counties and states seek to save money through the use of community alternatives to incarceration.

When incarceration is deemed necessary, offenders become part of a cycle that is often difficult to break. Although at least 95% of all state prisoners in the United States will be released from prison, many are re-arrested and re-incarcerated. The U.S. Bureau of Justice Statistics (BJS) tracked over 400,000 offenders released from prisons in 30 states in 2005 (Durose, Cooper, & Snyder, 2014). Seventy-seven percent were rearrested within five years. Fifty percent of offenders released in 2005 were reincarcerated within three years, and 55% were back in prison in five years (Durose et al., 2014). Given the revolving door of corrections that has been in existence for decades, rehabilitation and reentry programs are necessary to help break the cycle of recidivism.

It should be clear by now that the correctional setting was not meant to serve as mental health treatment centers, and the conditions inside corrections facilities can make symptoms of mental illness worse. Diversion programs can keep some offenders from being exposed to the stress and negative environment inside prisons and jails, while transition planning has the potential to help people remain in the community after release from incarceration. There are, of course, other potential benefits to diversion and transition planning, particularly for corrections populations. Inmates who suffer from mental illness are frequent targets of abuse while incarcerated (Pare & Logan, 2011; Wood, 2013), as other inmates see them as easy marks, and officers may become frustrated with their inability to follow commands. Another potential benefit is cost saving, and I will provide examples of this later in the chapter.

This chapter diverges from the rest of the book a bit, in that I do not specifically focus on suicide and self-harm here. Instead, I discuss programs designed to divert offenders with mental illness from prison and jail and, when incarceration is unavoidable, to prepare inmates to successfully reenter society. These programs can aid corrections agencies by keeping offenders who tend to be at an elevated risk for self-harm and suicide from entering prison or jail and by helping those who are already incarcerated make a successful transition into the community.

PRINCIPLES OF EFFECTIVE INTERVENTION

Before I start to describe diversion and reentry programs, I want to review what are now considered to be the four principles of effective correctional intervention. These are:

1. The risk principle: Treatment should target high-risk offenders;
2. The needs principle: Treatment should focus on criminogenic needs;
3. General responsivity: Treatment should be based on cognitive-behavioral strategies; and
4. Specific responsivity: Treatment delivery plans should account for clients' culture and environment (Cullen & Jonson, 2012; Latessa et al., 2014).

These four factors make up the risk-needs-responsivity (RNR) model.

Researchers have identified specific risk factors that predict recidivism. Andrews and Bonta (1996) pinpointed eight major correlates of criminal conduct: antisocial/pro-criminal attitudes; pro-criminal associates with isolation from anti-criminal people; temperamental/personality factors (e.g., impulsivity, weak socialization, psychopathy); history of antisocial behavior; family factors (e.g., abusive relationships, criminal involvement among family); low levels of educational, vocational, personal, or financial achievement; little involvement in prosocial leisure activities; and substance abuse. What is particularly interesting about this list is that mental illness is not included as being associated with offending. Does this mean that mental health treatment should not be the focus of rehabilitation and reentry programs?

Proponents of the "direct cause" model of offending believe that individuals' mental illness is directly responsible for their illegal behavior. If the direct cause model explains offending behavior, then programs that aim to improve clients' clinical outcomes should be associated with reductions in recidivism. There is little evidence to support this (Skeem et al., 2014). It is likely that, for a small proportion of the offending population, addressing mental health issues is enough to help them stay out of legal trouble. For most people, however, this is unlikely to be the case (Skeem, Manchak, & Peterson, 2011). Skeem and colleagues (2014) studied offenders with serious mental illness, defined as being diagnosed with schizophrenia, some other psychotic disorder, major depression, or bipolar disorder, and compared them to similar parolees who lacked such a diagnosis. Parolees with the aforementioned diagnoses tended to have more criminogenic needs than the comparison group of offenders without a serious mental illness.

Does this mean that mental health treatment is unnecessary when working to reduce recidivism? Absolutely not. As I mentioned earlier, there is a subset of the population of individuals with mental illness whose legal troubles can be directly attributed to their illnesses, so treatment of that one issue will likely be effective. For the majority of people with mental illness, however, Skeem and colleagues (2011) suggested that we view the role of mental illness in criminality as a "moderated mediation" effect, meaning that mental illness may impact criminality, but the relationship to offending is indirect. Osher, D'Amora, Plotkin, Jarrett, and Eggleston (2012) supported Skeem and colleagues' (2011) explanation and noted that, while mental illness is not a primary risk factor for recidivism, it is something that could interfere with individuals' ability to function productively. Osher et al. used the example of someone with severe depression who may be unable to focus on and accept treatment to address his or her antisocial attitudes until the depression symptoms are managed. In essence, while research has not found mental illness to be a risk factor for criminal behavior in most people, it appears to be an important responsivity factor that does need attention.

As severity of mental illness increases, the chances that it will become a factor in recidivism increases as well. Bales, Nadel, Reed, and Blomberg (2017) studied recidivism among inmates released from Florida prisons. To measure severity of mental illness, the researchers placed everyone with a serious mental illness, defined here as schizophrenia, major depressive disorder, bipolar disorder, and nonschizophrenic psychotic disorders, into one group. The second group consisted of inmates who were considered mentally ill and had any Axis I or II disorder other than those previously mentioned.

The third group was released inmates with no Axis I or II disorders. Bales et al. found that inmates with mental health diagnoses were more likely to be rearrested, reconvicted, and reincarcerated, but inmates with serious mental illness were at an even higher risk than inmates with all other types of mental illness. Baillargeon and associates (2009b) found that parolees with co-occurring disorders were twice as likely as other released offenders to have their parole revoked due to a technical violation and three times more likely to commit a new offense. Baillargeon et al. did speculate that the higher rate of technical violations might have been a product of parole officers using the violations to get parolees with mental illness into treatment.

When considering these results, it is important to bear in mind that Bales and colleagues (2017) did take into account some, but not all, risk factors and criminogenic needs, while Baillargeon et al. (2009b) did not include any criminogenic needs except for substance abuse. This is significant, because without these factors involved in the analyses, we cannot conclude whether there was a direct relationship between mental illness and recidivism or if the relationship would have been mediated by the inclusion of criminogenic needs. Skeem et al. (2014) found that serious mental illness was associated with higher recidivism rates but only for technical violations rather than new offenses. Offenders with mental illness tend to be sent back to prison at greater rates than other offenders for technical violations of their parole conditions. One possibility for this finding is that the mental illness interferes with offenders' ability to obey the terms of their parole. Another explanation could be that parole officers are more cautious with parolees who are mentally ill and are less inclined to give them additional chances in the community.

What does this all mean for diversion and reentry programs? Mental illness certainly needs to be addressed for the well-being of offenders, because untreated mental illness can interfere with their capability of participating in treatment, and it is likely to hamper offenders' abilities to comply with rules of probation or parole. Treating mental illness without addressing any of the known risk factors for offending, however, is likely to improve clinical outcomes but unlikely to make much of an impact on offending behavior.

Correctional staff need to collect information on inmates' risks and needs through assessment. Osher and colleagues (2012) developed a Criminogenic Risk and Behavioral Health Needs Framework that included suggestions for integrating mental health issues into assessments that focus on offenders' risks and criminogenic needs. The framework calls for assessment based on three levels of sorting. First, classification staff should assess all offenders for criminogenic risk. This risk assessment should involve static risk factors (age, offending history, age at first arrest, etc.), as well as dynamic risk factors, including the eight major correlates of criminal conduct discussed earlier. The second level of sorting involves determining if the inmate has a substance abuse problem, and, if so, determining the severity of it and the level of need the inmate has. The third sorting level involves assessment of the presence and severity of mental health disorders. Inmates receive a classification of low, medium, or high risk for each of these three levels, and those scores are combined to place inmates into groups numbered 1 to 8, with group 1 being low risk for criminogenic risk, substance abuse, and mental health disorders, and 8 being high risk for all three categories.

Assessment of offenders' risks and needs can be conducted by court, probation, jail, prison, and/or treatment providers. These data should then be used to guide decisions of whether to divert people and then, regardless of that decision, their treatment plans. For transition planning, inmates should be assessed at the start of their incarceration to allow treatment staff to begin reentry plans immediately. Reassessments are important and should be done if inmates spend months or years incarcerated, as it is possible that inmates' attitudes and other dynamic risk factors may have changed.

DIVERSION

The purpose of diversion programs is to limit some individuals' exposure to the criminal justice system. Diversion became popular in the 1970s, primarily for use with juveniles as a way to avoid the label of "offender" and being exposed to negative influences in juvenile facilities (Blomberg & Lucken, 2007). Since there are potential benefits to using diversion programs with other nonserious offenders, these programs have expanded in some jurisdictions to involve individuals with mental illness and/or people with substance abuse problems. Steadman, Morris, and Dennis (1995) identified the components of diversion programs for people with mental illness as:

> Specific programs that screen defined groups of detainees for the presence of a mental disorder; use mental health professionals to evaluate those detainees identified in screening; negotiate with prosecutors, defense attorneys, community-based mental health providers, and the courts to produce a mental health disposition as a condition of bond, in lieu of prosecution, or as a condition of a reduction in charges (whether or not a formal conviction occurs); and link the detainee directly to community-based services. (pp. 1630–1631)

Offenders can be sent into a diversion program at various points during their processing through the criminal justice system. For example, pre-booking diversion programs begin before formal charges are brought against the person. Clients are typically identified by the police, and such a program involves cooperation and frequent interaction between the police and community mental health and substance abuse agencies. For this type of program, police generally receive additional training in identifying and working with people with mental illness, and the jurisdiction creates a 24-hour drop-off center with a no-refusal policy for anyone brought in by the police. Postbooking diversion programs are more common in the United States. Persons are first arrested, then identified as meeting the criteria for the division program, and then diverted. Depending on the program, diversion can take place after booking but before charges are filed, upon release from pretrial detention, prior to case disposition, at the time of disposition or sentencing, or following a probation violation (U.S. Department of Health and Human Services, 2007; Steadman et al., 1995).

The National GAINS Center is part of the U.S. Department of Health and Human Services, Substance Abuse, and Mental Health Services Administration. The focus of the center is "on expanding access to community-based services for adults diagnosed with co-occurring mental illness and substance use disorders at all points of contact with the justice system" (U.S. Department of Health and Human Services, 2007). GAINS stands for *G*athering information, *A*ssessing what works, *I*nterpreting and integrating the facts, *N*etworking, and *S*timulating change. The center has a helpful website with important information about diversion programs, and this includes a list of essential elements of diversion programs:

1. Define the target population.
2. Identify persons appropriate for diversion as soon as possible to limit their exposure to incarceration.
3. Establish collaboration between mental health and criminal justice practitioners to negotiate treatment plans for individuals while considering the resources available in each community.
4. Implement the program (U.S. Department of Health and Human Services, 2007).

Steadman and colleagues (1995) conducted a national survey of jails in the United States and asked them to identify key characteristics of successful diversion programs. Respondents identified the following features:

1. *Integrated services*: Agencies within the criminal justice system and mental health system should regularly coordinate services.
2. *Meetings of key personnel*: Regular meetings should be held, and key representatives from each participating agency should be present to discuss issues of funding and staffing. Direct service providers should also have

frequent meetings to discuss individual treatment plans and other day-to-day activities of the program.

3. *Boundary spanners*: Boundary spanners are staff members who manage interactions between the correctional, mental health, and judicial staff and should be present in diversion programs, as they are vital to maintaining the lines of communication between the agencies.
4. *Strong leadership*: Some promising programs that are outstanding on paper have failed due primarily to the absence of strong leadership.
5. *Early identification*: Personnel need to identify arrestees or jail detainees with mental health treatment needs who meet the diversion program's criteria as soon as possible to limit the individuals' exposure to incarceration.
6. *Case management*: Case managers in diversion programs should have experience working with both criminal justice and mental health agencies and clients (Steadman et al., 1995).

The features identified in Steadman et al.'s (1995) survey are important, as diversion programs are unlikely to succeed without boundary spanners and strong leadership. The respondents did not discuss the importance of including components of the RNR model in diversion programming. The RNR model was in its infancy at the time of Steadman et al.'s survey, but readers of this book should remember that adherence to the RNR model is likely to improve criminal justice outcomes among diversion participants.

For diversion programs that focus on diverting people in the community from ever entering the jail, the challenges that police encounter with individuals who are mentally ill rarely coincide with regular business hours. Having 24-hour community resources, while difficult to run and possibly expensive, is vital to diversion efforts. This type of resource, especially if it has a no-decline policy for those delivered by the police, can save cities and counties money in the form of reduced hospitalizations (Sheridan & Teplin, 1981) and jail stays (Lamb, Shaner, Elliott, DeCuir, & Foltz, 1995).

Examples and Evaluations of Diversion Programs

Police-Led Diversion

Some jurisdictions have established partnerships between mental health staff and police departments to reduce further criminal justice involvement of individuals with mental illness. Since the police are typically the first to be called to a scene to address a problem with someone behaving abnormally, partnerships at this level have the potential to produce positive outcomes for both the criminal justice and medical fields. There are three types of partnerships between police and mental health staff. The first is the police-based specialized police response. A good example of this is Crisis Intervention Training (CIT). The second is police-based mental health response, where police hire mental health staff to assist with crisis calls to police. The third is mental health-based specialized responses, such as mobile crisis units (Compton, Bahora, Watson, & Olivia, 2008). All of these provide police with resources to help to de-escalate problems and to provide individuals with appropriate in-patient or out-patient services, in many cases in lieu of further criminal justice involvement. These programs have the potential to prevent some people with mental illness from going to jail.

One might wonder why these partnerships are necessary, as police have access to hospitals everywhere. Shouldn't police just recognize mental health problems and seek medical help when appropriate? This is unlikely for two reasons. First, police receive little training on mental illness, so they may not recognize the nature of the problem when encountering it. Second, in their work with police, researchers have noted that police rarely take independent initiative to seek a medical or mental-health outcome in lieu of a criminal justice option (Laberge & Morin, 1995). One possible reason why is that police are a part of the criminal justice system, so it may seem natural to seek in-system solutions to a problem. Another reason why police might hesitate to seek a medical solution is that taking people to the hospital can be difficult and time-consuming. Police have experienced long waits and have had to deal with complicated admissions procedures, resistance from hospital staff who are facing their own crowding problems, and frustration about the hospitals frequently discharging people who seemingly need extensive psychiatric attention (Laberge & Morin, 1995).

In response to negative interactions between the police and individuals with mental illness, city and county law enforcement agencies began establishing crisis intervention teams approximately 30 years ago. The most widely imitated model is the Memphis CIT program. The Memphis CIT model was developed following a police shooting of an unarmed man who was suffering from mental illness. CIT models typically involve two components: a small group of trained police officers and partnerships with community agencies. The community agencies' representatives work with the police to provide noncriminal justice resources to help people who are mentally ill (Slate, 2009). Following the implementation of the program in Memphis, the city noticed a 40% reduction in injuries to individuals with mental illness who were involved in encounters with police. The reduction in injuries among officers was even more dramatic, with an 85% drop in officer injuries during these incidents. As part of the CIT program, law enforcement began working with court personnel to divert people with mental illness from incarceration and into treatment. For people who could not be immediately diverted or were facing serious charges, jail staff worked to provide treatment for inmates (Kerle, 2016).

The National Association of Counties (NACo) obtained funding from the National Institute of Mental Health (NIMH) to help local criminal justice systems adopt the CIT model. The funding helped to cover training for police and sheriff's departments so that officers would have a better understanding of how they should approach calls for service involving people with mental illness. What is particularly important about the CIT programs is that, when done properly, police, courts, and corrections staff are all brought to the table, along with social service agencies, as the hope is to foster collaboration between all parties. The collaboration is helpful when it comes time for police to reach out to social services agencies or when prosecution and defense want to work out a plan to ensure that defendants receive much-needed treatment. Part of the Memphis model includes suicide prevention and treatment training for all participants. Trainees are taught about warning signs of suicide attempts, how to properly respond, and what resources are available to assist suicidal individuals (Kerle, 2016). Crisis intervention teams rapidly spread across the country, and currently over 2,700 agencies are involved in CIT programs worldwide (Taheri, 2016).

Is it necessary, or even wise, to require all correctional staff members to engage in CIT training? Those familiar with this program say no, and some even go far enough to suggest that providing training for all "bastardizes" CIT (Slate et al., 2013). First, it is not necessary to have everyone trained in this, just as it is not necessary to have every officer trained for special cell extractions or sharp shooting. What is essential is that there are enough trained staff to call upon during each shift should a problem arise. Second, not everyone has the proper skill set to be effective at CIT. Sworn police officers who tend to be more confrontational are unlikely to excel in de-escalation, so it would be more efficient and effective to train and utilize those best suited for this work.

While the use of CIT is widespread in the community, there are few methodologically rigorous evaluations of its effectiveness. Most of the evaluations lack adequate comparison groups or data for criminal justice outcomes (e.g., arrests, etc.) prior to program implementation. Taheri (2016) conducted a systematic review of the use of CIT among police and found little evidence that it reduces arrests or officer use of force. Studies that involved surveys of officers who were CIT-trained tended to produce positive findings, as these officers reported that they were less likely to arrest or use force with people with mental illness. Studies that relied on police records, however, did not find differences in police behavior when CIT-involved officers were compared to their non-CIT counterparts. Taheri suggested that, rather than abandoning CIT, researchers should work with agencies to produce more methodologically sound research that can provide more insight into the effectiveness of these programs.

Supporters of CIT have also recommended using it in the corrections setting, as corrections officers are typically the first to respond to situations involving inmates in psychological crises. Corrections-based programs may help officers throughout the facility, but especially in booking, detect signs of mental illness upon inmates' entry into the jail (Slate, 2009). CIT officers throughout the facility can assist other officers in recognizing when behavioral problems might stem from mental illness, and they can help to de-escalate tensions when they start to rise. CIT training helps to reintroduce the subject of treatment and informs participants about resources that may be available to help. Since sworn officers are not mental health specialists, it is important to emphasize in training that it is not their responsibility to diagnose and treat a problem. Instead, they need to simply be able to realize that a problem exists and take steps to communicate that issue to the proper outlets (Slate et al., 2013).

Los Angeles County adopted a different approach to working with individuals with mental illness in the community. Rather than adopting CIT, they developed the Systemwide Mental Assessment Response Team (SMART) to link police with mental health staff when responding to calls involving people experiencing psychiatric problems. Of the 101 referrals to this team, only two people were taken to jail. Most people were put on involuntary 72-hour holds or taken to the hospital. It is notable that only two people were "criminalized" by being incarcerated. In the six months following contact with the police, only 24% of the individuals were later arrested (Lamb et al., 1995).

Pre- or Postbooking Diversion

Steadman and Naples (2005) conducted an evaluation of both pre- and post-booking programs in nine different states. The four prebooking and five postbooking programs were responsible for screening and assessing nearly 2,000 persons with co-occurring mental illness and substance abuse disorders. Approximately 1,000 of these persons were diverted from involvement in the criminal justice system. The results indicated that the diverted and nondiverted participants were significantly different at the start of the study in that the diverted group members were more likely to have a primary diagnosis of schizophrenia or mood disorders with psychotic features, to indicate higher life satisfaction, and to have higher scores on the Colorado Symptom Inventory (indicating better mental health). The diverted group was also less likely to have been previously arrested and to have spent time in jail. Both groups were interviewed at the beginning of the program, three months later, and twelve months later. The diverted group spent an average of two months longer in the community after their initial contact with the criminal justice system than the comparison group. Both groups, however, had similar numbers of arrests during the one-year study period. The diverted group received significantly more mental health treatment during the study period, but both groups saw improvements in their mental health symptoms during the year. With regard to cost effectiveness, findings were mixed. Some jurisdictions saved money by operating a diversion program while others did not (Steadman & Naples, 2005; National GAINS Center, 2004). The results of this study should be considered with caution. While the researchers found that the diversion group fared better in that they were able to spend more time in the community, this could be a result of the fact that the two groups were different in their diagnoses and overall mental health status prior to the intervention.

Connecticut has developed a statewide diversion program for people with mental illness who come into contact with the criminal justice system (Frisman, Sturges, Baranoski, & Levinson, 2001). Diversion clinicians have arraignment lists faxed to them each day, and they identify clients who have been receiving mental health care. The diversion team also offers assistance to defendants who are identified by the judge, public defender, sheriff, or prosecutor as needing assistance. Staff drafts a treatment plan and, if the client consents, the plan is shared with the judge. If the judge approves, the defendant is released from jail, but he or she has to promise to participate in the program and reappear in court at a later date. At the next hearing, the case can be dropped, continued, or, if there is reason to believe that the person will not continue to participate voluntarily, the judge can place the person on probation with treatment as a condition. A 90-day review of the participants found that those who were diverted spent an average of 14.3 days in jail compared to 29.8 days for those who were not diverted. This amounted to a savings of $2,497.00 per client. The arrest rates for both groups over the 90-day period were similar, but it is important to note that the diverted group spent more time in the community and, therefore, had more opportunity than the nondiverted group to get arrested.

Connecticut also introduced a jail diversion program specifically for female offenders who have histories of both trauma and substance use disorders. The program staff receive referrals from court, and eligible participants can participate in the 90- to 180-day program in lieu of further criminal justice processing. Participants experienced some positive changes, including reduced use of alcohol and drugs, increased employment, and improvements in overall physical and mental health (Pollard, Schuster, Lin, & Frisman, 2007).

The New York City Department of Health and Mental Hygiene hosts the NYC-LINK diversion program for offenders with co-occurring alcohol and/ or drug problems and serious mental illness. This program serves inmates who are housed at the Rikers Island jail. Since the New York City jail population is so large, there were not enough spaces for every inmate who qualified for this program. In order to qualify, inmates had to be diagnosed with a "serious and persistent mental illness." Inmates with both felony and misdemeanor charges were eligible, but serious offenses such as murder and manslaughter were grounds for exclusion. Violent offenders were only admitted to the program on a case-by-case basis. Some inmates who were released from the jail on nondiversion status were permitted to participate in some of the programs, but they were not mandated to do so. In other words, there were no legal ramifications for poor performance or lack of attendance for this group. Researchers conducted interviews at three months and again at twelve months after the start of the diversion program (Broner, Mayrl, & Landsberg, 2005). Those who were subjected to the mandatory diversion program in New York fared better in terms of reducing the number of days incarcerated over the twelve-month period, increasing the number of days spent in the community, reducing drug use during the year, and increasing the time spent in treatment. The researchers also noted that, regardless of whether the treatment was mandated, the most successful inmates were those who acknowledged that they did have a mental illness. Thus, these programs are likely to be most successful with those offenders who are at the point when they are willing to recognize that they have a problem (Broner et al., 2005).

Case, Steadman, Dupuis, and Morris (2009) evaluated a multisite post-booking diversion program and found that participants had 75% fewer arrests during the postenrollment period compared to the preenrollment period. One particularly important factor here was homelessness, with people who were able to maintain housing over the course of a year having fewer arrests than others. This is important to remember, as housing tends to be a major obstacle to the success of justice-involved people with mental illness.

Incarceration can be expensive, and one of the advantages to diversion programs is that they can save cities, counties, and states money. Douglas County, Nebraska, established a voluntary postbooking diversion program for individuals diagnosed with either a serious mental illness or a mental illness with a co-occurring substance use disorder. The county saved approximately $38,000 through reductions in the use of incarceration (Boganowski, 2011).

Specialized Probation Caseloads

Jurisdictions are increasingly employing probation officers with the intention of having specialized caseloads with smaller numbers of clients per officer and with an increased emphasis on treatment. Specialized probation officers are trained specifically to understand symptoms of mental illness and how these symptoms can result in behavior that is counterproductive to compliance with the conditions of probation. The presence of such a caseload in a jurisdiction might encourage judges to recommend probation rather than incarceration for people with mental illness. Manchak, Skeem, Kennealy, and Louden (2014) evaluated the outcomes of specialty-probation, focusing on mental health caseloads compared to a general probation caseload. The probationers on the mental health-specific caseload were twice as likely than individuals on the traditional probation caseload to receive a formal probation violation report. A possible explanation for this was the expanded roles that the mental health probation officers adopted. Compared to regular probation officers, the specialty officers tended to span boundaries more and present their clients with more positive compliance strategies. They were also more likely to be able to access psychiatric and dual diagnosis services for their clients. While the presence of these services is a positive development, more services also mean more opportunities for probationers to receive a technical violation due to lack of compliance. Specialized probation caseloads are promising in that they present an opportunity for offenders with mental illness to receive greater access to treatment. It is important to remember, however, that providing only treatment for mental illness and not criminogenic needs is unlikely to produce substantial reductions in recidivism.

Mental Health Courts

Specialized courts, such as mental health and drug courts, are forms of diversion programs whose popularity soared in the early 2000s. Federal funds became available to jurisdictions looking to establish mental health courts or mental-health diversion programs following Congress's passage of America's Law Enforcement and Mental Health Project Act in 2000 (Judge David L. Bazelon Center for Mental Health Law, 2003). As with just about all diversion programs, mental health courts are designed to work mostly with people who commit minor offenses.

Mental health courts are similar to some of the postbooking mental health diversion programs that I already discussed. One notable difference is that the judge acts as the leader of the treatment team in mental health courts. The judge and other involved staff members receive training in understanding and working with defendants who are mentally ill (Frisman et al., 2001). Staff from the Judge David L. Bazelon Center for Mental Health Case Law (2003) have provided recommendations for effective mental health courts. They recommend that program participation be voluntary but, once offenders have consented to participate, they should not be permitted to withdraw. The penalties for noncompliance should be clearly written out in a treatment plan and should be signed by the defendant. Additionally, they recommend that the court deal with more serious offenders rather than minor offenders. The justification for this recommendation is out of concern that if the court accepts responsibility for people with minor misdemeanors, the court will become a dumping ground for all those abandoned by the mental health system. Additionally, best practices in rehabilitation call for providing the most services for high-risk offenders, as including very low risk individuals in correctional programming could actually be detrimental, as their exposure to high-risk offenders can prompt additional offending (Latessa et al., 2014). The duration of judicial supervision should be based on the treatment plan but should never exceed the typical sentence and probationary period for the criminal charge.

Do mental health courts work? Evaluation results have been mixed, but they are certainly promising. Some researchers have reported no impact on clinical or criminal justice outcomes. For example, Boothroyd, Mercado, Poythress, Christy, and Petrila (2005) compared defendants from a mental health court with similar defendants who were processed through a traditional court. The researchers did not study recidivism, but they did measure signs of clinical changes. They did not find any differences in clinical outcomes for the two groups of defendants. The researchers did caution, however, that the courts had little control over the types of services the mental health court defendants were receiving in the community, so it is possible that quality control issues in the community impacted the results. Cosden, Ellens, Schnell, and Yamini-Diouf (2005) reported clinical improvements in defendants participating in a California mental health court but no differences in likelihood to recidivate.

Most of the other studies on mental health court outcomes provided encouraging results. Researchers have reported reductions in likelihood of arrest (Burns, Hiday, & Ray, 2013; Herinckx, Swart, Ama, Dolezai, & King, 2005; Ray, 2014), increased time spent in the community without incurring new charges (McNeil & Binder, 2007), and reduced likelihood of violating probation (Herinckx et al., 2005). Honegger (2015) reviewed 15 articles that involved evaluations of mental health courts in terms of their impact on recidivism, and 13 of the studies reported recidivism reductions.

Mental health courts are not without challenges. There is wide variation in eligibility criteria and operation plans for mental health courts nationwide, and the variability makes it difficult to draw conclusions about the efficacy of the model as a whole (Honegger, 2015; Steadman, Davidson, and Brown, 2001). One concern about mental health court and other community-based criminal justice mental health initiatives is whether these jurisdictions are actually increasing the availability of services in the community, or if they are simply taking the court participants and putting them in line in front of nonoffending members of the community who also need assistance.

Earlier in this chapter, I discussed the importance of the RNR model when considering the development and functioning of offender treatment programs. Addressing mental health problems is definitely an important component of treatment, but programs must also target criminogenic needs to maximize the chances of reducing recidivism. Campbell et al. (2015) studied a mental health court in Canada to learn about the extent to which RNR principles were embedded in the program. The mental health court model was originally inspired by the drug court model, not the RNR paradigm. For this particular mental health court, higher-risk defendants were provided with more intensive interventions than medium- or low-risk clients. Researchers did find modest reductions in recidivism for program completers as well as improvements with the criminogenic needs of substance abuse, employment and education, family relations, leisure and recreation, and pro-criminal and antisocial attitudes. Following this evaluation, the court formally adopted a RNR model, but the court was closed in 2013, without researchers having the opportunity to evaluate the new design.

Mental health courts and other diversion programs can be cost-effective ways to provide services to people in need while improving public safety through crime reduction. Not all existing programs are effective, and there is a great deal of variation in the types of diversion programs offered, even within individual models such as mental health courts. Most of the aforementioned programs discussed did help people in need get access to mental health treatment. One major step that these programs should take, if they have not already done so, is to incorporate the RNR model into their plans so that they can address individual characteristics associated with criminal offending while also working to stabilize offenders' mental health.

TRANSITION/REENTRY PLANNING

Due to the extensive reliance on incarceration in the United States, diversion is not going to be available for the thousands of inmates with mental illness whose crimes are deemed worthy of incarceration. Their psychiatric conditions become just one of several hurdles that they will have to overcome in order to return to the community successfully. Education, employment, housing, and criminogenic needs—including substance abuse, family and peer associations, and antisocial attitudes—are other factors that will likely require attention. Approximately 22% of jail inmates have some level of learning disability (Maruschak, 2006), and 60% do not have a high school diploma or GED (Freudenberg, 2006). Finding housing is especially difficult for returning offenders. The fact that federal law bars many offenders from public housing and federally assisted housing programs means that some of these inmates will not be able to return to their family's homes (Travis, Solomon, & Waul, 2001). For those who were homeless prior to incarceration, Metraux and Culhane (2004) found that they were more likely than other returning inmates to utilize homeless shelters after their release from prison, and they were also more likely to wind up returning to prison. The Vera Institute of Justice found that prisoners released back to New York City who had to live in shelters were three times more likely to abscond from parole than those who had housing (Nelson, Dees, & Allen, 1999).

How to properly release inmates and provide them with appropriate services is an issue that has received court and media attention over the past 20 years. The landmark case of *Brad H. v. City of New York* (2000) publicized the lack of transition planning taking place in the New York City jail system. During the late 1990s, the discharge plan for Rikers Island consisted of a bus ride to a subway station sometime between 2am and 6am, two subway tokens or a two-fare Metro Card, and $1.50 cash. Released inmates generally were not provided with any mental health services or set up for any government assistance, nor were they given housing referrals or medication. If an inmate went to court during the day and was informed that he or she was free to go, that person had the option of walking out the door of the courthouse or going back to the jail to pick up his or her belongings. From that point, no services were offered. While this would be problematic in any jurisdiction, New York State's mental hygiene law made this practice illegal. According to the law, inmates with mental illness are to be involved in transition planning before they are released. The court recognized that the absence of transition planning at Rikers Island violated state law, was dangerous, and greatly increased the chances that released individuals with mental illness would become homeless or reincarcerated.

Based on the recommendation of the American Association of Community Psychiatrists and researchers in this field, the term "transition planning" seems appropriate to describe programs that aim to prepare inmates for their transition to living in the community. Other terms that are commonly used to describe these programs are "discharge planning" and "reentry planning." Some inmates will experience relapses during their transition, so this particular release from prison or jail may not be the final reentry or discharge from a corrections facility that they experience. Corrections staff and community service providers are preparing incarcerated persons for a transition to the community, and while it is hoped that this transition will be permanent, not all will succeed on the first try (Osher, 2007; Osher, Steadman, & Barr, 2003).

Transition planning is important for various reasons. First, as is evident from the preceding paragraphs, many inmates leave jail ill-prepared to succeed in the community. Second, corrections facilities have a moral and, in some states, legal obligation to conduct transition planning with inmates who are mentally ill. Third, transition planning is vital considering the research on the number of former inmates who commit suicide after release from custody. Haglund et al. (2015) tracked individuals released from prison in Sweden. Suicide comprised 14% of all postrelease deaths, and released inmates were found to have a risk of suicide that was 18 times higher than the nonconvicted general population of Sweden. The risk was highest in the first few months after release. Daigle and Naud (2012) studied suicides among released prisoners in Canada and also found a pattern of higher risk of death by suicide in the first month following release. Twenty percent of inmates who died by suicide did so in the first month, and 40% who committed suicide did so in the first year.

Similar results have been found among former prisoners in other countries. Binswanger et al. (2007) found that 40 of the 30,237 released prisoners from Washington State from 1999 through 2003 committed suicide, whereas only 12 would be expected for individuals in that age range. The suicide rate for those released prisoners was approximately 70 per 100,000 per year over the 4-year period but 136 in the first 2 weeks after release. In a similar study, Pratt, Piper, Appleby, Webb, and Shaw (2006) tracked inmates released from prisons in England and Wales from January 1999 through December 2002. While released prisoners accounted for only 0.2% of the population of England and Wales, they comprised 3% of all suicides between 2000 and 2002. Fifty-one percent of the released inmate suicides occurred within the first four months after release from incarceration. Females released from prisons in southern Australia were 14 times more likely to die from suicide than other females in the community. Released males were five times more likely to commit suicide than other males in the community (Sptittal, Frosyth, Pirkis, Alati, & Kinner, 2014). Transition planning programs that help soon-to-be-released inmates obtain medication for their first few days of release, work on reestablishing benefits, set up safe housing arrangements, and connect people to service providers in the community may help to ease the stress of reentry and help people manage their psychiatric problems.

Key Elements of Transition Planning

The National Commission on Correctional Health Care's (2015) accreditation standards call for prisons and jails to arrange for a reasonable supply of medication whenever inmates are scheduled to be discharged. Inmates should also leave the facilities with a list of resources in the community. If inmates have critical mental health needs, correctional staff should schedule appointments with community providers and share clinically relevant medical information with those providers.

Osher and colleagues (2003) published a best-practice approach to transition planning for jails, specifically for inmates with co-occurring disorders in mind. This plan also seems applicable to the prison setting and for work with inmates who lack co-occurring diagnoses. The authors referred to this plan as the APIC model. APIC stands for *A*ssess, *P*lan, *I*dentify, and *C*oordinate. The first step is assessment. Staff must assess inmates' clinical and social needs as well as their public safety risks. Osher and colleagues recommend testing all inmates who have either a substance abuse or mental health problem for co-occurring disorders, given the high prevalence of co-occurring disorders in this population. While working on assessment, the staff should get the inmates' perspectives on their needs, as this helps to increase the probability that inmates will engage with staff and cooperate with the plan. During this step, correctional staff should begin to research the types of services that will be available in the community to which the inmate plans to return.

Some inmates might be eligible for veterans' benefits, disability income, or other benefits. Activation or reactivation of these benefits after a person has been incarcerated takes time, so it is important, especially in a jail setting, to begin this process as soon as possible (Osher et al., 2003). Medicaid approval can take a few months, so the application should be filled out well before the inmates are expected to be released (McVey, 2001). While payments from the Social Security Administration will be stopped upon an inmate's incarceration, some jails have made agreements with the administration to set up a swift reactivation process (Osher et al., 2003).[1] Out of appreciation for the importance of reactivating benefits, the Connecticut Department of Corrections provided funding to employ two full-time staff members in the state's Medicaid office to work exclusively on applications coming from corrections transition planning staff (Frisman, Swanson, Marin, & Leavitt-Smith, 2010).

Second, the staff should work on a treatment plan that will meet the inmates' needs identified during assessment. Input from and collaboration with inmates' families can be helpful, and transition personnel should try to obtain it if possible. Families have the potential to play an important part in the inmates' transition. In a study of prisoners returning home to the Cleveland, Ohio area, released inmates tended to rely on housing and employment assistance from family members. One-quarter of the men identified family support as the most important factor keeping them out of prison (Visher & Courtney, 2007). Taylor (2016) surveyed released prison inmates and found that higher levels of family support predicted reductions in recidivism. Instrumental support, such as financial, housing, and job assistance, however, was not associated with recidivism in this study. Taylor recommended that transition planning staff remain cognizant of the existing or lacking emotional support for soon-to-be-released inmates and attempt to provide additional counseling or mentoring for those who appear to lack such connections and support on the outside. Facilitating visitation during incarceration may help to maintain or improve ties between inmates and their families and has been found to be associated with reduced recidivism (Bales & Mears, 2008). Orrick and colleagues (2011) did not find social support to be associated with recidivism. What should we make of these mixed findings? The helpfulness of social support may depend on the inmates, their families, and the type of support they are receiving. Visher and Travis (2003) cautioned that continued contact and association with the support system from home could help returning prisoners, but it could also facilitate their return to offending and substance use. Social support from home might be complicated due to the offenders victimizing their relatives in the past and due to family and friends' own criminal behavior. Additionally, while social support might not be associated with recidivism, Jenkins, Dammer, and Raciti (2017) found that it was related to better quality of life, better health, and less of a need for shelter.

Third, it is necessary to identify the community and correctional programs that will administer any appropriate postrelease services in each offender's community. Referrals to homeless shelters should be used only as a last resort (Osher et al., 2003), given the very strong relationship between stable housing and recidivism. While it will not be possible to arrange for housing for everyone, every effort should be made to find discharged inmates a safe place to stay.

Fourth, the transition plan needs to be coordinated to ensure smooth implementation. In addition to housing, some issues that should be considered during the planning stages are arranging for mental health and substance abuse treatment, health care, employment referrals, and child care (Delaney, Ferguson, Nazon, & Bynum, 2016). The American Correctional Association and the National Commission on Correctional Health Care require all accredited facilities to have a written continuity of care plan that spans admission to discharge for each inmate (McVey, 2001). Continuity of care is a wonderful idea, but it is important to acknowledge that it is difficult in practice. McVey (2001) listed several obstacles facing corrections systems when they attempt to coordinate continuity of care plans. While jail inmates are usually incarcerated in a facility close to home, prison inmates could be housed hundreds of miles away from the communities to which they are set to return. Jail staff who are working on continuity of care plans have the obstacle of uncertainty of release dates. Staff members in both prisons and jails face problems with coordinating service delivery. Each community agency handles a particular issue—for example, employment—so it is important to have someone who is able to coordinate the provision of multiple services, since inmates are likely to need simultaneous assistance in more than one area. Jenkins and colleagues (2017) interviewed inmates who participated in transition planning at a local jail, and one theme that emerged during these interviews was the need for a greater connection between the facility's substance abuse treatment program and the services offered in the community.

Anticipating how released inmates will actually get to their appointments is essential, as reentry staff and community service providers have reported substantial drop-off in program participation shortly after release. Inmates might seem interested while they are incarcerated, as they are eager to resume life on the outside, have good intentions, and are not yet faced with any of the distractions that they might experience on the street. Once they are released, however, it is a very different story. The Urban Institute interviewed prisoners who returned from prison to the Chicago area. Only 22% of these individuals either contacted a community service provider or accessed these services using the referrals that they received while incarcerated. The researchers also reported that the ex-prisoners were much less likely to participate in drug treatment outside prison compared to when they were incarcerated (La Vigne, Visher, & Castro, 2004). Community providers specializing in working with released prisoners with HIV/AIDS reported that, once inmates were released from prison or jail, they rarely heard from them again (Nelson et al., 1999). Even inmates with the best of intentions might have a difficult time once released due to family-related complications. Child care and transportation problems are common obstacles to post-release program participation. While the inmates are still incarcerated, the inmates, case managers, and service providers should discuss how these issues will be resolved so the released inmates will have a viable plan to make their appointments in the community.

Practitioners and researchers have set up programs with the goal of preventing attrition upon release to the community. One technique that transition planning programs have been implementing is in-reach. Researchers with The Urban Institute defined in-reach as "The process of community-based agencies working with offenders during their period of incarceration in a jail or prison setting" (Crayton, Ressler, Mukamal, Janetta, & Warwick, 2010, p. 6). The idea is that the community service providers might be able to develop a positive working relationship and communicate the importance of continuing to receive treatment and services to hopefully increase the chances of people following up in the community. It is important that correctional administrators play an active role in drawing service providers into the facilities to facilitate the continuum of care (Christensen, 2006).

The Auglaize County jail in Ohio has a reentry program that involves in-reach. Case managers help to establish reentry plans, and the jail staff work with service providers in the community to help with employment placement, drug and alcohol treatment, education plans, and mental health counseling. In a study of the reentry program, participants were compared to a similar group of inmates who were eligible for the program but were not admitted due to a lack of space. The only factor that was associated with recidivism was program participation, with the inmates in the program being less likely to recidivate in the first year after release (Miller & Miller, 2010).

The Rikers Island jail in New York developed the Rikers Island Discharge Enhancement (RIDE) program in 2004. The RIDE program gives inmates transportation to postrelease services directly from the jail as a way to prevent program attrition. Participants are then provided with postrelease services for 90 days. White, Saunders, Fisher, and Mellow (2012) evaluated the program and found that program completion was associated with an average of 46 more days spent in the community before recidivating.

Another transition planning factor for corrections staff to consider is the community to which inmates plan to return. There is evidence that the community of return is related to the chances of offenders' success. Taylor (2016) found that the neighborhood of return can increase the chances of recidivism between 7% and 18%. Wright, Pratt, Lowenkamp, and Latessa (2012) tracked inmates released from halfway houses in Ohio with the goal of researching the impact of concentrated disadvantage in neighborhoods on recidivism. They measured concentrated disadvantage as the percentage of family below the poverty line, families receiving public assistance, female-headed households, and African Americans in the community. The treatment provided by the halfway house programs was less effective at reducing recidivism for inmates released to communities with higher levels of concentrated disadvantage or lower affluence. It appears that more affluent communities are able to absorb returning offenders without many detrimental effects, possibly because return to such areas likely indicates a degree of financial support, housing, and/or employment support from friends and families. Areas of concentrated disadvantage tend to house people who, themselves, are struggling, and they may be unable to provide much assistance to returning inmates. These findings suggest that inmates who are set to return to certain communities may be at a greater disadvantage, and additional resources might be necessary to increase returning inmates' odds of success.

Since housing has been found to be one of the most important issues to be resolved in transition planning programs, Lutze, Rosky, and Hamilton (2014) studied the Residential Housing Pilot Program in Washington State. This program provided up to a year of housing support to qualifying offenders, provided that they engaged in treatment, worked toward self-sustainability, and secured employment. Program participants were compared to a similar group of high-risk offenders who were released from incarceration to a community supervision program. Program participants were less likely to become homeless during the follow-up period than the members of the comparison group. Program participation was also associated with reductions in reconvictions and readmission to correctional facilities but was not related to technical violations.

Clark (2016) studied housing and community type to examine the impact of both factors on inmates' chances of recidivating. Clark gathered data from files of inmates leaving prison in Minnesota and found that the type of housing where individuals were set to live after prison predicted recidivism. Specifically, released inmates who went to go live in a private dwelling were less likely to recidivate. Stays at correctional-based housing and shelters were associated with increased chances of recidivism. In this study, poverty and disadvantage levels of the cities where inmates were set to return were not related to the odds of recidivism once individual housing plans were included in the analysis.

Transition Planning Issues Specific to the Jail Setting

People may be incarcerated in jail anywhere from a few hours to several years. The uncertainty of pretrial inmates' release dates and times adds a challenge to transition planning not seen in prisons. A quick or unexpected release from jail may impact staff members' ability to make arrangements for inmates who require assistance in the community. The Correctional Association of New York and the Urban Justice Center wrote *Prisons and Jails: Hospitals of Last Resort* in response to the problems at Rikers Island (Barr, 1999). They noted the danger of stabilizing an inmate on medication while in jail and then releasing that inmate into the community without any more medication or any way to obtain it. The two agencies recommended arranging for safe housing, establishing a clear plan for getting inmates with mental illness who are about to be released into mental health treatment in the community, providing inmates with a supply of medication and an appointment to see a doctor, and assisting inmates with applications for social services prior to their release. By the time of the inmate's release, he or she should have been linked to a social service provider in the community to assist with case management and crisis intervention. Since jails have the unique situation that some of their inmates are released from court at a moment's notice, the New

York Correctional Association and the Urban Justice Center suggested that the courthouse should have an office specifically for released defendants who are mentally ill. That office should be able to provide inmates with access to mental health services, benefits, and housing assistance (Barr, 1999). Of course, not every inmate released directly from court will take advantage of these services. It is important, however, to offer the services, since they could assist inmates in making a successful transition to the community.

Osher (2007) made suggestions for working specifically with individuals who may be released from jail quickly. Inmates who are expected to be in the jail for 72 hours or less can be identified as needing to be put on a "fast track" for reentry services. The National GAINS Center has produced a reentry checklist to assist corrections personnel who are working to identify the needs of inmates with mental illness. It is a quadruplicate document that can provide reentry staff information on the needs of inmates in ten domains: mental health services, psychotropic medications, housing, substance abuse services, health care services, health care benefits, income support/benefits, food/clothing, transportation, and "other." This form includes space for correctional personnel to write notes about each topic. Copies of the documents should be given to the correctional staff, the inmate, and community providers. Osher also recommends having an updated resource manual in the jail that can be given to inmates who are suddenly released without having the opportunity to spend time with a case manager.

Transition Planning in the Prison Setting

Most of the examples offered thus far in this chapter have come from research of jail transition programs, but transition planning also occurs in the prison setting. All states have some type of prison-based prerelease program that attempts to prepare inmates for the transition back into society, but the scope and success of these programs differ (Austin, 2001). Prison staff members have an advantage over jail staff in that they tend to have a good idea of the approximate date that the inmate is set to be released into the community. Additionally, since inmates are typically in prisons longer than they are in jails, staff members may engage inmates in long-term programs. The following paragraphs will provide examples of existing prison transition planning programs that deal with inmates who are mentally ill or who have co-occurring disorders.

The Oklahoma Department of Corrections set up a program to target offenders with mental illness identified as high risk for reoffending. Some inmates may have a very unrealistic and rather romanticized vision of how life will be upon reentry. Staff reliance on what inmates say will happen can result in the transition plan collapsing as soon as the inmates leave prison. For example, some inmates will confidently state that they have a place to stay, as they think that a friend, significant other, or relative is willing to accept them. That is not always reality, however, and the absence of housing makes just about every other aspect of the reentry process difficult or impossible to accomplish. That is why staff in this program call the person whom the inmate thinks will provide housing to confirm that this is the case. Discharge managers meet with any inmates willing to participate in this process to discuss housing options and other transition planning goals. About 90 days before release, staff work to put inmates in touch with the Social Security Administration, and they submit Medicaid applications about 30 days before release. This increases the chances that released inmates will be able to receive Social Security and Medicaid benefits once they leave prison. Once inmates are released, staff members are available 24 hours a day to help with day-to-day needs and provide some funding for temporary housing and necessities (clothing, bus passes, etc). One issue that seems to be especially difficult for people with mental illness is keeping up with the fines, fees, and other legally necessary responsibilities, so the staff members help them to work on that. These services can last for up to a year but will end earlier if the individual is demonstrating the ability to live independently (Mann, Bond, & Powitzky, 2011).

The Oklahoma program has produced some very positive outcomes. Inpatient hospitalization among released offenders decreased from 9% to 2%, while rate of service engagement increased from 12% to 65%. The percent of inmates receiving Social Security benefits increased, while return to prison in the first year decreased from 32% to 17% (Mann et al., 2011).

Minnesota created the Minnesota Comprehensive Reentry Program (MCORP) to reduce recidivism among inmates leaving prison. They began with a pilot program (Phase 1) and then rolled out the full program (Phase 2). Phase 1 began when inmates were several months away from their release date, but once the staff was able to implement Phase 2, they started enrolling inmates shortly after prison admission. The program used the Level of Service Inventory—Revised, a highly regarded assessment instrument that helps to identify risk level and needs. Staff members use motivational interviewing and evidence-based rehabilitation practices to prepare inmates for their eventual return to society. Duwe (2014) conducted a randomized experiment on the MCORP program where inmates were assigned either to the program or to a control group. The offenders in the program were less likely to recidivate and stayed in the community longer before recidivating relative to the control group. There was also a difference between inmates who participated in the full program and those in the shortened pilot program. This is important to consider, as reaching inmates shortly after admission to prison and working with inmates throughout their sentences provided the best outcomes. In addition, Duwe estimated that the program saved approximately $4,300 per inmate and $1.8 million overall over the 18-month follow-up period.

While not designed specifically for offenders with mental illness, Bourgon and Armstrong (2005) identified an effective prison reentry program that can also be useful with inmates with mental illness. The reentry program at the Rideau Correctional and Treatment Center in Ontario, Canada is a cognitive-behavioral program based on the RNR principle. Offenders in the program are classified according to risk and criminogenic needs and then placed in programs of three different lengths: 100 hours of treatment over 5 weeks, 200 hours over 10 weeks, or 300 hours over 15 weeks. The inmates' number of criminogenic needs and their treatment levels were both predictors of recidivism. The shorter programs appeared to be appropriate for the lower risk offenders, but inmates with high levels of risk and high needs were most successful if they received the 15-week program when compared to inmates of the same risk and need level who received only five weeks of treatment. These results suggest that not only is program type important, but corrections and treatment staff need to use assessment results to place inmates into programs that will supply the correct amount of treatment to maximize program effectiveness (Bourgon & Armstrong, 2005). This program targets criminogenic needs rather than mental illness. This type of program is likely to be useful to all types of inmates, as addressing RNR is associated with recidivism reduction.

USE OF ASSERTIVE COMMUNITY TREATMENT AND FORENSIC ASSERTIVE COMMUNITY TREATMENT FOR DIVERSION OR REENTRY

Assertive Community Treatment (ACT) is a mental health program that aims to help people with severe mental illness function in the community setting. Specifically, ACT works to help these individuals, typically 24 hours a day, to decrease rates of homelessness and psychiatric hospitalizations (Slate et al., 2013). ACT programs have been used to help people make the transition from psychiatric hospitalization to living in the community (Davis, Fallon, Vogel, & Teachout, 2008). Forensic Assertive Community Treatment Programs (FACT) are based on the ACT model but tend to focus more on justice-involved individuals with mental illness. ACT and FACT can be used independent of the criminal justice system or as part of diversion or a criminal sanction. When used in the criminal justice system, these programs aim to use therapeutic leverage to require mental health treatment participation in lieu of criminal penalties. The use of the ACT model in the criminal justice system is rather controversial, as some mental health advocates argue that the original ACT programs were never intended to be coercive (Slate et al., 2013). While ACT and FACT programs have been adopted by some local, county, and state jurisdictions as part of interventions with justice-involve people, these programs have mostly been found to be ineffective in achieving reductions in offending. Skeem et al. (2011) believe that the reason behind this lack of success is the programs' lack of attention to criminogenic needs, as many of the case management approaches tend to focus on mental health treatment and provision of services but not much on the behaviors associated with criminal offending. Instead, ACT and FACT programs are more likely to produce improvements in clinical outcomes, such as reductions in hospitalizations.

Cosden and colleagues (2005) evaluated a mental health court that used ACT as a model for their case management services. Case managers were expected to be "assertive" in working with clients and motivating them to use services, such as job placement, housing, medical care, and medication management. Eligible participants must have been charged with either a felony or misdemeanor, have a diagnosis of serious mental illness, live in a particular county, and have at least one prior booking. The program did not have any impact on participants' criminal activity when compared to other offenders who participated in the regular criminal justice processing. The mental health court offenders did experience improvements working on drug addiction, decreasing levels of psychological distress, and improving overall quality of life. The authors did speculate that the services offered to the treatment group might have bled into the comparison group, so the lack of differences between the two groups may be a product of both getting some level of treatment. Another possibility is that the ACT component of the program did not address any of the offenders' criminogenic needs.

Staff at four prisons in New Zealand introduced an in-reach model reentry program with a focus on ACT. The program's goal was to improve the continuity of care and provide 24-hour per day services for psychiatric emergencies upon release. The program improved the frequency of contact with mental health professionals in the community, and there were modest reductions in reoffending (McKenna et al., 2015). Davis and colleagues (2008) studied an ACT program that was used in conjunction with a jail aftercare program. The ACT staff members provided services 24-hours per day, assisted people with tasks of daily living, and worked with them to make their criminal justice-related appointments. Program participation did reduce the number of days people spent in jail during the follow-up period but had no impact on arrests.

ACT and FACT can be useful components of criminal justice interventions that involve people with mental illness and co-occurring disorders. Components of ACT and FACT, such as motivational interviewing, 24-hour availability of psychiatric assistance, mental health care, and assistance with navigating the requirements of any necessary criminal justice responsibilities, are welcome services. They do have the potential to be enough to help anyone whose criminality is solely the product of an untreated mental illness, but for the majority of offenders with mental illness who have multiple criminogenic needs, they will require additional programming specifically targeting those needs in order for there to be meaningful reductions in recidivism.

BARRIERS TO IMPLEMENTATION OF DIVERSION AND TRANSITION PLANNING PROGRAMS

Implementation of rehabilitation programs and social services has been a challenge since the inception of prisons and jails. The staff working in these facilities, as well as all personnel in the criminal justice system, must always be concerned about balancing public safety and security needs with the needs of offenders. Roskes (2001) notes that, although it may seem that these two missions are at odds, they are, in a way, complementary. If the treatment needs of offenders are addressed, this could prevent them from committing future offenses which, in turn, increases public safety. Nevertheless, suggestions for collaboration between criminal justice staff and mental health treatment professionals are sometimes met with skepticism or outright hostility from both groups. Roskes (2001) states that the negative stereotypes of both groups—criminal justice personnel just want to "lock-em-up" while treatment staff members have "bleeding hearts"—can lead to reluctance of the two groups to trust each other. Cross-training to help both groups understand information from the other side's point of view could help the groups move past their mistrust and develop a greater understanding of each other (Farabee et al., 1999).

The political climate of each jurisdiction is another potential barrier to both diversion and transition planning programs. Programs that emphasize treatment over punitiveness are subject to criticism by get-tough politicians and members of the public who believe that this amounts to coddling criminals. This attitude makes it difficult to establish and maintain funding. While there seemed to be a change to this attitude during the George W. Bush and Barak Obama administrations, with Bush's advocacy for the Second Chance Act and Obama's visit to a federal prison, the legacy of the Trump White House when it comes to support for rehabilitation has yet to be determined. The

Trump administration has sent mixed signals, with the appointment of War on Drugs supporter Jeff Sessions as his first attorney general, but then the administration has also been willing to discuss the possibility of meaningful reforms for federal prisoners.

An additional problem confronting correctional agencies is the partial or misapplication of programs, resulting in ineffective practices. The history of corrections is littered with examples of programs being modified so they are cheaper, easier to run, or involve less political risk taking, but the price of these changes is a loss of effectiveness (Cowles & Dorman, 2001; Farabee et al., 1999; Rhine, Mawhorr, & Parks, 2006; Tartaro, 2002, 2006; Wilson & Davis, 2006). Lowenkamp, Latessa, and Smith (2006) assessed the quality of halfway house programs in Ohio in fiscal year 1999, for example, and found that over two-thirds of the programs were not operating in ways that would maximize their chances of being successful.

Quality control is important and can be the difference between successful and failing programs. A good starting point is to look at what the program is intending to target. Throughout this chapter, I have discussed the importance of targeting offenders' criminogenic needs and helping to resolve important issues such as housing, reactivation of benefits, and continuation of medication. Setting appropriate goals is important, but so is program implementation. Lowenkamp et al. (2006) found a correlation between program integrity and recidivism reduction when analyzing rehabilitation programs.

CONCLUSION

Both diversion and reentry programs are promising strategies, as they aim to reduce the use of incarceration. Diversion shortens, and sometimes eliminates, incarceration time for individuals who are not considered to be a danger to the community and who are potentially treatable. Treatment in the community is both cheaper and can be less damaging compared to the often counterproductive environments inside of prisons and jails. Reentry programs may be able to help keep offenders in the community, if not permanently, then at least for a longer period than they would have without assistance. I conducted an evaluation of diversion and reentry services offered by Jewish Family Services, a local nonprofit that assists justice-involved individuals with mental illness. The offenders whom they treated tended to be at a higher risk for reoffending than the comparison group, as was evidenced by their more extensive criminal histories prior to treatment. After intervention, the treatment group remained in the community for an average of 495 days prior to reincarceration compared to 278 days for the comparison group. Incarceration cost $80 per day per inmate at the time of the study, so this reduction of incarceration resulted in an average savings of $17,360 per treatment participant (Tartaro, 2015).

The quality, thoroughness, and aims of diversion and transition planning programs vary to a great extent. Reentry became a buzzword in the early 2000s, and problem-solving courts, including mental health courts grew rapidly and with little standardization. The result is that many jurisdictions offer these programs, but they are not all necessarily effective. What is evident from this chapter is that proper staffing, availability of resources, targeting of appropriate needs, and provision of the proper amounts of treatment are key factors in the success of these programs. Without boundary spanners and strong program leaders, efforts to reduce recidivism are likely to fail, as both diversion and reentry require the establishment and maintenance of relationships between criminal justice and health care/social service providers. A disconnect between these groups can doom a program to failure. Both diversion and transition plans can be wonderful on paper, but unless the communities actually have services available for these populations, the offenders are unlikely to succeed.

Programs need to address specific needs. Mental health treatment is very important, as is housing and employment assistance, but they alone are unlikely to impact recidivism unless they are accompanied by attention to criminogenic needs. The extent of treatment that inmates need depends on their risk level. Assessment tools will help to inform staff of each person's level of risk.

NOTE

1. Jails in Maryland have established an agreement with Medicaid whereby inmates' benefits will be suspended, but not terminated, upon incarceration. Even if the incarceration lasts over thirty days, the inmates will be able to reactivate their Medicaid membership promptly upon release from jail. The jail in Lane County, Oregon, has a similar agreement with Medicaid (Judge Bazelon Center for Mental Health Law, 2006).

Chapter Nine

Litigation Issues

When inmate suicides occur, the decedent's family is often, understandably, frustrated and confused about how their relative could have succeeded in committing suicide while being supervised by correctional staff. Families who believe that the staff failed in their duty to properly screen, monitor, and treat the inmate may file suit in federal or state court. Schlanger (2003a) surveyed all 50 state prison systems and all jails listed in the National Institute of Corrections' Large Jail Network and found that suicides ranked seventh among reasons why these institutions were sued during the three years prior to survey distribution in 2001. Thirty-six of the 50 responding facilities reported having to respond to a lawsuit over suicide prevention issues.

The purpose of this chapter is to discuss the legal options for plaintiffs following an attempted or completed suicide of an incarcerated individual and to review defenses available to corrections agencies. This chapter covers both federal civil rights claims and state wrongful death cases. I will summarize potential legal remedies for family members of inmates who died by suicide and review the significant court decisions relating to suicides in custody.

LEGAL OPTIONS FOR PLAINTIFFS

The families of deceased inmates, or the inmates themselves in the event of a suicide attempt, who are looking for relief in civil court have the option of filing a tort claim or a civil rights claim. A tort is some injury or wrong for which a court provides damages or compensation (Anderson & Dyson, 2001), and this type of claim is heard in state courts. Wallace and Roberson (2000) identified two areas where torts apply to corrections officials. The first

197

category is *intentional torts* in which the plaintiff alleges that officials intentionally inflicted harm, and this includes cases involving false imprisonment, assault, or emotional distress. Second, *negligence torts* involve injuries that occurred due to corrections officials acting carelessly or providing substandard care. Successful tort actions involve a demonstration of three elements: (1) a legal duty owed to the plaintiff by the defendant, (2) a breach of that duty, and (3) an injury due to that breach (Anderson & Dyson, 2001; Wallace & Roberson, 2000). A successful tort action will result in a financial award to the plaintiff in the form of compensatory damages for any injuries and/or punitive damages to punish the defendant for improper conduct (Wallace & Roberson, 2000). A drawback to tort claims is that attorney fees will not be awarded, nor is any injunctive relief available, meaning that plaintiffs will not be able to have the court order corrections administrators to change the way the facility operates (Anderson & Dyson, 2001). Tort claims for suicide, however, tend to be easier for plaintiffs to win than federal civil rights claims, since they generally require proof of negligence, while civil rights claims require proof of deliberate indifference.

The other option for inmates seeking relief in court is Title 42, Section 1983, of the U.S. Code, commonly referred to as "Section 1983." This is the provision that allows inmates and their families to sue government entities for a constitutional violation (Magun, 2017). Section 1983 lawsuits deal with conditions of the inmates' confinement. Judges, in deciding the case of *Monell v. Department of Social Services* (1978), established that a civil rights violation under Section 1983 occurred when (1) a person was deprived of a right, privilege, or immunity guaranteed under the Constitution and federal laws; and (2) the deprivation resulted from official policy or custom of a local government entity (Wallace & Roberson, 2000). Section 1983 lawsuits can be filed against sworn and civilian staff in their individual capacity when their action or inaction resulted in a constitutional violation. The other option is for plaintiffs to file a claim against an entire entity, such as a municipality. In that case, the plaintiffs must prove that problematic policy or custom was the "moving force" behind the constitutional violation (Magun, 2017). An advantage of Section 1983 claims over tort claims is that, in addition to monetary awards, it is possible to win an injunction that may force the corrections department to change their policies and/or procedures. Additionally, it is possible for plaintiffs to be awarded attorneys' fees (Anderson & Dyson, 2001).

Section 1983 cases often involve allegations that inmates have been denied constitutional rights, usually pertaining to the 8th Amendment. The 8th Amendment, however, pertains only to inmates who have been convicted, as it protects individuals against cruel and unusual punishment. Specifically, the 8th Amendment, as interpreted today, gives convicted inmates the right to adequate medical care and the right to be free from the substantial risk of serious harm (Magun, 2017). Pretrial detention is not considered punishment and, therefore, is not covered by the 8th Amendment. Instead, pretrial inmates can sue using the 14th Amendment's Due Process Clause. The 14th Amendment requires that the rights afforded to pretrial detainees be at least as great as those provided to convicted offenders (see *Bell v. Wolfish*, 1979; *Cavalieri v. Shepard*, 2003 and *City of Revere v. Massachusetts General Hospital*, 1983). In other words, the 14th Amendment requires correctional agencies to extend protections of the Bill of Rights to pretrial detainees.

TYPES OF RULINGS IN FAVOR OF DEFENDANTS

Before I provide more details about state and federal court proceedings for correctional suicide cases, I will explain rulings that the defense can request to have the case dismissed.

Summary Judgment

Section 1983 suicide litigation cases are frequently dismissed before they reach trial due to a grant of summary judgment. Summary judgment is granted if the court decides that "the plaintiff has failed to prove that a genuine issue of material fact exists between the parties" (C. Johnson, 2002, p. 1241). The purpose of summary judgment is to allow courts to discard claims that are not supported by the facts, even when viewed in light most favorable to the plaintiffs, before they proceed to a jury trial (C. Johnson, 2002).

Immunity

Government officials are immune from litigation under certain circumstances. Judges, for example, have absolute immunity, protecting them from all lawsuits pertaining to their work (Anderson & Dyson, 2001). Corrections officials are not eligible for such comprehensive protection, but they may make a successful argument for qualified immunity under certain circumstances. Government employees tend to be eligible for qualified immunity unless they are found to be violating clearly established constitutional rights of which a reasonable person should be aware. If there was a violation of inmates' rights, the next question for the courts to determine is whether the employee knew or should have known that the action in question violated inmates' rights. Officials can claim to be operating in good faith if they can demonstrate that they were working to adhere to prison regulations and constitutional protections (Anderson & Dyson, 2001).

The standard for qualified immunity for government employees was articulated in a case involving the work of school officials. In *Wood v. Strickland* (1975), the U.S. Supreme Court justices heard arguments about whether school administrators who expelled students for bringing alcohol to school should be granted qualified immunity for performing their duties in good faith. The court decided that, in determining good faith, both objective and subjective standards should be used. Specifically, Justice White wrote in the majority opinion that:

> The official himself must be acting sincerely and with a belief that he is doing right, but an act violating a student's constitutional rights can be no more justified by ignorance or disregard of settled, indisputable law on the part of one entrusted with supervision of students' daily lives than by the presence of actual malice. To be entitled to a special exemption from the categorical remedial language of § 1983 in a case in which his action violated a student's constitutional rights, a school board member, who has voluntarily undertaken the task of supervising the operation of the school and the activities of the students, must be held to a standard of conduct based not only on permissible intentions, but also on knowledge of the basic, unquestioned constitutional rights of his charges. (*Wood v. Strickland*, 1975, p. 322)

To summarize, the professional is expected to have a general knowledge of basic rights for the population that he or she is supervising.

In another case, this one involving senior aides to President Nixon, the Supreme Court stated that public officials could not be held civilly liable provided that "their conduct does not violate clearly established statutory or constitutional rights to which a reasonable person would have known" (*Harlow v. Fitzgerald*, 1982, p. 815). Although this decision does provide public officials, including corrections officers, with some protection from lawsuits, they cannot plead ignorance to recent changes in inmates' rights indefinitely (*Harlow v. Fitzgerald*, 1982).

The work of corrections personnel is characterized to a certain degree by obeying orders and practicing in accordance with policy, but there is also a great deal of discretion involved. For example, when should an inmate be taken off suicide watch? Should the staff member responsible for making such a decision be sued if the inmate commits suicide after being removed from suicide watch? The aforementioned *Harlow v. Fitzgerald* (1982) case, which set the requirements for filing civil suits against federal officials for unconstitutional conduct indicates the "government officials performing discretionary functions generally are shielded from liability for civil damages insofar as their conduct does not violate 'clearly established' statutory or constitutional rights of which a reasonable person would have known" (pp. 815–816).

State courts have also routinely held that correctional staff members are immune from prosecution while performing discretionary functions but not ministerial functions. Ministerial functions are those that require a staff member to complete a specific duty in accordance with explicit directions. For example, officers who are ordered to check an inmate every 15 minutes must do so. The Georgia Court of Appeals ruled on a case that provides a good illustration of ministerial duties in the course of suicide prevention. During a pretrial court hearing for a defendant, the judge ordered that the inmate be held on suicide watch and in protective custody at the jail. At that time, the county had a main jail and another facility that they were using to alleviate crowding. The disposition recorder working in the records office of the main jail wrote down the judge's protective custody order but not the requirement of suicide watch. The inmate was housed on suicide watch in the first jail, but upon transfer to the second facility, he was placed in an attorney's booth to keep him separated from other inmates, but no suicide precautions were taken. The court hearing this case ruled that the jail staff member responsible for the failure to record the court order should be denied qualified immunity. Additionally, the employee who placed the suicidal inmate in the attorney's booth should be denied qualified immunity, as both staff members failed to complete tasks that were "simple, absolute, and definite, arising under conditions admitted or proved to exist, and requiring merely the execution of a specific duty" (*Hill v. Jackson*, 2016, p. 689).

Since discretion is such a key part of criminal justice work, staff members are granted qualified immunity if they are performing tasks that require their discretion. One example of a discretionary function becoming the basis for qualified immunity is from the Michigan state court system. A captain in a Michigan jail interviewed an inmate for 30 to 45 minutes before deciding that the inmate should be placed in one of the holding cells instead of an observation cell. The inmate later committed suicide in the holding cell. The court ruled that the captain's actions were discretionary; therefore the court granted the defendants summary judgment (*Harvey v. Nichols*, 2003). In another example, the family of a deceased pretrial inmate in Missouri filed lawsuits in both federal and state courts following a suicide. The plaintiff argued that the jail staff knew about the inmate's history of suicide attempts and were aware that he was very upset about a recent breakup. In response to concerns about self-harm, the staff placed him in a cell with a roommate, thinking that this supervision and companionship might help to prevent a suicide. In the initial interview following the discovery of Jereme Hartwig's body, the officer responsible for doing hourly rounds could not recall seeing him in his cell during the last check. The officer later amended her statement and said that she recalled seeing Hartwig alone in his cell. The court ruled that the officer had fulfilled her ministerial function by completing the check, even if she only briefly glanced inside the cell. The court then determined that the officer's inaction after finding Hartwig alone, even when the staff specifically placed him with an inmate so he might be less likely to commit suicide, was a discretionary function that was protected by qualified immunity (*A. H. v. St. Louis County, Missouri*, 2018).

SECTION 1983 CASES AS
THEY PERTAIN TO CUSTODIAL SUICIDE

The history of federal courts' treatment of Section 1983 claims, particularly those involving concerns about health care and suicide, can be broken down into four time periods: (1) pre–*Estelle v. Gamble* (1976), (2) *Estelle v. Gamble* but before *Farmer v. Brennan* (1994), (3) *Farmer v. Brennan* but before *Kingsley v. Hendrickson* (2015), and (4) post–*Kingsley v. Hendrickson*.

Pre–*Estelle v. Gamble*

Prior to the 1960s, members of the judiciary were hesitant to involve themselves in matters concerning the treatment of inmates, as operation of prisons and jails falls under the executive branch of government. While the courts did rule on some cases about prisoners' conditions of confinement (Blomberg & Lucken, 2007), few of these resulted in significant changes to correctional policy. It was not until the 1960s that the federal courts, and specifically the U.S. Supreme Court with Chief Justice Earl Warren at the helm, became active participants in extending the protections of the Bill of Rights to inmates.

Estelle v. Gamble

The landmark case establishing inmates' rights to medical treatment was decided in 1976. In *Estelle v. Gamble* (1976), the court recognized that the withholding of medical care can be an 8th Amendment violation under certain circumstances. The U.S. Supreme Court determined that, for a court to rule in favor of an inmate alleging a violation of the 8th Amendment due to denial of medical care, the plaintiff must demonstrate that the corrections personnel exhibited "deliberate indifference" toward that person's medical needs. The justices explained that:

> deliberate indifference to a prisoner's serious medical needs constituted cruel and unusual punishment under the Eighth Amendment and gave rise to a civil rights cause of action under 42 USCS 1983, regardless of whether the indifference was manifested by prison doctors in their response to the prisoner's needs

or by corrections officers in intentionally denying or delaying access to medical care or intentionally interfering with treatment once prescribed (*Estelle v. Gamble*, 1976, pp. 104–105).

The justices did note that inmates would not succeed in all cases alleging poor medical treatment, since a violation of the 8th Amendment required a "wanton infliction of unnecessary pain." If it was a matter of simple malpractice or an unintentional misdiagnosis, it did not constitute a civil rights violation. While *Estelle* involved a question about the quality of care for a physical ailment, corrections departments remained uncertain about their legal duty to provide mental health care. In the *Bowring v. Godwin* (1977) case the court clarified that inmates' rights to medical care extends to psychological ailments.

The *Estelle* court recognized deliberate indifference as the standard for determining a violation of the 8th Amendment, but it did not provide specific guidance to the lower courts on what is required to establish deliberate indifference. Following the *Estelle* ruling, some of the lower courts used the objective standard, where plaintiffs needed to prove that either the defendant actually knew or *should have known* of the risk to the individual, yet the officials failed to act. Other districts used the subjective standard, dismissing cases unless the plaintiffs showed either that the defendants had knowledge of risk to a specific individual or knowledge of a general risk to all prisoners in a given situation (Magun, 2017). The U.S. Supreme Court put an end to this divergence with *Farmer v. Brennan* (1994).

Farmer v. Brennan

Farmer v. Brennan (1994) involved an inmate-inmate assault rather than a suicide. Farmer was a biological male who was in the process of transitioning to a woman. She had already undergone estrogen therapy, received silicone breast implants, submitted to an unsuccessful testicle-removal surgery, and had been taking hormonal drugs that she smuggled into the prison. In addition to the biological changes, Farmer also wore her clothes in a feminine manner. Farmer spent most of her sentence housed in segregation for her own safety. She was transferred to another prison for disciplinary reasons, where she was placed among the general population of males. Farmer voiced no objections to her placement in the general population. Within two weeks of the transfer, Farmer claimed to have been beaten and raped by another inmate in her cell.

Farmer sued, claiming that her placement in the general population constituted deliberate indifference, since the prison administrators should have known that someone with her physical characteristics would be in danger if placed in the general population. The U.S. Supreme Court did not rule in favor of Farmer but did explain under what conditions a prison official can be held responsible for injury to an inmate. Justice Souter, who wrote the majority opinion, stated:

> A prison official cannot be found liable under the Eighth Amendment for denying an inmate humane conditions of confinement unless the official knows of and disregards an excessive risk to inmate health or safety; the official must both be aware of facts from which the inference could be drawn that a substantial risk of serious harm exists, and he must also draw the inference (*Farmer v. Brennan*, 1994, p. 837).

The *Farmer* case determined that it is not enough for there to be a risk that correctional personnel should have been able to detect. There must be evidence that (1) the risk existed, (2) correctional personnel were aware of and understood the risk, and (3) they purposefully ignored that risk. *Farmer* ended the debate among the lower courts about the standard to use when considering whether staff members were deliberately indifferent to an inmate's risk or need. All of the lower courts began adopting this subjective standard and continued to apply it for decades.

Kingsley v. Hendrickson

Like *Farmer*, *Kingsley v. Hendrickson* (2015) did not involve an inmate suicide or even an instance of self-harm. Kingsley was a pretrial inmate in a county jail. An officer ordered him to remove a piece of paper that was covering his cell window. Kingsley refused, and officers entered the cell to cuff and remove him. Kingsley was uncooperative and made it difficult for the officers to move him by refusing to stand on his own and tensing up his arm muscles to resist being cuffed. Officers moved him to a new cell, and Kingsley claimed that officers became abusive, slamming his head against a concrete slab and tasering him. This case made it to the Supreme Court, where the justices ruled in favor of Kingsley, using an objective standard. Prior to this case, the standard for determining whether force crossed the line to abuse was the subjective standard. In *Kingsley*, the court decided that, since he was a pretrial inmate, the objective standard was more appropriate. The justices ruled that the plaintiff needed only to demonstrate that the force was objectively unreasonable. It was not necessary to provide evidence of the officers' state of mind.

Kingsley is significant for two reasons. First, it allows use-of-force cases for pretrial inmates to be handled differently than those involving convicted inmates. Application of the objective standard would ultimately provide more protections for pretrial inmates than their convicted counterparts. Second, and germane to this chapter, is the possibility that federal courts will begin to apply the objective standard to cases involving suicides and attempted suicides, access to medical care, and conditions of confinement for pretrial inmates. I will return to this issue later, but first I will discuss how difficult it is for plaintiffs to win suicide cases under the subjective standard set by *Farmer v. Brennan*. The *Farmer* standard still applies to cases involving convicted inmates and, as of this writing, it is unclear whether *Farmer* or *Kingsley* will guide litigation following suicides of pretrial detainees.

DEFENSES FOR SECTION 1983 SUICIDE LAWSUITS POST-*FARMER*

While the *Farmer* ruling was about the question of staff members' duty to protect inmates from other inmates, the subjective deliberate indifference standard established in this case became the standard for custodial suicide cases. Justice Souter, in his opinion on the aforementioned *Farmer v. Brennan* (1994) case, acknowledged that three possible defenses for prison administrations would arise from the decision. The first defense is that staff members were unaware of the facts indicating that the inmate was in danger. Assuming that this first defense is not possible, the second defense is that, while acknowledging being aware of the facts, the individuals believed that the risk was either insubstantial or nonexistent. Third, officials can claim that they (1) knew of the facts, (2) interpreted them properly, and (3) provided a reasonable response to the risk, but the injury occurred anyway. Examples of each of these defenses, successful and unsuccessful, are provided below.

Defense 1: The Defendant Was Unaware of the Facts Indicating That the Inmate Was in Danger.

The *Farmer* precedent that plaintiffs have to demonstrate that the defendant was actually aware of a threat against a specific inmate was disappointing to inmates' rights advocates, as this is a hard standard to meet. While this was a setback, the *Farmer* court did provide some hope for future cases. The court indicated a willingness to rule in favor of the plaintiff upon demonstrating the presence of a general risk to inmates. The lower courts had been reluctant to rule in favor of defendants attempting to demonstrate a general risk (Magun, 2017), but *Farmer* seemed to signal an end to exclusive reliance on the "individual-specific" rule. In an analysis of the impact of the *Farmer* case on custodial suicide liability cases, Robertson (2004) stated that, if an official is pleading ignorance of a risk, the court can conclude that the risk was so clear that the official must have been aware of the danger. For example, risk of assault for an inmate can be derived from more general information, such as evidence that a given area inside the jail is a known trouble spot for violence, rather than specific threats against a particular inmate (*Hale v. Tallapoosa County*, 1995).

While prisoners' rights advocates might have been somewhat hopeful when the *Farmer* court indicated a willingness to accept general risk of harm as evidence, the lower courts have been inconsistent in their rulings (Hanser, 2002). *Hale v. Tallapoosa County* (1995) is an example of the lower courts adhering to the removal of the individual-specific rule in an inmate-inmate assault case. Inmate Hale, who was being held for failing to appear on a marijuana charge, was locked in a cell with several inmates, some of whom were charged with violent offenses. The correctional administration had no knowledge of any threat specific to Hale, yet he was beaten by his cellmates. Hale sued, arguing that jail staff were deliberately indifferent to the risk of violence present in that part of the jail. When the corrections officials filed to have the case dismissed, the court declined to do so. The court ruled that, although the administration had no knowledge of specific threats against Hale, violence had been a regular occurrence in that part of the jail, so the jail was aware of a generalized risk to Hale and any other inmates housed there. Despite awareness of this risk, the administrator did not take any action to prevent violence in that part of the jail, and that raised the question whether the jail was deliberately indifferent to Hale's safety.

Contrary to the *Hale v. Tallapoosa* (1995) ruling, in *Frake v. City of Chicago* (2000), the court required evidence of a threat to a specific inmate, even though there seemed to be evidence of a general risk for suicide. Following Robert Frake's suicide, his family sued the city, noting that there were 20 suicides and 163 suicide attempts, all by hanging, in the jail from December 4, 1990 through November 18, 1997. Horizontal metal bars in the cells were frequently used by suicidal inmates to attach ligatures, and given the number of suicides and attempts, the corrections staff clearly knew how these bars were being used. Regardless of the repeated use of the bars for suicide attempts, the court ruled in favor of the defendants, citing the lack of evidence that corrections personnel were aware that Frake, specifically, was suicidal.

A jail staff person's claim of being unaware of a risk to a specific inmate can be a successful defense for a county or municipality, even if the government entity was violating a consent decree at the time of the inmate's death. Cynthia Cagle filed a Section 1983 claim when her brother, Danny Ray Butler, committed suicide in the Winston County Jail. The jail was court-ordered to have two full-time officers on duty from 5pm to 8am daily in the cell block where Butler was housed. Only one staff member was on duty on the night of Butler's death. The plaintiff sued, claiming that the jail was aware of a supervision problem in that part of the facility. The defendants were granted summary judgment, because the court noted that the jail was ordered to have two officers present due to the known risk of escapes, not suicides, and that the jail had no knowledge that Butler was suicidal (*Cagle v. Sutherland*, 2003). In a similar case, an inmate committed suicide while housed on a floor that was supposed to be monitored by an officer 24 hours a day. Despite the court order that the officer be on the floor at all times, supervisors let the officer leave for meals, for breaks, and to move inmates. An inmate committed suicide while the officer was off the floor. When the family of the deceased sued, the court ruled in favor of the defendants. Lawyers for the jail argued that suicidal people are usually placed on a different floor of the jail, and, had they known that the inmate was suicidal, he would have been housed elsewhere (*Wade v. Tompkins*, 2003).

Even examples of the county jail failing to abide by state standards may not be enough for plaintiffs to prevail unless they can demonstrate that the county knew specifically that a particular inmate was suicidal. Charles Jernegan denied being suicidal during booking, but during his screening, he did admit to feelings of paranoia, hearing voices, feeling nervous or depressed, and taking prescribed medication for a mental health problem. By the jail's standards, his answers should have prompted a more thorough assessment by a mental health professional, but that never happened. The following day, Jernegan submitted a medical request to "speak to someone about problems." He received an automated response the next day, stating that someone would see him in the next 48 to 72 hours. He hanged himself two days later, before anyone from the mental health staff was able to speak with him. The state of Oklahoma conducted an investigation in the wake of the incident and cited the jail for three deficiencies: (1) improperly detaining the inmate, (2) failing to house him in an area offering more frequent observation and medical evaluations (prisoners with mental illness in Oklahoma are supposed to be separated from the general population), and (3) using a mental health care management policy that conflicted with the state standards. Regardless of the state finding that the county violated facility and state policy, the 10th Circuit Court of Appeals granted the defendants summary judgment in the absence of proof that anyone at the jail knew that Jernegan was suicidal (*Cox v. Glanz*, 2015).

To summarize, although the *Farmer v. Brennan* ruling in 1994 appeared to signal the end of the individual-specific rule, the descriptions of the aforementioned cases show that the federal courts continue to apply that rule to federal correctional suicide lawsuits. Although this part of the *Farmer* ruling appeared to be a positive change in case law for plaintiffs, it is not being reflected in the lower court decisions.

Defense 2: The Defendant Acknowledged Being Aware of the Facts Indicating Possible Danger, but He/She Believed that the Risk Was Either Insubstantial or Nonexistent.

Corrections officials sometimes become aware of past suicide attempts or threats of an upcoming attempt and, for a variety of reasons, do not interpret that information as an immediate threat to the inmate's safety. Robertson (1993) noted that case law requires a four-prong test for satisfying the "awareness" factor for deliberate indifference. The four facts that plaintiffs need to establish are (1) the inmate previously threatened or attempted suicide, (2) the prior threat or attempt was known to the defendants, (3) the prior threat or attempt was somewhat recent, and (4) the prior threat or attempt appeared genuine.

Donald Ray Terry committed suicide by hanging in the Montgomery County Jail in Crawfordsville, Indiana. He had a history of suicide attempts during previous stays at that jail. During his last stay, Terry was noncompliant with his psychiatric medication. Three weeks before his suicide, he cut his wrist and fought with the officers. That behavior prompted a transfer to the state's Reception and Diagnostic Center (RDC), where he was placed on suicide watch, and a psychiatrist increased his medication. Terry was transferred back to the jail six days later for what appeared to be financial, and not treatment, reasons. The jail staff neglected to review his medical file upon his reentry to the jail, so they did not see that his medication was supposed to increase. On his last day, Terry appeared irrational when visiting with his mother, and he received news from home that his girlfriend was leaving him. The defendants requested summary judgment on the grounds that they were unaware that Terry was at risk for suicide (*Terry v. Rice*, 2003). In denying the defendants summary judgment, the court cited *McGill v. Duckworth* (1991), noting "Going out of your way to avoid acquiring unwelcome knowledge is a species of intent. Being an ostrich involves a level of knowledge sufficient for conviction of crimes requiring specific intent" (p. 44).

In *Turney v. Waterbury* (2004), Turney told officers in the Pennington County Jail that he was going to "hang it up." When he was transferred to the Bennett County Jail three days later, the sheriff who conducted the inmate transport told the supervisor at the Bennett County Jail about the threat of suicide. The sheriff also informed the supervisor about Turney's comment that, if he received a long prison sentence, he would kill himself and someone else. Before leaving for the night, the supervisor told an officer to keep an eye on Turney but advised that officer to avoid entering Turney's cell alone for any reason. The officer was not given an explanation for this warning. When the officer later found Turney hanging in his cell, he heeded his supervisor's warning and refrained from entering the cell to cut down Turney and start

CPR. The court denied summary judgment to the defendants due to the fact that corrections officials were aware of the suicidal risk, yet they did not pass that information on to those left watching the inmate.

The U.S. Court of Appeals for the 7th Circuit heard the case of *Cavalieri v. Shepard* (2003) and concluded that the arresting officer (Shepard) was deliberately indifferent in neglecting to inform the jail staff that Cavalieri was suicidal. Shepard was at the crime scene when Cavalieri was holding his girlfriend hostage, and Cavalieri threatened to kill her and himself. When they arrived at the jail, Cavalieri asked Shepard if he could speak to a counselor. Despite Shepard's assurances that he would arrange that, it never happened. Additionally, Shepard was told by Cavalieri's mother that her son was in a fragile mental state and had called the crisis hotline the night before. She also told the officer that her son had been on suicide watch at the jail during the previous month. Shepard claimed that, after conducting interviews with Cavalieri, the inmate seemed fine. He was later placed in a cell with a telephone and a strong cord. The inmate wrapped the cord around his neck, and this suicide attempt left him in a vegetative state. The court ruled that Shepard should not have relied exclusively on his impressions of the inmate during the interviews but should have used the information obtained at the crime scene and from Cavalieri's mother. The information from the crime scene and the information provided by the inmate's mother was enough to demonstrate that at least one government official involved in this case was aware of the suicide risk.

William Scott Salter committed suicide in a county jail while he was housed there as a pretrial detainee. Salter's mental health history and history of suicide attempts were well known to most of the jail staff. He was placed on suicide watch and later removed and placed on a lower level of supervision (health watch) by the facility's general physician. Jail staff were aware of his very agitated state, self-harming behaviors during the current incarceration, and his suicide attempt a few days before being incarcerated. The jail allowed a general practitioner rather than a mental health specialist to remove Salter from suicide watch (a violation of institutional policy). Following Salter's suicide, the court granted the staff members summary judgment on the basis that Salter's behavior was typical of an individual with mental illness, and the court assumed that this is why staff did not draw the inference that his behavior was a warning sign of a suicide (*Salter v. Mitchell,* 2017).

The courts will only consider a previous suicide attempt a warning sign of an impending attempt if the prior act of self-harm occurred recently. In *Holland v. City of Atmore* (2001), Holland was taken to a hospital for a suicide attempt in December 1997. He was arrested and placed in jail in February 1998, where he was put on suicide watch for banging his head against the bars. In July 1998, he committed suicide in the local jail. The officer who handled the 911 call for the 1997 suicide attempt was also the jailer on the night of Holland's suicide in July 1998. The officer was unaware of the February 1998 head-banging incident, but he did know about the December 1997 incident. The court found that the December suicide attempt did not make the risk so obvious as to require a special duty of care for the inmate. The court concluded that:

> An individual that threatens to attempt suicide has unequivocally expressed an immediate desire or intent to end his life, and that desire or intent may readily be assumed to persist only until the passions provoking it have cooled sufficiently for reason and self-love to regain primacy. A strong likelihood of self-annihilation may remain for periods of a few hours or even a few days after a suicide attempt or threat, but the plaintiffs have identified no support for the proposition that an individual may remain on the brink of suicide for months at a time, much less that Holland did so (*Holland v. City of Atmore*, 2001, p. 1314).

In a similar case, the court granted officers and screening staff summary judgment even though they had knowledge of the inmate's suicidal history and violated jail policies by failing to place the inmate on suicide watch. During intake in 2011, Kristina Prochnow told the screening officer of her prior diagnoses of depression and bipolar disorder, her current feelings of hopelessness, and a suicide attempt the previous year. Had the staff looked at her inmate record, they would have seen that she was placed on suicide watch in 2008. They did not look at the record, nor did they place her on suicide watch. The lower court granted summary judgment, and the appeals court affirmed noting that the jail records that the staff failed to examine would have shown that Prochnow survived previous, recent incarcerations in the general population, so the evidence of previous placement on suicide watch might not have prompted placement on suicide this time (*Grabow v. County of Macomb*, 2014).

In another case where previous records were not consulted, the jail had a policy that inmates who had previously been on suicide watch needed to go right back onto watch upon re-incarceration. The staff did not examine Demittarus Pernell Burden's files, so during his 2007 incarceration, they were unaware of his 2005 stay on suicide watch. The court granted the defendants summary judgment arguing "simply because Burden had been on suicide watch in the jail in 2005 did not put defendants on notice that he was suicidal in March 2007" (*Smith v. Atkins*, 2011, p. 965). The knowledge that staff violated their own suicide prevention policy was not enough to establish deliberate indifference.

While correctional staff members are responsible for checking inmates' files for their previous incarcerations, the courts have indicated that the staff should be given a reasonable amount of time to do this. John Stewart was arrested on July 7, 2002, for violating probation. The officer screened him and noted that he appeared intoxicated and despondent. He was placed in a detox cell, since there was no evidence of suicidal ideation. The officers were unaware at that time that Stewart had been in that jail six weeks ago and was noted to be suicidal. He committed suicide before the staff members had an opportunity to look at his records. Stewart was found hanging 90 minutes after he entered the jail. The defendants were granted summary judgment, since the court agreed that the officers did not have the opportunity to review his file (*Stewart v. Waldo County,* 2004).

Defense 3: The Defendant Did Provide a Reasonable Response to the Risk, but the Injury Occurred Anyway.

Corrections departments might be able to clear themselves of wrong-doing, at least in federal court,[1] by demonstrating that, while they were not successful in preventing the suicide attempt, they did provide some response to the inmate's suicide risk. Derald William Jorgensen was incarcerated in a jail in Iron County, Utah. His wife died two weeks after his arrest. He was placed on suicide watch twice following her death, but during the second time, the supervisor failed to provide instructions to staff about how frequently he needed to be monitored. Jorgensen talked to a counselor at 8:30pm the night of his death, and the counselor told the supervising officers that Jorgensen "would be all right." The supervising officer conducted a variety of tasks, including the inmate count and report writing, while leaving Joregnsen in the booking area and assuming that other staff would watch him. Jorgensen hanged himself sometime during the 80 minutes when he was unsupervised. Despite the officer's knowledge that Jorgensen was suicidal and her lack of proper implementation of protocol, the court granted her summary judgment, ruling that, while she might have been negligent, her response to the suicide risk was not enough to be considered deliberately indifferent (*Bame v. Iron County, Utah,* 2014).

Another example of the defense successfully arguing that they did provide the inmate enough treatment to not be considered deliberately indifferent can be found in *Serafin v. City of Johnstown* (2003). Joseph Serafin was put on suicide watch, and, in this particular facility, suicide watch meant that the clerk would monitor the inmate through closed-circuit television (CCT) while attending to her usual clerical duties at her desk. The clerk was monitoring Serafin and other inmates by periodically switching the channel on the television to check on each inmate. When the clerk switched to check on Serafin, she found him hanging in his cell. He suffered severe brain damage. Serafin's family sued, claiming deliberate indifference, but the U.S. Court of Appeals,

3rd Circuit granted the defendants summary judgment. The court stated that, while the jail's prevention policy could have been better, the staff did follow the policy, and the injury occurred despite the staff's efforts.

As was noted earlier, failure to follow the facility's suicide prevention policy is not always enough to establish deliberate indifference. The Dodge County Jail in Nebraska assigned a new staff member who had not yet had any suicide prevention training to handle the screening and much of the interactions with Troy Sampson. Shortly after his arrest, Sampson's family called the jail to inform them that he attempted suicide two weeks earlier and that he was on antipsychotic medication. He was initially put on suicide watch but moved to the general population a few days later. The same untrained staff member who handled the suicide screening failed to ensure that Sampson was medicated in compliance with the doctor's orders. The case went to trial, and the jury found for the plaintiffs, but the appeals court vacated the award, stating that while there seems to have been poor judgment and even negligence, the failures did not amount to deliberate indifference. The court specifically noted that the staff kept Sampson on 30-minute watch during his entire incarceration as a precaution, despite their belief that he was not suicidal (*Luckert v. Dodge County*, 2012). The court interpreted that 30-minute watch as staff effort to prevent the suicide.

What if there is a flawed suicide prevention policy or even a lack of one? This does not guarantee a victory for plaintiffs. The 11th Circuit Court of Appeals, when discussing qualified immunity in a suicide case, stated that with the standard of deliberate indifference "perfect efforts are not required of jailers, and where the jail has standard operating procedures to protect at-risk detainees, these usually will be sufficient to confer qualified immunity even when aspects of the system are imperfect" (*Bearden v. Anglin*, 2013, p. 921). The 11th Circuit also noted that the lack of a written suicide prevention policy alone does not impose liability automatically (*Bearden v. Anglin*, 2013).

There are some examples of cases where the courts determined that violations of the facilities' policies were sufficient enough to rise to the level of deliberate indifference. Scotty Ray Sisk's mother called Shawnee County (Kansas) Department of Corrections Sergeant Joel Manzanares to express her concern that her son was suicidal. Sgt. Manzanares ordered one of his officers to search Sisk's cell, and the officer found a tear-stained suicide note. The sergeant ordered Sisk removed from his cell and put on "hard lockdown," meaning that he was to be put in a cement cell that had no protrusions that could be used to attach a noose. This was contrary to facility custom, since suicidal inmates were typically put in rubber cells, and the only time "hard lockdown" was used was when the rubber cells were already occupied. The cell where Sisk was placed did have a metal plate attached to the wall. Also contrary to custom, the sergeant ordered that the inmate be given a woolen blanket, rather than a tear-away paper shroud or a suicide-prevention blanket (the department's stock of suicide prevention blankets had run out). The cell where Sisk was placed could not be viewed completely from its window, but the officers could see the entire cell with the security camera. No one was scheduled to watch the security monitors on third shift, and the officers did not do their 15-minute wellness checks. The inmate was able to move the metal plate in the cell, attach the blanket to it, and hang himself. The court denied the defendants summary judgment. While the staff did take steps in response to the inmate's risk of self-harm, the court decided that the question of whether they responded to that risk in a reasonable manner should be subject to a jury trial (*Sisk v. Manzanares, 2002*).

The case of *Martin v. Somerset County* (2005) had similar results, since the jail staff members appeared to have violated their own protocol. The jail staff members were aware that Joseph Hayes was suicidal since he had a record of past suicide attempts, his mother had called the jail to say that he could be suicidal, and he told a case worker that he had attempted to hang himself while in the jail. Despite all of this information, he was put in a holding cell instead of on suicide watch. The jail policy dictates that the shade in the control room overlooking the holding cells must be up at all times, but the officer had the shade down. That shade prevented the officer from observing Hayes as he committed suicide. According to jail policy, suicidal inmates are to be checked every 15 minutes, but Hayes was left alone for 2.5 hours. The court denied the defendants summary judgment for the federal and state claims due to the repeated violations of the jail's own policies.

Correctional Medical Services (CMS) was ordered to pay 1.75 million dollars in compensatory and punitive damages in 2004 for failing to follow its own written suicide prevention policies (*Woodward v. Correctional Medical Services*, 2004). Justin Farver committed suicide in the Lake County Jail in Illinois. During the trial, two nurses testified that CMS routinely had a month-long backlog of intake evaluations of inmates. When Farver was incarcerated, a nurse who had never done an intake screening before was told to do it. The nurse had not completed a single element of the nurse orientation checklist, nor did she complete the 90-day orientation program. Farver was forthcoming about his current suicidal ideation, previous suicide attempts, and mental health history. The nurse did not note any of this in the intake summary, nor did she notify the shift commander or refer him for a mental health evaluation. During Farver's time at the jail, both the social worker and psychiatrist who treated him also noted that the inmate was suicidal, but neither worked to have him put on suicide watch. The court concluded that, had the staff followed its own policies, the inmate would have received mental health treatment and would have been properly supervised.

Billy Wade Montgomery committed suicide in the Reception and Guidance Center in Southern Michigan shortly after being removed from suicide watch. A psychologist (McCrary) put him on suicide watch but did not put the report in the inmate's file. When Montgomery received a routine physical the next day, the physician took him off suicide watch, because he did not see the psychologist's report. After the inmate was removed from suicide watch, McCrary met with Montgomery again. Montgomery said that he was no longer suicidal. Despite McCrary's belief that he was suicidal the previous day and his knowledge that Montgomery was having trouble with other inmates, he chose to keep him off suicide watch. Following Montgomery's death by suicide, the 6th Circuit Court of Appeals ruled that the case should proceed to a jury trial, since the inmate was removed from suicide watch without the psychologist making any "reasoned assessment or evaluation of the patient's suicide risk" (*Comstock v. McCrary*, 2001, p. 710).

THE IMPACT OF *FARMER* ON SUICIDE CASES AND POTENTIAL IMPACT OF *KINGSLEY*

The above examples of defenses emanating from the subjective deliberate indifferent standard set by *Farmer* indicate that it is quite difficult for plaintiffs to make it past the motions phase into trial. Magun (2017) provided data to illustrate the impact that *Farmer* has had on custodial suicide litigation. Prior to *Farmer*, plaintiffs won 29% of cases involving a suicide in a prison, jail, or police station detention area, but after *Farmer,* that figure decreased to 17%.

The Supreme Court's *Kingsley v. Hendrickson* (2015) decision was a significant departure from *Farmer* and lower court rulings pertaining to inmates' protection from self and others. Will *Kinsgley* set a new standard that lower courts will apply to correctional cases involving safety matters outside of excessive use of force? At the time of this writing, it is too early to tell. If the lower courts decide to apply the objective standard used in *Kingsley*, then it is likely to have a profound effect on conditions of confinement and suicide cases in jails and police lockups (Levinson, 2017; Shapiro, 2016). As of now, the federal district courts differ with regard to their application of the objective standard to cases involving pretrial detainees who allege constitutional violations other than use-of-force.

The 4th, 5th, 8th, and 11th Districts have heard cases involving conditions of confinement for pretrial inmates since the *Kingsley* decision, but all have continued to use the subjective standard (*Miranda v. County of Lake*, 2018). The 5th Circuit Court of Appeals heard the case of Jason Hyatt's suicide in police custody. Hyatt's wife called the police because he was missing, and she was concerned that he was suicidal. The police located him and promptly placed him under arrest for driving while intoxicated. When the police called Hyatt's wife to tell her about the arrest, she reminded the police that he was suicidal. During screening, Hyatt admitted to feeling "very depressed" and having attempted suicide twice two months earlier, but he denied current suicidal ideation. The screener observed that Hyatt was intoxicated but in otherwise good spirits. He was not placed on suicide watch, but the screener assigned him to a cell without bed sheets, since the sheets had been previously used in suicides at that facility. Hyatt was given a standard jail uniform and placed in a cell monitored by CCTV, but there was a known blind spot to give inmates privacy while on the toilet. He used that blind spot to commit suicide undetected. After the lower court granted the jail staff qualified immunity, the 5th Circuit Court of Appeals affirmed that decision, with the justification that there was no evidence that the jail staff drew the inference that the deceased was suicidal (*Hyatt v. Thomas*, 2016).

The 8th Circuit Court of Appeals cited *Kingsley* when discussing a case involving the death of a pretrial detainee by suicide, but only to assert that *Kingsley* did not apply here. Normal Witney Jr. was arrested but then taken to the hospital for an irregular heartbeat. He attempted to escape from the hospital and, when caught, Witney told the officers that he would take his life rather than go back to prison. He was placed on suicide watch at the hospital and then removed upon apparent improvement of his emotional state. Two days after being taken back to the jail, Witney was placed in the medical wing due to physical ailments. He was being monitored with CCTV and, upon the supervising officer failing to watch the monitor for 14 minutes, hanged himself and died. The appeals court upheld the district court's decision to grant the defendants' motion to dismiss on account that the plaintiff could not prove that the officers knew that Witney was at risk for suicide. The court chose to apply the subjective standard rather than objective (*Witney v. City of St. Louis*, 2018).

The 2nd and 9th Circuits have applied the *Kingsley* standard to cases outside the realm of use-of-force. The 9th Circuit decided that the objective standard is appropriate in determining whether staff should be held liable for an incident of inmate-inmate violence where a pretrial detainee was the victim (*Castro v. County of Los Angeles*, 2016). The 2nd Circuit applied the new standard to a conditions of confinement case where pretrial detainees were being held in overcrowded and very unsanitary conditions at a pre-arraignment center (*Darnell v. Piniero*, 2017).

Use of the objective standard rather than subjective has the potential to have a tremendous impact, not only on plaintiffs' chances of prevailing in federal court, but it could serve to improve suicide prevention programs in jails and lockups throughout the country. *Farmer* had a chilling effect on the ability of plaintiffs to win in federal court, and this includes cases in jails, typically involving pretrial detainees. Prior to *Farmer*, 25% of jail cases were won by plaintiffs, but that was reduced to just 16% after *Farmer* (Magun, 2017). If facilities holding pretrial inmates know that they are less likely to win in federal court, it is possible that government entities will be more inclined to provide the funding for staff, training, and even upgrades to the design of a facility in order to safeguard themselves from costly lawsuits. Even if correctional administrations fail to do so, the lawsuits can result in injunctions that will force change.

NEGLIGENCE CLAIMS IN STATE COURT

The above examples illustrate the very high standards that federal courts set for plaintiffs to meet when establishing deliberate indifference. While the recent ruling in *Kingsley* may ultimately benefit some pretrial inmates, that remains to be seen, plus there is no relief in sight for convicted inmates. Civil litigation in state courts, however, only requires the establishment of negligence on the part of the custodial staff for plaintiffs to prevail. The *Farmer* (1994) court made the differentiation between negligence and deliberate indifference by stating that the latter "describes a state of mind more blameworthy than negligence" (p. 1978), since negligence includes inadvertent behavior on the part of corrections officers (Kappeler, Vaughn, & Del Carmen, 1991).

When a plaintiff brings a negligence claim to state court, it is not necessary to demonstrate that the staff knew about the inmates' needs and then deliberately displayed indifference to those needs. Instead, to establish negligence, the court needs to determine whether the officer's act or failure to act created an unreasonable risk to the detainee (Kappeler et al., 1991). Negligence cases allow for a broader definition of who is owed protection from themselves due to suicide risk, and the negligence laws attach a higher standard of care in discharging that duty (Robertson, 1993). These cases are handled in state courts, and the laws of each state differ. Generally, four elements must be considered in this determination: legal duty, breach of duty, proximate cause of injury, and actual injury (Kappeler et al., 1991). The following sections explain legal duty, breach of duty, and proximate cause of injury. In all cases described here, actual injury is the attempted or completed suicide.

Legal Duty

State courts have commonly recognized an officer's responsibility to provide a general duty of care to inmates. To meet this requirement, officers are expected to keep detainees free from harm, treat them humanely, and provide medical assistance whenever necessary (Kappeler, 1993; Kappeler et al., 1991). However, certain circumstances may arise when a special duty of care is necessary. Special duties arise when an officer has reason to believe that the person under supervision poses a risk to himself or herself. Kappeler and colleagues identified two types of detainees whose incarceration results in officers having to perform a special duty of care: those who suffer from a disturbed state of mind and, therefore, have a diminished ability to protect themselves; and those who are under the influence of drugs and alcohol. Courts have noted that a special duty of care is warranted when officers can reasonably anticipate that a detainee may cause injury or damage. The issue of foreseeability is crucial here. When a reasonable person is able to see the potential for injury, jail staff must take steps to prevent the injury from occurring (Kappeler et al., 1991). Several factors have been determined by courts to be indicators of the need of a special duty:

1. Previous suicide attempts while in custody;
2. Detainee's statement of intent to harm himself/herself;
3. Detainee's history of mental illness;
4. Health care professional's determination of suicidal tendencies;
5. Emotional state and behavior of detainee;
6. Circumstances surrounding detainee's arrest; and
7. Detainee's level of intoxication or drug dependence[2] (Kappeler, 1993).

The presence of any of these factors can be viewed by courts in most states[3] as a foreseeable indicator of an inmate's plan to commit an act of deliberate self-harm, provided that the information (e.g., knowledge of previous attempts) was accessible to the jail staff (Kappeler et al., 1991).

Breach of Duty

Once the type of duty owed to the plaintiff is established, the next question is whether there was a breach of that duty. Courts may find that an officer has committed a breach of duty when there has been a failure to follow agency rules and regulations, properly supervise a suicidal or incapacitated detainee, provide a safe facility, and/or provide for or call for medical assistance (Kappeler et al., 1991). Anthony Stapleton was placed on suicide watch while in the Shawnee County Jail (Kansas). During screening, he told staff that he had attempted suicide a few months earlier, believed that he had "lost everyone," and wanted to die. After being on suicide watch for a few days, Stapleton was moved from suicide observation to close observation. In close observation, Stapleton became belligerent. According to the facility's suicide prevention policy, he should have been moved back to suicide watch, as such a behavioral change is a potential warning sign. An officer decided, without doing a formal screening, that Stapleton did not need to be moved. Another inmate testified that Stapleton stated that he intended to kill himself while standing 15 feet from another corrections officer, but the officer did not hear him because he was not paying attention. After Stapleton was found dead in his cell, the officers found three suicide notes. According to the jail's suicide prevention policy, officers were supposed to sweep the cells to check for such materials once per shift, but the logs do not reflect that this was done. The court ruled that the jail staff had a legal duty to protect him but there appears to have been a breach of that duty (*Thomas v. County of Commissioners of Shawnee County*, 2009).

Plaintiffs may succeed in establishing a negligence claim even if they fail to demonstrate that a special duty of care was required, provided that they can show that there was a breach of the general duty of care. Philip Edward Hott was found dead in the Hennepin County Jail in Minnesota. Hott committed suicide by hanging and was not found until several hours after his death. While the lower court granted the defendants summary judgment, the appeals court reversed that decision, since there was evidence that the general duty owed to inmates was violated. Officers were required to conduct wellness checks on all inmates every 30 minutes, but Hott clearly had not been checked for hours (*Hott v. Hennepin County*, 2001).

Jeffrey Ray Belden appeared to be well-adjusted for the first six weeks of incarceration, but his behavior changed after he received an upsetting letter from home. Belden placed paper over his cell window, disobeyed an order to remove the paper, and threatened to harm anyone who attempted to enter the cell. The deputy called the off-duty sergeant for advice, and the sergeant told the officer to get back up and move Belden to a suicide prevention cell that was also used in various situations when enhanced supervision was necessary. The sergeant specifically ordered the deputy to move Belden without his personal belongings. Inmates are only moved to that special observation cell without belongings when they are suicidal. While the deputy claimed that he called for backup and never received it, there is nothing in the logbook to support this assertion. Belden remained in the cell with paper over his door for an additional 90 minutes. After that time, the deputy entered the cell and found that Belden was dead. The Kansas State Court of Appeals denied the deputy and sergeant their requests for summary judgment. The court noted that the sergeant's order to move Belden to the special observation cell without belongings was an indicator that he believed Belden was suicidal, yet the sergeant failed to follow-up or emphasize the importance of this move to the deputy. The deputy was aware of the jail policies and knew that the only justification for stripping inmates of belongings without any type of disciplinary procedures would be for one's own protection, and he was ordered to take this step with Belden yet failed to do so. This is a potential breach of duty (*Estate of Belden v. Brown County*, 2011).

Proximate Cause of Injury

This requirement establishes the relationship between the detainee's injury and the actions of staff members. For negligence to be determined, the employee's action or inaction must be proven to be the proximate cause of the inmate's death. When establishing proximate cause, Kappeler (1993) recommended asking the question: "but for the officer's conduct, would the detainee have sustained the injury?" (p. 157). In the aforementioned *Hott v. Hennepin County* (2001) case, the appeals court overruled the lower court's ruling of summary judgment for the defendants, suggesting that the lack of health checks was the proximate cause of Hott's death. The court ruled that more frequent health checks could have prevented the suicide.

If an inmate wanted to die, should the responsibility of the incident lay with the individual? This concept, called contributory negligence, cannot be used in custodial suicide cases. In Washington State, a jury found in favor of the defendants, since they believed that the jail staff members were negligent in failing to screen an emotionally unstable inmate and placing him alone in a cell, but that the negligence was not the proximate cause of death—the inmate hanging himself was the proximate cause. The Court of Appeals reversed the decision and ordered a new trial, since a defense of contributory negligence is not permissible in such cases (*Gregoire v. City of Oak Harbor*, 2017).

IMPACT OF THE PRISON REFORM
LITIGATION ACT ON SUICIDE LITIGATION

The Prison Reform Litigation Act (PRLA) was passed in 1996 in response to the public's perception that the courts were being clogged by frivolous inmate lawsuits. As a result of this legislation, indigent inmates are now required to pay a $150 filing for federal lawsuits, a fee that poor non-inmates do not have to pay. Inmates who lose their cases might have to pay the defendants costs associated with the case. Inmate plaintiffs who have had three prior cases dismissed as frivolous or malicious have to pay additional court costs in order to proceed with future lawsuits. These rules, however, do not apply to deceased inmates or their families, so the PRLA does not directly relate to federal lawsuits involving inmate suicides (Schlanger, 2003b).

THE ROLE OF JAIL STANDARDS IN SUICIDE LITIGATION

As I have discussed throughout this book, there are a few professional organizations that have written standards for treatment of incarcerated individuals, including the National Commission on Correctional Health Care, the American Correctional Association, the American Psychiatric Association, and the Commission on Accreditation of Law Enforcement Agencies. The standards address specific issues of mental health and substance abuse treatment, suicide prevention, and reacting to suicide attempts. Unfortunately, accreditation is optional for most prisons and jails, and it is up to each individual state to determine whether there will be statewide standards for correctional institutions. As of 2004, only 18 states had adopted mandatory statewide jail standards for suicide prevention, and 6 states had voluntary standards (Hayes 2004b). State standards and accreditation are not legally binding but can contribute to favorable outcomes for the defendants (see *Yellow Horse v. Pennington County*, 2000). It is important to remember that many accreditation processes do not involve continuous monitoring of facilities, so an accredited facility could revert to operating in a way that is contrary to the standards once accreditation is achieved. Accreditation standards also do not cover every aspect of inmate care, so it is possible for facilities to be in compliance with accreditation standards and still be found liable for an inmate's suicide (Friedmann, 2014). For these reasons, there is no guarantee that the courts will side with the defense in cases involving 8th Amendment claims just because the facility is accredited (*Grenning v. Miller-Stout*, 2014).

There have been instances where the presence of statewide jail standards has helped the defendants argue that the jail and its staff were working to prevent suicides. In a federal Section 1983 case, jail personnel in Illinois were able to point to the county jail standards to show that what the staff did on the night of an inmate's suicide exceeded what was mandated by the state. According to the Illinois County Jail Standards, officers are expected to conduct checks on suicidal inmates every 30 minutes, but officers in this particular case had been checking on the suicidal inmate every 15 minutes. The judges referred to the jail standards when they ruled that the county was entitled to summary judgment (*Rapier v. Kankakee County, Illinois*, 2002).

As was noted earlier, findings that a facility violated state standards does not guarantee that facility staff will be held legally responsible, particularly in federal court. In *Harvey v. County of Ward* (2005) the plaintiff was able to demonstrate that the county jail violated statewide standards. The court acknowledged that the violations of the standards might help to prove negligence, but the violation itself was not enough to meet the federal standard of deliberate indifference. There was a similar outcome in the previously discussed *Cox v. Glanz* (2015) case.

CONCLUSION

While plaintiffs stand to gain more by pursuing litigation in federal courts, the standard of deliberate indifference is a hurdle that is difficult to overcome. Demonstrating that a person or persons actually knew something and then ignored the risk to an inmate's life on purpose would be difficult in any setting. The problem is only compounded by the key witness often either dying or becoming incapacitated during the suicide attempt. It is possible that there is a change coming at the federal level, with the *Kingsley* case presenting the lower courts with the opportunity to revisit the appropriate standard for cases involving pretrial detainees. Only time will tell whether the lower courts decide that suicide cases should use the objective, rather than subjective, standard. Even if the lower courts choose to adopt the more plaintiff-friendly objective standard, this will not impact cases involving deaths of sentenced prisoners.

The previous chapters of this book have provided advice for best practices for screening and treating inmates in crisis and adjusting the corrections environment to promote a more positive, less stressful setting. All of these are practices that I encourage every correctional institution to adopt. Is doing so a guarantee that the administration will either avoid lawsuits or win them? No. Lawsuits are very common in corrections, and relatives of deceased inmates are likely to at least contemplate filing suit. It is understandable that the decedent's relatives would want answers and harbor resentment toward the correctional administration. Taking steps to be proactive with suicide prevention planning can, however, reduce the number of suicides and lawsuits stemming from such incidents. Most importantly, these steps can save lives and spare other inmates, the correctional staff, and the inmates' families the trauma and grief of having to deal with such terrible loss.

Pursuit of accreditation can be a positive step for corrections agencies, since the institutions and their staff members have to demonstrate that they are in compliance with best practices, at least at the time of the review. Accreditation can prompt agencies to hire and retain employees who have the proper credentials and to develop and, hopefully, maintain appropriate training programs for staff. Accreditation programs that involve suicide prevention will also require the facilities to draft a prevention program that, if followed, will prevent most suicides. If a suicide does occur despite the staff adhering to the prevention program, courts are likely to find in favor of the defendants.

NOTES

1. The federal court distinction is made here, because suing for negligence in state court is easier for the plaintiff. For negligence, state laws generally allow for a broader definition of "who is owed a duty to be protected from suicide" and "it also requires a higher standard of care in discharging that duty" (Robertson, 1993, p. 828).

2. Melvin Pretty on Top was arrested for public intoxication, but he was composed, able to walk, and able to speak well. He was placed in a jail cell, and he committed suicide by stabbing himself. The inmate did not have a previous suicide attempt, and he was not extremely intoxicated. Pretty on Top's family sued for wrongful death, but the defendants were granted summary judgment on the grounds that the inmate did not demonstrate "special circumstances" that would have elevated the jail's duty of care (*Pretty on Top v. City of Hardin,* 1979).

3. Each state has different laws pertaining to wrongful death. Alabama has a very narrow definition of what conditions amount to a foreseeable circumstance requiring a special duty of care for jail inmates. In Alabama, the suicide is only deemed foreseeable if the inmate was brought into the facility for an incident involving the inmate attempting suicide or that the inmate had a history of suicide attempts AND the jail knew of that history (*Williams v. Lee County, Alabama*, 1996).

Chapter Ten

Suggestions for Suicide Prevention

Many suicides that occur in correctional facilities are preventable. The more correctional staff know about predictors of suicides, how they tend to occur, and the locations and circumstances in which they occur, the better prepared staff will be to recognize the signs of an impending suicide and to take action. The development of and adherence to a strong suicide prevention policy can reduce the probability that staff and inmates will have to share in the trauma that follows suicide. In this chapter, I will summarize what is known about suicides in custody and provide recommendations for suicide prevention.

WHAT WE KNOW

There have been several consistent trends in correctional suicide research over the past few decades. First, there are known predictors of inmate suicide. Current suicidal ideation, a history of self-harm (intended to be suicidal or not), mental illness and especially active symptoms of mental illness, drug/alcohol addiction, and difficulty coping (especially when manifesting in aggression toward self or others) are associated with an increased probability of a suicide attempt. Second, there are high-risk times for suicides, attempted suicides, and NSSI among people in custody. Days preceding or following court dates, preceding or following transfers, the first few days of a new incarceration, after receipt of bad news from home, after receipt of news regarding one's legal status, and following a humiliation or rejection, are all associated with increases in suicide and self-harm. Third, suicides in custody are more likely to occur when people are alone. Fourth, most suicides in custody will occur by hanging or by asphyxiation.

There will be exceptions, of course. Occasionally, there will be an inmate who will show no signs of mental illness, lack a history of suicidal ideation and self-harm, and at least appear to be coping satisfactorily with incarcerated life and other matters, yet this person will attempt suicide. There will also be individuals who bypass hanging or asphyxiation and utilize less conventional methods to commit suicide, such as ingesting foreign objects. There have been a few instances of inmates who are out on the tier and suddenly jump over the second-floor railing, falling headfirst onto the first floor. Most suicides, however, will involve people who were alone, in one of the aforementioned risk groups, and/or are experiencing one of the previously mentioned high-risk periods. Our knowledge of suicide in custody can help us formulate policies that will save lives and help promote effective facility management.

RECOMMENDATIONS FOR PREVENTION

Custodial suicide prevention programs should be multifactored. Such plans should include detailed protocols for screening, staff communication, housing and supervision, therapeutic interventions, regular staff training, addressing a suicide attempt in progress, investigating an event after it occurs, and counseling and debriefing for all involved after a suicide. Plans need to include clear descriptions of responsibilities for custodial, mental health, and medical staff, and there should also be guidelines for communication with nonstaff members. Police officers, court personnel, case workers and counselors in the community, and even family and friends of inmates, are potentially vital sources of information. I included examples throughout the book where a breakdown in communication or a loss of continuity of care resulted in preventable deaths. Suicide prevention plans should also include nonambiguous instructions about the role that each office and staff member plays in the communication of information regarding inmates who appear to be at risk.

Screening

Screening is an essential component of effective suicide prevention programs. It presents an opportunity to gather self-report information about an individual's current emotional state and psychiatric history. Inmates who have an incarceration history will have records on file, and part of the screening and assessment process should be a review of that information to check for any evidence of a history of self-harm or psychiatric problems. Earlier in this chapter, I mentioned the factors that need to be included in screening, specifically current suicidal ideation, current mental health status and history, drug and alcohol use and history, and current emotional state. In addition to checking medical records for inmates who have been incarcerated before, staff should work to gather information about history of suicide attempts, self-harm, and psychiatric history from the inmates themselves. Screening forms should be appropriate for use with correctional populations, and facility staff should be trained in multicultural sensitivity. The cultures making up an inmate population should also be considered when selecting screening forms and developing screening procedures. Jails that tend to house Native Americans, for example, should be cognizant of the limitations of conventional screening programs and work to establish protocol for effectively communicating with all inmates.

Screening needs to be completed quickly, so a triage setup is likely to help maintain a balance between safety and efficiency. While the ideal situation would be for all inmates to be immediately screened by mental health professionals, this is difficult for many facilities, particularly jails that do intake 24-hours a day. There are screening forms that can be administered by properly trained corrections personnel, but those screenings that reveal red flags must be brought to the attention of the mental health staff for further assessment in a timely fashion. "Timely" should be determined by the seriousness of the situation. Per ACA Standards (2002), follow-up should occur in a maximum of 72 hours, but perhaps even sooner if there is great concern. Inmates who appear to be at risk need to be properly supervised between the time of initial screening and the more in-depth assessment.

Screening should never be considered a one-time procedure that only occurs upon an inmate's initial entry into the corrections system. Screening should occur repeatedly, especially following transfers to new facilities or even transfers to different housing units. Escort forms should be given to transferring officers so they can pass on information about any troubling incidents or statements that should be brought to the attention of the mental health and custodial staff.

Finally, the results of screening assessments need to be used to inform housing, supervision, and treatment decisions. There is little purpose to this exercise unless the information is going to be used to guide custody and treatment decisions.

Housing and Treatment Options for Suicidal Inmates

Discerning inmates' motives when they discuss or commit self-harm should never be the responsibility of custody staff. That is a much more appropriate task for qualified mental health clinicians. Custody staff should take proper precautions to safeguard an inmate regardless of whether the talk or actions appear to be manipulative, attention-seeking, or linked to an apparent attempt to die. Even people who are self-harming for manipulative motives often have at least some degree of lethal intent, and regardless of intent, a suicidal gesture that is meant to manipulate can accidentally turn deadly. Men and women who self-harm in custody should be subjected to suicide prevention protocols under the supervision of mental health staff, regardless of the apparent intent. It is tempting to make suicide prevention procedures humiliating for inmates in order to deter malingering, but doing so could also discourage those who truly need help from seeking it. Additionally, taking those who already have a degree of suicidal intent and making their current life circumstances even worse is unlikely to be productive in the long-term.

Custodial and social service staff should always seek assistance from appropriately qualified mental health authorities when working with an individual who is suicidal or otherwise self-harming. Appropriately qualified mental health professionals should sign off on any housing, medication, and treatment plans for inmates before they are implemented. Changes in housing assignments have been associated with suicide attempts, particularly if the change is punitive in nature. Isolation and other forms of restrictive housing should be used with caution, given that these settings are associated with higher rates of suicide. Inmates who are both a danger to themselves and others may need to be placed in isolation, at least for a short time. Isolation is convenient in that it prevents inmates from harming others, but it also substantially increases the opportunity, and even motivation, for self-harm. If at-risk inmates are going to be alone without constant face-to-face supervision, it will be necessary to use suicide-resistant cells and to limit clothing and belongings that can be used to make ligatures. Mental health staff need to assess inmates who are being moved, especially if segregation is being used for disciplinary or administrative purposes. If it is determined that the individuals are likely to psychologically deteriorate in segregation, mental health staff should work with custody to arrange for alternative housing and treatment plans. While segregation might be unavoidable for a short period of time, it should never be considered anything more than a very temporary solution. It is unreasonable to expect any individual to learn positive coping skills or other prosocial behaviors if the primary "treatment" given to them is removal from all social contact for days, weeks, months, or even years.

Inmates who are in an acute suicidal crisis need constant, face-to-face supervision. If it is safe enough for someone to be in the cell with them, a trained inmate can serve as a companion and provide constant supervision. If the inmates need to be housed alone, then a staff member or trained inmate should be stationed outside of the cell where he or she can see the inmates without the assistance of a camera. Using CCTV to monitor suicidal inmates has failed at times and resulted in the facilities simply having a video recording of the suicide taking place. Constant supervision serves the dual purposes of reducing opportunity for self-harm and reducing one's sense of isolation. Intermittent observation can be used, per the advice of qualified mental health staff, as inmates' conditions improve, but this remains a risky procedure. Suicide by hanging or asphyxiation can easily be accomplished in under 15 to 30 minutes, and those are the usual enhanced-risk observation times set by correctional facilities.

Since corrections facilities were never intended to be psychiatric institutions, general population and most of the restrictive housing settings are not conducive to working with people who are in crisis. Some state corrections departments have developed in-custody housing options that should provide safer housing and more intensive mental health treatment for inmates who are unable to function well in general population. This is a welcome and likely much safer alternative to the overuse of restrictive housing as the solution to inmates who are difficult to manage elsewhere. Inmates whose mental health still makes it too difficult for them to live productively in these more treatment-oriented settings should be considered for transfer to a secure psychiatric institution.

For inmates who enter jail while intoxicated or will be incarcerated long enough to detox, facilities should have written detoxification protocols that involve close medical supervision and special housing. Inmates who are in detox need enhanced supervision, as their physical health is in jeopardy, and it is also considered a high-risk time for suicide attempts.

There are some promising programs that can serve as therapeutic options for inmates who are having difficulty coping with incarceration. Mental health staff working in a custody environment should be trained in crisis intervention to help guide inmates through the most difficult times and work with them to focus on ways to overcome challenges. Cognitive behavioral therapy programs (CBT) have been implemented both inside and outside of correctional facilities and have worked to address a number of behavioral problems, including maladaptive coping, suicide attempts, and self-harm. Dialectical behavior therapy appears to help individuals who self-harm, particularly those with borderline personality disorder. Both CBT and DBT can be offered within the general population of a corrections facility or in part of a separate unit focusing exclusively on inmates who need extra assistance.

Changes to the Entire Correctional Environment

Suicide is just one problem that corrections administrations work to prevent each day. Assaults, transference of contraband, property damage, and other forms of misconduct are always a possibility within correctional settings.

Environmental and managerial factors can impact the frequency of these incidents. The design of correctional facilities can hurt or hinder inmate supervision. The older, linear cell blocks seen in many correctional facilities are difficult to manage, as officers typically cannot see what is happening in cells down the hall. The podular designs have improved sight lines, but it might be difficult to see inside cells with solid doors. Podular direct supervision facilities place officers in the pods with the inmates, putting them much closer to the cell doors. While this can help with supervision, the much more substantial benefit should be the officers' presence in and effective management of the living areas. The new generation jail management involves a combination of changes to the physical environment to improve sight lines and make the living areas less institutional-looking while also including a different approach to officer-inmate interactions. The improved physical appearance of the jail and the amenities available on the living units (telephones, televisions, a microwave, etc.) is expected to give inmates an incentive to behave, as misbehavior can result in curtailment of privileges or movement to a less desirable part of the jail. The officers are trained in communication skills and are expected to interact with the inmates in the pod, conveying the message that the space is controlled by the officers who expect them to behave. When done properly, this approach can lead to reduced violence, property damage, stress, and even reduced suicides and suicide attempts. The goal is to generate a culture shift in the facility where good behavior is expected and rewarded, while bad behavior is punished. This is a change from the more traditional approach of expecting, and then reacting to, bad behavior in the absence of any rewards for compliance.

Correctional facilities are expensive to build and renovate, so there are hundreds of prisons and jails that are old and have outdated designs. Working with a poor design certainly makes management more difficult, but not impossible. It is still feasible to use evidence-based practice and effective management strategies to improve the functioning of an institution. Behavior management units are a good example of the use of research to inform management techniques to generate positive change.

The Role of Leadership in Suicide Prevention

Strong leadership is an essential component to all successful suicide prevention programs. Subordinates take cues from management, and when they sense that management lacks full commitment to initiatives, line staff have little reason to buy-in to the work. Management must communicate the importance of the interdisciplinary aspects of suicide prevention to line-level workers. Lack of leadership can also exacerbate problems in the event of litigation, as regular behavior on the part of leaders can be considered facility custom by the courts (Wallace & Roberson, 2000).

For programs to be effective, custody, mental health, medical, and social services staff must communicate and share responsibility for various aspects of the prevention programs. As I discussed in Chapter 5, the British Home Office (1999) investigated the Prison Service's responses to positive mental health screens and found a lack of coordination between staff members, sometimes resulting in no action being taken despite the inmates' apparent need for services. Whether it is suicide prevention programs for inmates in custody, diversion programs for individuals with mental illness, or re-entry programs for inmates needing to transition back into society, strong leadership is needed to help coordinate work between the various agencies involved. Management should identify specific boundary-spanners who can take responsibility for combating fragmentation and lack of continuity in programs.

The Role of Accreditation in Suicide Prevention

Accreditation provides standards for criminal justice agencies, and adherence to these standards will improve operations. Unfortunately, being accredited is not a guarantee that the institution is living up to those standards on any particular day. Accredited agencies must submit periodic reports and open their institutions to occasional site-visits by reviewers. After the reviews, the accrediting bodies render their decisions regarding accreditation and then do not visit the facilities again for some time. During that time between visits, it is entirely up to the administration and staff members to adhere to the accreditation standards. Accrediting bodies will not be aware of violations of these standards until the next site visit, so it is possible for an accredited prison or jail to be operating in violation of one or more of the mandatory or essential standards. Strong facility leadership during the years between accreditation review is essential to keep institutions in compliance with the standards at all times.

One additional word of caution about accreditation is that it is no guarantee of protection against litigation. The courts have generally looked favorably upon accreditation and often consider it evidence of facility management taking steps toward keeping inmates safe from harm. For the reasons mentioned in the previous paragraph, though, accreditation is not proof that the staff was abiding by the appropriate policies at the time that a suicide occurred.

REDUCING OFFENDERS' EXPOSURE TO INCARCERATION

Even in the United States, the world's leader in incarceration, there have been efforts to divert some groups of offenders from prisons and jails. Individuals with mental illnesses are among the groups who have been targeted for diversion from traditional criminal justice processing. The decentralized nature of criminal justice systems throughout the country has resulted in each jurisdiction taking a different approach to working with justice-involved people with mental illness. Some police departments have partnered with mental health agencies to secure treatment alternatives for people whose mental illnesses are making it difficult for them to manage in the community. Other jurisdictions are working to divert people after arrest but before, during, or even after a criminal trial. Many of these programs offer mental health treatment as one of their services, and this is a positive development. It is important, however, that these programs don't stop there. Most offenders with mental illness have as many or more criminogenic needs than offenders without mental illness. Unless those issues are addressed, diverted offenders are likely to experience clinical improvements but remain at risk for future criminal behavior.

Individuals who are ineligible for diversion and are incarcerated will need assistance with transitioning back into the community. The breadth and depth of reentry services vary, as some people will be in custody for just a few hours, while others will remain there for years. Transition programing should start upon initial incarceration, as the goal of incarceration should be preparing people to reenter the community and remain there. Programs should include working with inmates to reactivate their benefits and setting them up with treatment and other services in the community. Mental health treatment should be included whenever appropriate, but as with diversion programs, inmates' criminogenic needs should be addressed in order to reduce recidivism. Both diversion and reentry programs should adopt the risk-needs-responsivity model to maximize their effectiveness at reducing reoffending.

CONCLUDING THOUGHTS

In Chapter 1, I cited Hanson's (2010) application of a public health framework to suicide prevention in custody. There were three levels: tertiary, secondary, and primary. Tertiary involved intervening in a suicide attempt and preventing death. Secondary prevention included identifying those at risk for suicide attempts through screening and then safeguarding these individuals through observation, careful selection of housing assignments, and therapeutic programs. Primary prevention practices included environmental and management adjustments to entire facilities or units to make the institution one in which fewer of its inhabitants would progress to the point where they are at risk for self-harm.

Tertiary responses seem to be the methods for which most jail officers are prepared. Requiring CPR and first aid certification is standard for first responders, and tools to cut ligatures have become common equipment in many correctional facilities. Although there have been a few exceptions, most corrections officers follow not only their training but their instincts to preserve life and immediately work to save someone who has attempted suicide. Over the past 30 years, corrections facilities have also made great strides in the development and implementation of secondary prevention techniques. Screening for suicidal ideation and previous suicide attempts is now commonplace, as is the presence of at least rudimentary suicide prevention programs. While there have been improvements in these areas, one only needs to read about lawsuits involving custodial suicides to find examples of subpar policies and poor implementation of them. Much work still needs to be done in this area.

As with some public health initiatives, it can be difficult to convince stakeholders of the importance of primary prevention. For example, the United States is in the midst of an opioid epidemic. Needle exchange programs have been found to improve participants' health, reduce medical care costs (Nguyen, Weir, Jarlais, Pinkerton, & Holtgrave, 2014), and increase drug treatment referrals (Normand, Vlahov, & Moses, 1995), but there is still resistance to such programs due to their "soft" stance on drug users. Critics of these programs often argue that such endeavors are not a wise use of money, when in fact, they have been found to have a $7.58 return on every dollar invested (Nguyen et al., 2014), and they facilitate addicts' entry into drug treatment programs (SAMHSA, 2017).

I have been studying suicide in correctional facilities for 20 years. One unfortunate fact that I have learned over the course of my research is that arguing that primary (and sometimes even secondary) prevention policies will save lives and spare survivors pain and suffering is not always enough to convince decision-makers and the taxpaying public. More than once, I have been told by laypeople that we should just let inmates kill themselves rather than putting the money and effort into prevention programs. When the issue of more primary prevention arises, a typical response is that we need prisons and jails to be uncomfortable, and instead of paying money to make them nicer, we should spend less and try to make them worse. Besides the moral and possible constitutional problems with these sentiments, what some people fail to understand is that this approach is likely to be costly.

Former Sheriff Joe Arpaio of Arizona built a career on catering to those who believe we should do whatever we can to make incarceration as difficult as possible. He ran for Sheriff of Maricopa County, vowing not to improve conditions in the jails but to make them worse. He argued that people were in jail because the jails were so comfortable that they were attractive places to live. If we made jails worse, he argued, incarceration rates would plummet (Pearce, 2017). His supporters assumed that Arpaio's way would not only give people in jail the hard time that they deserved, but the county would save millions in reduced recidivism costs. Arpaio was wrong about his assumption. Incarceration rates in his jurisdiction did not decrease, and instead of saving money, taxpayers were faced with having to pay 40 million dollars in litigation costs for instances where the jail was found to be violating the constitutional rights of inmates through abuse and other types of mistreatment (Roberts, 2018).

It can be very difficult to convince stakeholders to utilize precious taxpayer resources on the incarcerated population in a way that would seem to benefit inmates. Doing so, however, is likely to actually save the government and taxpayers in the long run if the money is used to make improvements rooted in evidence-based practice. Providing resources to foster better management and the creation of an environment where both corrections staff and inmates feel safe, where inmates can engage in productive programming, and where officers have a mixture of both punishments and rewards at their disposal can save money. If the moral and constitutional arguments are ineffective at swaying opinions about primary and secondary prevention methods, perhaps the possibility of saving taxpayer money will help. The use of best practices to prevent suicides will go a long way in saving both lives and money. That possibility should appeal to everyone.

References

Abram, K. M., Choe, J. Y., Washburn, J. J., Teplin, L. A., King, D. C., Dulcan, M., K., & Bassett, E. D. (2014). *Suicidal thoughts and behaviors among detained youth.* United States Department of Justice, Office of Juvenile Justice and Delinquency Prevention.

Aldape, C., Cooper, R., Haas, K., Hu, X. A., Hunter, J., Shimizu, S., Kalb, J., & Resnik, J. (2016). Rethinking "death row": Variations in the housing of individuals sentenced to death. *Yale Law School, Public Law Research Paper No. 571.* New Haven, CT: Yale University.

American Correctional Association (2002). *Performance-based standards for correctional health care in adult correctional institutions (5th ed.).* Alexandria, VA: American Correctional Association.

———. (2010). *Core jail standards.* Alexandria, VA: American Correctional Association. American Psychiatric Association.

American Psychiatric Association. (2000). *Psychiatric services in jails and prisons (2nd ed.).* Washington, DC: American Psychiatric Association.

———. (2016). *Psychiatric services in correctional facilities (3rd ed.).* Washington, DC: American Psychiatric Association.

Anderson, J. F. & Dyson, L. (2001). *Legal rights of prisoners.* Lanham, MD: University Press of America.

Anderson, R. E., Geier, T. J., & Cahill, S. P. (2015). Epidemiological associations between posttraumatic stress disorder and incarceration in the National Survey of American Life. *Criminal Behaviour & Mental Health*, DOI: 10.1002/cbm.1951.

Andrade, J. T., Wilson, J. S., Franko, E., Deitsch, J., & Barboza, S. (2014). Developing the evidence base for reducing chronic inmate self-injury. *Corrections Today, 76*(6), 31–40.

Andrews, D. & Bonta, J. (1996). *Psychology of criminal conduct.* Cincinnati, OH: Anderson Publishing.

Applebaum, K. L., Savageau, J. A., Trestman, R. I., & Baillargeon, J. (2011). A national survey of self-injurious behavior in American prisons. *Psychiatric Services, 62*(3), 285–290.

Applegate, B. K. & Sitren, A. H. (2008). The jail and the community: Comparing jails in rural and urban contexts. *The Prison Journal, 88*(2), 252–269.

Austin, J. (2001). Prisoner reentry: Current trends, practices and issues. *Crime & Delinquency, 47*, 314–334.

Austin, A. E., van den Heuvel, C., Byard, R. W. (2014). Prison suicides in south Australia: 1996–2010. *Journal of Forensic Sciences, 59*(5), 1260–1262.

Baggio, S., Getaz, L., Tran, N. T., Peigne, N., Pala, K. C., Golay, D., Heller, P., Bodenmann, P., & Wolff, H. (2018). Association of overcrowding and turnover with self-harm in a Swiss pre-trial prison. *International Journal of Environmental Research and Public Health, 15,* 601–606.

Baillargeon, J., Penn, J. P., Thomas, C. R., Temple, J. R., Baillargeon, G., & Murray, O. J. (2009a). Psychiatric disorders and suicide in the nation's largest state prison system. *Journal of the Academy of Psychiatry & the Law, 37*, 188–193.

Baillargeon, J., Williams, B. A., Mellow, J., Harzke, A. J., Hoge, S. K., Baillargeon, G., & Greifinger, R. B. (2009b). Parole revocation among prison inmates with psychiatric and substance use disorders. *Psychiatric Services, 60*(11), 1516–1521.

Bales, W. D. & Mears, D. P. (2008). Inmate social ties and the transition to society: Does visitation reduce recidivism. *Journal of Research in Crime and Delinquency, 45*, 287–321.

Bales, W. D., Nadel, M., Reed, C., & Blomberg, T. G. (2017). Recidivism and inmate mental illness. *International Journal of Criminology and Sociology, 6,* 40–51.

Barboza, S. & Wilson, J. S. (2011). Behavior management plans decrease inmate self-injury. *Corrections Today, 73*(5), 34–37.

Barker, E., Kolves, K., & De Leo, D. (2014). Management of suicidal and self-harming behaviors in prisons: Systematic literature review of evidence-based activities. *Archives of Suicide Research, 18,* 227–240.

Barr, H. (1999). *Prisons and jails: Hospitals of last resort.* New York: The Correctional Association of New York and the Urban Justice Center.

Bartoli, C., Berland-Benhaim, C., Tuchtan-Torrents, L., Pascal, K., Georges, L., & Pelissier-Alicot, A. (2018). Suicide by medication overdose in prison: A study of three cases. *Journal of Forensic Sciences, 63*(4), 1316–1320.

Bayens, G. J., Williams, J. J., & Smykla, J. O. (1997a). Jail type makes difference: Evaluating the transition from a traditional to a podular, direct supervision jail across ten years. *American Jails, 11*(2), 32–39.

Bayens, G. J., Williams, J. J., & Smykla, J. O. (1997b). Jail type and inmate behavior: A longitudinal analysis. *Federal Probation, 61*(3), 54–62.

Beck, A. T., Steer, R. A., & Brown, G. (1996). *Manual for the Beck Depression Inventory-II.* San Antonio, TX: Psychological Corporation.

Bell, D. (1999). Ethical issues in the prevention of suicide in prison. *Australian & New Zealand Journal of Psychiatry, 33,* 723–728.

Bentham, J. (1789 [1948]). *On the principals of morals and legislation.* New York: Kegan Paul.

Binswanger, I. A., Stern, M. F., Deyo, R. A., Heagerty, P. J., Cheadle, A., Elmore, J. G., & Koepsell, T. D. (2007). Release from prison. *New England Journal of Medicine, 356*, 157–165.

Blaauw, E. (2005). Bullying and suicides in prisons. In J. L. Ireland (Ed.), *Bullying among prisoners* (pp. 44–61). Devon, UK: Willan Publishing.

Blaauw, E., Arensman, E., Kraaij, V., Winkel, F. W., & Bout, R. (2002). Traumatic life events and suicide risk among jail inmates: The influence of types of events, time period and significant others. *Journal of Traumatic Stress, 15*(1), 9–16.

Blaauw, E., Winkel, F. W., & Kerkhof, J. F. M. (2001). Bullying and suicidal behavior in jails. *Criminal Justice & Behavior, 28*(3), 279–299.

Blomberg, T. G. & Lucken, K. (2007). *American penology: A history of control (2nd ed.).* New York: Aldine de Gruyter.

Boganowski, C. A. (2011). Douglas County's mental health diversion program. *American Jails, 25*(4), 9–14.

Boothroyd, R. A., Mercado, C. C., Poythress, N. G., Christy, A., & Petrila, J. (2005). Clinical outcomes of defendants in mental health court. *Psychiatric Services, 56*(7), 829–834.

Borrill, J. (2002). Self-inflicted deaths of prisoners serving life sentences 1988–2001. *British Journal of Forensic Practice, 4*(4), 30–35.

Borrill, J., Burnett, R., Atkins, R., Miller, S., Briggs, D., Weaver, T., & Maden, A. (2003). Patterns of self-harm and attempted suicide among white and black/mixed female prisoners. *Criminal Behaviour & Mental Health, 13,* 229–240.

Borum, R. & Rand, M. (2000). Mental health diagnostic and treatment services in Florida's jails. *Journal of Correctional Health Care, 7,* 189–207.

Boston Congress of Correction Policies and Resolutions (2016). *Corrections Today, 78*(6), 72–76.

Bourgon, G. & Armstrong, B. (2005). Transferring the principles of effective treatment into a "real world" prison setting. *Criminal Justice & Behavior, 32,* 3–25.

British Home Office (1999). *Suicide is everyone's concern.* London, England: Home Office.

Broner, N., Mayrl, D. W., & Landsberg, G. (2005). Outcomes of mandated and non-mandated New York City jail diversion for offenders with alcohol, drug and mental disorders. *Prison Journal, 85*(1), 18–49.

Brown, D. (2016). *Counselors' perceptions of suicide in Texas jails.* Doctoral Dissertation. Texas Tech University.

Brown, M., Comtois, A., & Linehan, M. (2002). Reasons for suicide attempts and nonsuicidal self-injury in women with borderline personality disorder. *Journal of Abnormal Psychology, 111*(11), 198–202.

Burns, P. J., Hiday, C. A., & Ray, B. (2013). Effectiveness 2 years post-exit of a recently established mental health court. *American Behavioral Scientist, 57*(2), 189–208.

Butler, A., Young, J. T., Kinner, S. A., & Borschmann, R. (2018). Self-harm and suicidal behavior among incarcerated adults in the Australian capital territory. *Health & Justice, 6,* 13–19.

Butterfield, F. (1998, March 5). By default, jails become mental institutions. *New York Times.* Retrieved from www.nytimes.com/yr/mo/day/early/030598prisons-mental-health.html.

Byrne, J. M., Lurigio, A. J., & Pimentel, R. (2009). New defendants, new responsibilities: Preventing suicide among alleged sex offenders in the federal pretrial system. *Federal Probation, 73*(2), 40–44.

Camilleri, P. & McArthur, M. (2008). Suicidal behavior in prisons: Learning from Australian and international experience. *Law & Psychiatry, 31*, 297–307.

Campbell, M. A., Canales, D. D., Wei, R., Totten, A. E., Macaulay, W. A., & Wershler, J. L. (2015). Multidimensional evaluation of a mental health court: Adherence to the risk-need-responsivity model. *Law & Human Behavior, 39*(5), 489–502.

Canadian Centre on Substance Abuse (2006). *Self-harm among criminalized women.* Ottawa, ON: Canadian Centre on Substance Abuse.

Carson, E. A. (2018). *Prisoners in 2016.* Washington, DC: United States Department of Justice, Office of Justice Programs, Bureau of Justice Statistics.

Casiano, H., Bolton, S., Hildahl, K., Katz, L. Y., Bolton, J., & Sareen, J. (2016). A population-based study of the prevalence and correlates of self-harm in juvenile detention. *PLoS ONE, 11*(1), 1–9.

Case, B., Steadman, H., Dupuis, S. A., & Morris, L. S. (2009). Who succeeds in jail diversion programs for persons with mental illness? A multi-site study. *Behavioral Sciences & the Law, 27,* 661–674.

Centers for Disease Control (2015). *Suicide: Facts at a glance.* Atlanta, GA: Centers for Disease Control. Retrieved from https://www.cdc.gov/violenceprevention/pdf/suicide-datasheet-a.pdf.

Chapman, A. L., Gratz, K. L., & Brown, M. Z. (2006). Solving the puzzle of deliberate self-harm: The experiential avoidance model. *Behaviour Research & Therapy, 44*, 371–394.

Charles, D. R., Abram, K. M., McClelland, G. M., & Teplin, L. A. (2003). Suicidal ideation and behavior among women in jail. *Journal of Contemporary Criminal Justice, 19*(1), 65–81.

Chen, G. & Gueta, K. (2017). Lifetime history of suicidal ideation and attempts among incarcerated women in Israel. *Psychological Trauma: Theory, Research, Practice, and Policy, 9*(5), 596–604.

Christensen, G. E. (2006). Our system of corrections: Do jails play a role in improving offender outcomes? *Jail Reentry Roundtable.* Washington, DC: The Urban Institute.

Chui, V. (2018). Correcting correctional suicide: Qualified immunity and the hurdles to comprehensive inmate suicide prevention. *Boston College Law Review, 59*(4), 1397–1432.

Clark, V. A. (2016). Predicting two types of recidivism among newly released prisoners: First addresses as "launch pads" for recidivism or reentry success. *Crime & Delinquency, 62*(10), 1364–1400.

Clarke, R.V. (1997). Introduction. In R. V. Clarke (Ed.), *Situational crime prevention: Successful case studies (2nd ed.)* (pp. 2–43). New York: Harrow and Heston.

Clarke, R.V. & Lester, D. (1989). *Suicide: Closing the exits*. New York: Springer-Verlag.

Compton, M. T., Bahora, M., Watson, A. C., & Olivia, J. R. (2008). A comprehensive review of extant research on Crisis Intervention Team (CIT) Programs. *Journal of American Academy of Psychiatry & the Law, 36,* 47–55.

Condelli, W. S., Bradigan, B., & Holanchock, H. (1997). Intermediate care programs to reduce risk and better manage inmates with psychiatric disorders. *Behavioral Sciences & the Law, 15,* 459–467.

Cook, T. B. & Davis, M. S. (2012). Assessing legal strains and risk of suicide using archived court data. *Suicide & Life-Threatening Behavior, 42*(5), 495–506.

Cornish, D. B. & Clarke, R. V. (1985). Modeling offenders' decisions: A framework for research and policy. In M. Tonry & N. Morris (Eds.), *Crime and Justice (Vol. 6)* (pp. 147–180). Chicago: University of Chicago Press.

Cornish, D. B. & Clarke, R. V. (1987). Understanding crime displacement: An application of rational choice theory. *Criminology, 25*(4), 933–947.

Correia, K. M. (2000). Suicide assessment in a prison environment. *Criminal Justice & Behavior, 27,* 581–599.

Cosden, M., Ellens, J., Schnell, J., & Yamini-Diouf, Y. (2005). Efficacy of a mental health treatment court with assertive community treatment. *Behavioral Sciences & the Law, 23,* 199–214.

Cowles, E. L. & Dorman, L. A. (2001). *Despite the best of intentions: The problems of implementing a residential substance abuse treatment therapeutic community in a juvenile correctional institution.* Paper presented at the Annual Meeting of the Academy of Criminal Justice Sciences, Washington, DC.

Cox, J. F., McCarty, D. W., Landsberg, G., & Paravati, M. P. (1988). A model for crisis intervention services within local jails. *International Journal of Law & Psychiatry, 11,* 391–407.

Crayton, A., Ressler, L., Mukamal, D., Janetta, J., & Warwick, K. (2010). *Partnering with jails to improve reentry.* Washington, DC: The Urban Institute.

Crighton, D. & Towl, G. (1997). Self-inflicted deaths in prison in England and Wales. *Issues in Criminological and Legal Psychology, 28,* 12–20.

Cull, J. G. & Gill, W. S. (1998). *Suicide Probability Scale (SPS) manual.* Los Angeles: Western Psychological Services.

Cullen, F. T. & Jonson, C. L. (2012). *Correctional theory: Context and consequences.* Thousand Oaks, CA: Sage Publications.

Cummings, D. L. & Thompson, M. N. (2009). Suicidal or manipulative? The role of mental health counselors in overcoming a false dichotomy in identifying and treating self-harming inmates. *Journal of Mental Health Counseling, 31*(3), 201–212.

Cunningham, M. D., Reidy, T. J., & Sorensen, J. R. (2015). Wasted resources and gratuitous suffering: The failure of a security rationale for death row. *Psychology, Public Policy, & the Law, 22*(2), 185–199.

Curtin, S. C. & Warner, M. (2016). *Suicide rates for females and males by race and ethnicity: United States, 1999 and 2014.* Atlanta, GA: National Center for Health Statistics.

Curtin, S. C., Warner, M., & Hedegaard, H. (2016). *Increase in suicide in the United States, 1999–2014.* Atlanta, GA: National Center for Health Statistics.

Daeid, N. N. & Lynch, J. (2000). Are prison staff effective in recognizing the suicidal prisoner? *Journal of the Irish College of Physicians & Surgeons, 29,* 135–137.

Daigle, M. & Cote, G. (2006). Nonfatal suicide-related behavior among inmates. *Suicide & Life-Threatening Behavior, 36,* 670–681.

Daigle, M. S., Labelle, R., & Cote, G. (2006). Further evidence of the validity of the suicide risk assessment scale for prisoners. *International Journal of Law & Psychiatry, 29,* 343–354.

Daigle, M. S. & Naud, H. (2012). Risk of dying by suicide inside or outside prison: The shortened lives of male offenders. *Canadian Journal of Criminology and Criminal Justice, 54*(4), 511–528.

Davis, K., Fallon, J., Vogel, S., & Teachout, A. (2008). Integrating into the mental health system from the criminal justice system: Jail aftercare services for persons with a severe mental illness. In D. Phillips (Ed.), *Probation and parole: Current issues* (pp. 217–231). New York, NY: Haworth Press.

DeAmicas, A. (2017). Alternative housing and mentally ill inmates: An essential need. *American Jails, 31*(2), 13–16.

Deane, F. P., Skogstad, P., & Williams, M. W. (1999). Impact of attitudes, ethnicity and quality of prior therapy on New Zealand male prisoners' intentions to seek professional psychological help. *International Journal for the Advancement of Counseling, 21,* 55–67.

Dear, G. E., Slattery, J. L., & Hillian, R. J. (2001). Evaluations of the quality of coping reported by prisoners who have self-harmed and those who have not. *Suicide & Life-Threatening Behavior, 31,* 442–450.

Dear, G. E., Thomson, D. M., Hall, G. J., & Howells, K. (1998). Self-inflicted injury and coping behaviours in prison. In R. J. Kosky, H. S. Eshkevari, R. D. Goldney, & R. Hassan (Eds.), *Suicide prevention* (pp. 131–137). New York: Plenum.

Dear, G. E., Thomson, D. M., & Hills, A. M. (2000). Self-harm in prison: Manipulators can also be suicide attempters. *Criminal Justice & Behavior, 27*(2), 160–175.

Death in Custody Reporting Act of 2000–Pub. L. 106–297. 114 Stat. 1045, codified as amended at 42 U.S.C. 13704.

DeGroote, J. I. (2014). Weighing the eighth amendment: Finding the balance between treating and mistreating suicidal prisoners. *University of Pennsylvania Journal of Constitutional Law, 17,* 259–285.

DeHart, D., Smith, H. P., & Kaminski, R. J. (2009). Institutional responses to self-injurious behavior among inmates. *Journal of Correctional Health Care, 15*(2), 129–141.

Delaney, R., Ferguson, D., Nazon, M., & Bynum, R. (2016). Reentry and offenders with special needs: Mental illness and addressing criminogenic needs. *American Jails, 30*(2), 20–25.

Deliberto, T. L. & Nock, M. K. (2008). An exploratory study of correlates, onset, and offset of non-suicidal self-injury. *Archives of Suicide Research, 12,* 219–231.

Devilly, G. J., Sorbello, L., Eccleston, L., & Ward, T. (2005). Prison-based peer-education schemes. *Aggression & Violent Behavior, 10,* 219–240.

Dexter, P. & Towl, G. (1995). An investigation into suicidal behaviours in prison. *Issues in Criminological & Legal Psychology, 22,* 45–54.

de Wit, H. (2009). Impulsivity as a determinant and consequence of drug use: A review of underlying processes. *Addiction Biology, 14*(1), 22–31.

Dhaliwal, R. & Harrower, J. (2009). Reducing prisoner vulnerability and providing a means of empowerment: Evaluating the impact of a Listener scheme on the Listeners. *British Journal of Forensic Practice, 11*(3), 35–43.

Doty, S., Smith, H. P., & Rojek, J. (2012). Self-injurious behaviors in corrections: Informal social control and institutional responses in a state prison system. *Victims & Offenders, 7,* 30–52.

Drum, J. D., Brownson, C., Burton Denmark, A., & Smith S. E. (2009). New data on the nature of suicidal crises in college students: Shifting the paradigm. *Professional Psychology: Research and Practice, 40*(3), 213–222.

Durkheim, E. (1897 [1951]). *Suicide.* New York, NY: The Free Press.

Durose, M. R., Cooper, A. D., & Snyder, H. N. (2014). *Recidivism of prisoners released in 30 states in 2005: Patterns from 2005 to 2010.* Washington, DC: United States Department of Justice, Office of Justice Programs, Bureau of Justice Statistics.

Duthe, G., Hazard, A., Kensey, A., & Ke Shon, J. P. (2013). Suicide among male prisoners in France: A prospective population-based study. *Forensic Science International, 233,* 273–277.

Duwe, G. (2014). A randomized experiment of a prisoner reentry program: Updated results from an evaluation of the Minnesota Comprehensive Offender Reentry Plan (MCORP). *Criminal Justice Studies, 27*(2), 172–190.

Dye, M. H. (2010). Deprivation, importation, and prisons suicide: Combined effects of institutional conditions and inmate composition. *Journal of Criminal Justice, 38,* 796–806.

———. (2011). The gender paradox in prison suicide rates. *Women & Criminal Justice, 21*(4), 290–307.

Earthrowl, M. & McCully, R. (2002). Screening new inmates in a female prison. *Journal of Forensic Psychiatry, 13,* 428–439.

Eccleston, L. & Sorbello, L. (2002). The RUSH Program. *Australian Psychologist, 37,* 237–244.

Encrenaz, G., Miras, A., Contrand, B., Galera, C., Pujos, S., Michel, G., & Lagarde, E. (2014). Inmate-to-inmate violence as a marker of suicide attempt risk during imprisonment. *Journal of Forensic & Legal Medicine, 22,* 20–25.

Evans, C., Brinded, P., Simpson, A. I., Frampton, C., & Mulder, R. T. (2010). Validation of brief screening tools for mental disorders among New Zealand prisoners. *Psychiatric Services, 61*(9), 923–928.

Fagan, T. J., Cox, J., Helfand, S. J., & Aufderheide, D. (2010). Self-injurious behavior in correctional settings. *Journal of Correctional Health Care, 16*(1), 48–66.

Farabee, D., Prendergast, M., Cartier, J., Wexler, H., Knight, K., & Anglin, M. D. (1999). Barriers to implementing effective correctional drug treatment programs. *Prison Journal, 79*(2), 150–162.

Farbstein, J. & Wener, R. (1989). *A comparison of "direct" and "indirect" supervision correctional facilities.* Washington, DC: National Institute of Corrections.

Fatos, K., Sollimo, A., Graves, J., Glowa-Kollisch, S., Vise, A., MacDonald, R., Waters, A., Rosner, Z., Dickey, N., Angell, S., & Venters, H. (2015). Disparities in mental health referral and diagnosis in the New York City Jail mental health service. *American Journal of Public Health, 105*(9), 1911–1916.

Favril, L., Vander Laenen, F., Vandeviver, C., & Audenaert, K. (2017). Suicidal ideation while incarcerated: Prevalence and correlates in a large sample of male prisoners in Flanders, Belgium. *International Journal of Law & Psychiatry, 55,* 19–28.

Favril, L., Wittouck, C., Audenaert, K., & Laenen, V. (2018). A 17-year national study of prison suicides in Belgium. *Crisis.* DOI: 10.1027/0227-5910/a000531.

Fazel, S., Grann, M., Kling, S., & Hawton, K. (2011). Prison suicide in 12 countries: An ecological study of 861 suicides during 2003–2007. *Social Psychology & Psychiatric Epidemiology, 46*(3), 191–195.

Fazel, S. & Seewald, K. (2012). Severe mental illness in 33,588 prisoners worldwide: Systematic review and meta-regression analysis. *British Journal of Psychiatry, 200,* 364–373.

Federal Bureau of Prisons (n.d.) *About Our Facilities.* Retrieved from https://www.bop.gov/about/facilities/.

Felix, A., Barber, C., & Lesser, M. L. (2001). Serving paroled offenders with mental illness who are homeless: Collaboration between the justice and mental health systems. In G. Landsberg & A. Smiley (Eds.), *Forensic mental health* (pp. 11.1–11.11). Kingston, NJ: Civic Research Institute.

Felthous, A. R. (1994). Preventing jailhouse suicides. *Bulletin of the American Academy of Psychiatry & the Law, 2,* 477–488.

Florentine, J. B. & Crane, C. (2010). Suicide prevention by limiting access to methods: A review of theory and practice. *Social Science and Medicine, 70,* 1626–1632.

Franczak, M. & Dye, C. (2001). Treating offenders with mental disorders and co-occurring substance abuse disorders—the Arizona integrated treatment initiative. In G. Landsberg & A. Smiley *Forensic Mental Health* (pp. 10.1–10.21). Kingston, NJ: Civic Research Institute.

Freudenberg, N. (2006). Coming home from jail: A review of health and social problems facing US jail populations and of opportunities for reentry interventions. *Jail Reentry Roundtable.* Washington, DC: The Urban Institute.

Friedmann, A. (2014). How the courts view ACA Accreditation. *Prison Legal News, 25*(1), 18–20.

Frisman, L., Sturges, G. E., Baranoski, M. V., & Levinson, M. (2001). Connecticut's criminal justice diversion program: A comprehensive community forensic mental health model. In G. Landsberg & A. Smiley (Eds.), *Forensic mental health* (pp. 5.1–5.8). Kingston, NJ: Civic Research Institute.

Frisman, L. K., Swanson, J., Marin, M. C., & Leavitt-Smith, E. (2010). Estimating costs of reentry programs for prisoners with severe mental illness. *Correctional Health Care Report, 11*(6), 81, 90–96.

Frottier, P., Fruehwald, S., Ritter, K., Eher, R., Schwalzler, J., & Bauer, P. (2002). Jailhouse blues revisited. *Social Psychiatry & Psychiatric Epidemiology, 37,* 68–73.

Frottier, P., Konig, F., Matschnig, T., Seyringer, M. E., & Fruhwald, S. (2007). Suicide prevention in correctional institutions: The significance of solitary cell accommodation. *International Journal of Prisoner Health, 3*(3), 225–232.

Fruehwald, S., Frottier, P., Eher, R., Gutierrez, K., & Ritter, K. (2000). Prison suicides in Austria, 1975–1997. *Suicide and Life-Threatening Behavior, 30*(4), 360–369.

Fruehwald, S., Frottier, P., Matschnig, T., Koenig, F., Lehr, S., & Eher, R. (2003). Do monthly or seasonal variations exist in suicides in a high-risk setting? *Psychiatry Research, 121*, 263–269.

Gallagher, C. A. & Dobrin, A. (2005). The association between suicide screening practices and attempts requiring emergency care in juvenile justice facilities. *Journal of the American Academy of Child & Adolescent Psychiatry, 44*, 485–493.

Garroutte, E. M., Goldberg, J., Beals, J., Herrell, R., & Manson, S. M. (2003). Attempted suicide among American Indians. *Social Science & Medicine, 56*, 1571–1579.

Gastwirth, J. L. (2005). Case comment—*Boncher v. Brown County*: The need for an appropriate comparison of suicide rates. *Law, Probability, & Risk, 4*, 257–263.

Gates, M. L., Turney, A., Ferguson, E., Walker, V., & Staples-Horne, M. (2017). Associations among substance use, mental health disorders, and self-harm in a prison population: Examining group risk for suicide attempt. *International Journal of Environmental Research and Public Health, 14*(3), 315–331.

Gauthier, S., Reisch, T., & Bartsch, C. (2015). Swiss prison suicides between 2000 and 2010. *Crisis, 36*(2), 110–116.

Georgiou, M., Souza, R., Holder, S., Stone, H., & Davies, S. (2015). *Standards for prison mental health services.* London, UK: Royal College of Psychiatrists Centre for Quality Improvement.

Gerlinger, J. & Turner, S. F. (2015). California's public safety realignment: correctional policy based on stakes rather than risk. *Criminal Justice Policy Review, 26*(8), 805–827.

Gettinger, S. H. (1984). *New generation jails: An innovative approach to an age-old problem.* Longmont, CO: NIC Jails Division.

Gibbs, J. J. (1982). The first cut is the deepest: Psychological breakdown and survival in the detention setting. In R. Johnson & H. Toch (Eds.), *The pains of imprisonment* (pp. 97–114). Prospect Heights, Il: Waveland Press.

———. (1987). Symptoms of psychopathology among jail prisoners. *Criminal Justice & Behavior, 14*(3), 288–310.

———. (1992). Jailing and stress. In H. Toch (Ed.), *Mosaic of despair: Human breakdowns in prison (2nd ed.)* (pp. 177–202). Washington, DC: American Psychological Association.

Glaze, L. & Maruschak, L. (2008). *Parents in prison and their minor children.* Washington, DC: United States Department of Justice, Office of Justice Programs, Bureau of Justice Statistics.

Glowa-Kollisch, S., Lim, S., Summers, C., Cohen, L., Selling, D., & Venters, H. (2014). Beyond the bridge: Evaluating a novel mental health program in the New York City Jail System. *American Journal of Public Health, 104*(11), 2212–2218.

Gondles, E. F., Maurer, K. F., & Bell, A. (2017). A major challenge for corrections: National survey findings identify challenges in recruiting and retaining correctional health care professionals. *Corrections Today, 79*(1), 16–23.

Gooding, P. A., Tarrier, N., Dunn, G., Awenat, Y., Shaw, J., Ulph, F., Pratt, D. (2017). Psychological characteristics and predictors of suicide probability in high-risk prisoners. *Criminal Justice & Behavior, 44*(3), 321–335.

Goss, J. R., Peterson, K., Smith, L. W., Kalb, K., & Brodey, B. B. (2002). Characteristics of suicide attempts in a large urban jail system with an established suicide prevention program. *Psychiatric Services, 53*, 574–579.

Gould, C., McGeorge, T., & Slade, K. (2018). Suicide screening tools for use in incarcerated offenders: A systematic review. *Archives of Suicide Research, 22,* 345–364.

Greenfield, L. A. & Snell, T. L. (1999). *Women offenders.* Washington, DC: United States Department of Justice, Office of Justice Programs, Bureau of Justice Statistics.

Hagel-Seymour, J. (1982). Environmental sanctuaries for susceptible prisoners. In R. Johnson & H. Toch. *The pains of imprisonment* (pp. 267–284). Prospect Heights, IL: Waveland Press.

Haglund, A., Tidemalm, D., Jokinen, J., Langstrom, N., Lichtenstein, P., Fazel, S., & Runeson, B. (2015). Suicide after release from prison—a population-based cohort from Sweden. *Journal of Clinical Psychiatry, 75*(10), 1047–1053.

Hakansson, A., Bradvik, L., Schlyter, F., & Berglund, M. (2011). Variables associated with repeated suicide attempt in a criminal justice population. *Suicide & Life-Threatening Behavior, 41*(5), 517–531.

Hales, H., Davison, S., Misch, P., & Taylor, P. J. (2003). Young male prisoners in a young offenders' institution: Their contact with suicidal behaviour by others. *Journal of Adolescence, 26*, 667–685.

Hales, H., Edmondson, A., Davison, S., Maughan, B., & Taylor, P. J. (2015). The impact of contact with suicide-related behavior in prison on young offenders. *Crisis, 36*(1), 21–30.

Hall, B. & Gabor, P. (2004). Peer suicide prevention in a prison. *Crisis, 25,* 19–26.

Hannan, M., Hearnden, I., Grace, K., & Bucke, T. (2010). *Deaths in or following police custody: An examination of the cases 1998/99–2008/09.* London, UK: Independent Police Complaints Commission.

Hanser, R. D. (2002). Inmate suicide in prisons: an analysis of legal liability under 42 USC section 1983. *Prison Journal, 82*(4), 459–477.

Hanson, A. (2010). Correctional suicide: Has progress ended? *The Journal of the Academy of Psychiatry and the Law, 38*(6), 6–10.

Harris, T. L. & Molock, S. D. (2000) Cultural orientation, family cohesion and family support in suicide ideation and depression among African American college students. *Suicide & Life-Threatening Behavior, 30*, 341–353.

Hassine, V., Johnson, R., & Tabriz, S. (2011). *Life without parole: Living and dying in prison today.* New York, NY: Oxford University Press.

Haw, C., Hawton, K., Houston, K., & Townsend, E. (2003). Correlates of relative lethality and suicidal intent among deliberate self-harm patients. *Suicide and Life-Threatening Behavior, 33*(4), 353–364.

Hawton, K., Linsell, L. Adeniji, T., Sariaslan, A., & Fazel, S. (2014). Self-harm in prisons in England and Wales: An epidemiological study of prevalence, risk factors, clustering, and subsequent suicide. *The Lancet, 383,* 1147–1154.

Hayes, A., Senior, J., Fahy, T., & Shaw, J. (2014). Actions taken in response to mental health screening at reception into prison. *The Journal of Forensic Psychiatry and Psychology, 25*(4), 371–379.

Hayes, L. M. (1983). And darkness closes in. *Criminal Justice & Behavior, 10,* 461–484.

———. (1989). National study of jail suicides: Seven years later. *Psychiatric Quarterly*, *60*(1), 7–29.

———. (1994). Developing a written program for jail suicide prevention. *Corrections Today, 56*(2), 182–185.

———. (2003). Use of no-harm contracts and other controversial issues in suicide prevention. *Jail Suicide/Mental Health Update, 12*(2), 1–9.

———. (2004a). News from around the country. *Jail Suicide/Mental Health Update, 13*(1), 14–15.

———. (2004b). State jail standards and suicide prevention: A report card. *Jail Suicide/Mental Health Update, 13*(3), 8–10.

———. (2005). A practitioner's guide to developing and maintaining a sound suicide prevention policy. *Jail Suicide/Mental Health Update, 13(4),* 1–20.

———. (2009). *Juvenile suicide in confinement: A national survey.* Washington, DC: National Institute of Justice, Office of Juvenile Justice and Delinquency Prevention.

———. (2010). *National study of jail suicide: 20 years later.* Washington, DC: U.S. Department of Justice National Institute of Justice.

Hefland, S. J. (2011). Managing disruptive offenders. In T. J. Fagan & R. K. Ax (Eds.), *Correctional mental health* (pp. 309–326). Thousand Oaks, CA: Sage Publications.

Heney, J. (1990). *Report of self-injurious behaviour in Kingston Prison for Women.* Ottawa: Correctional Service Canada.

Herinckx, H. A., Swart, S. C., Ama, S. M., Dolezal, C. D., & King, S. (2005). Rearrest and linkage to mental health services among clients of the Clark County Mental Health Court Program. *Psychiatric Services, 56*(7), 853–857.

Hjelmeland, H., Nordvik, H., Bille-Brahe, U., De Leo, D., Kerkhof, J. F. M., Lonnqvist, J., Michel, K., Renberg, E. S., Schmidtke, A., & Wasserman, D. (2000). A cross-cultural study of suicide intent in parasuicide patients. *Suicide & Life-Threatening Behavior, 30*(4), 275–303.

Hochstetler, A., Murphy, D., & Simons, R. (2004). Damaged goods: Exploring predictors of distress in prison inmates. *Crime & Delinquency, 50,* 436–457.

Hockenberry, S., & Puzzanchera, C. (2015). *Juvenile Court Statistics 2013.* Pittsburgh, PA: National Center for Juvenile Justice.

Hoke, S. (2013). *Inmate behavior management: Northampton County Jail case study.* Washington, DC: National Institute of Corrections.

Home Office (1999). *Suicide is everyone's concern.* London, England: Home Office.

Honegger, L .N. (2015). Does the evidence support the case for mental health courts? A review of the literature. *Law & Human Behavior, 39*(5), 478–488.

Hopes, B. & Shaull, R. (1986). Jail suicide prevention. *Corrections Today*, *48*(8), 64–70.

Hounmenou, C. (2010). *Standards for monitoring human rights of people in police lockups*. Chicago, IL: Jane Addams Center for Social Policy and Social Work.

Hulbert, C. & Thomas, R. (2010). Predicting self-injury in BPD: An investigation of the Experiential Avoidance Model. *Journal of Personality Disorders, 24*(5), 651–663.

Humber, N., Piper, M., Appleby, L., & Shaw, J. (2011). Characteristics of and trends in subgroups of prisoner suicides in England and Wales. *Psychological Medicine, 41,* 2275–2285.

Humber, N., Webb, R., Piper, M., Appleby, L., & Shaw, J. (2013). A national case-control study of risk factors among prisoners in England and Wales. *Social Psychiatry Psychiatric Epidemiology, 48,* 1177–1185.

Hutchinson, V., Keller, K., & Reid, T. (2009). *Inmate behavior management: The key to a safe and secure jail.* Washington, DC: National Institute of Corrections.

Ireland, J. L. (2005). Bullying among prisoners: The need for innovation. In Jane L. Ireland (Ed.), *Bullying Among Prisoners* (pp. 3–21). Devon, UK: Willan Publishing.

Irwin, J. (1985). *The jail: Managing the underclass in American society.* Berkeley, CA: University of California Press.

Irwin, J. & Cressey, D. (1962). Thieves, convicts and the inmate culture. *Social Problems, 10*(2), 142–155.

Jackson, P. G. (1992). *Detention in transition: Sonoma County's new generation jail.* Rohnert, CA: Department of Criminal Justice Administration, Sonoma State University.

James, D. J. & Glaze, L. E. (2006). *Mental health problems of prison and jail inmates.* Washington, DC: United States Department of Justice, Office of Justice Programs, Bureau of Justice Statistics.

Jenkins, R., Bhugra, D., Meltzer, H., Singleton, N., Bebbington, P., Brugha, T., Coid, J., Farrell, M., Lewis, G., & Paton, J. (2005). Psychiatric and social aspects of suicidal behaviour in prisons. *Psychological Medicine, 35,* 257–269.

Jenkins, M. J., Dammer, H., & Raciti, D. (2017). "Built around failure": Improving county jail inmates' perceptions of reentry. *Corrections Today, 79*(4), 58–65.

Johnson, C. (2002). Mental health care policies in jail systems: Suicide and the eighth amendment. *University of California–Davis Law Review, 35,* 1227–1260.

Johnson, R. (2002). *Hard time (3rd Ed.).* Belmont, CA: Wadsworth.

Joiner, T. (2005). *Why people die by suicide.* Cambridge, MA: Harvard University Press.

Joiner, T., Walker, R., Rudd, M. D., & Jobes, D. (1999). Scientizing and routinizing the outpatient assessment of suicidality. *Professional Psychology: Research and Practice, 30,* 447–453.

Jones, R. M., Hales, H., Butwell, M., Ferrier, M., & Taylor, P. J. (2011). Suicide in high security hospital patients. *Social Psychiatry & Psychiatric Epidemiology, 46,* 723–731.

Joukamaa, M. (1997). Prison suicide in Finland, 1969–1992. *Forensic Science International, 89,* 167–174.

Judge David L. Bazelon Center for Mental Health Law (2003). Criminalization of people with mental illness: The role of mental health courts in system reform. *Jail Suicide/Mental Health Update, 12*(1), 1–11.

———. (2006). Best practices: Access to benefits for prisoners with mental illnesses. *Jail Suicide/Mental Health Update, 14*(4), 7–13.

Junker, G., Beeler, A., & Bates, J. (2005). Using trained inmate observers for suicide watch in a federal correction setting. *Psychological Services, 2*(1), 20–27.

Kappeler, V. E. (1993). *Critical issues in police civil liability.* Prospect Heights, IL: Waveland Press, Inc.

Kappeler, V. E., Vaughn, M. S. & Del Carmen, R. V. (1991). Death in detention: An analysis of police liability for negligent failure to prevent suicide. *Journal of Criminal Justice, 19*, 381–393.

Karishma, C. A., Simon, A. E., DeFrances, C. J., & Maruschak, L. (2016). *National survey of prison health care: Selected findings.* Atlanta, GA: National Health Statistics Reports.

Kerle, K. (2016). The mentally ill and crisis intervention teams: Reflections on jails and the U.S. mental health challenge. *The Prison Journal, 96*(1), 153–161.

Kiekbusch, R. G. (2017). Managing suicidal inmates in the jail setting. *Corrections Managers' Report, 23*(3), 33–34; 42–55.

Kirchner, T., Forns, M., & Mohino. S. (2008). Identifying the risk of deliberate self-harm among young prisoners by means of coping technologies. *Suicide & Life-Threatening Behavior, 38*(4), 442–448.

Klonsky, E. D. (2007). The functions of deliberate self-injury: A review of the evidence. *Clinical Psychology Review, 27*, 226–239.

Klonsky, E. D., May, A. M., & Glenn, C. R. (2013). The relationship between non-suicidal self-injury and attempted suicide: Converging evidence from four samples. *Journal of Abnormal Psychology, 122*(1), 231–237.

Knoll, J. L. IV. (2010). Suicide in correctional settings: Assessment, prevention, and professional liability. *Journal of Correctional Health Care, 16*(3), 188–204.

Kokorowski, F. & Freng, S. (2001). Posttraumatic stress disorder with co-occurring substance abuse: Implications for jails. *American Jails, 15*(2), 33–38.

Konchanek, K. D., Murphy, S. L., Xu, J., & Tejada-Vera, B. (2016). Deaths: Final data for 2014. *National Vital Statistics Report, 65*(4), 1–122.

Kovasznay, M. D., Miraglia, R., Beer, R., & Way, B. (2004). Reducing suicides in New York State correctional facilities. *Psychiatric Quarterly, 75*(1), 61–70.

Kroner, D. G., Mills, J. F., Grazia, A., & Talbert, K. O. N. (2011). Clinical assessment in correctional settings. In T. J. Fagan & R. K. Ax (Eds.), *Correctional mental health* (pp. 77–102). Thousand Oaks, CA: Sage Publications.

Laberge, D. & Morin, D. (1995). The overuse of criminal justice dispositions: Failure of diversionary policies in the management of mental health problems. *International Journal of Law & Psychiatry, 18*(4), 389–414.

Lamb, R. H., Shaner, R., Elliott, D. M., DeCuir, W. J., & Foltz, J. T. (1995). Outcome for psychiatric emergency patients seen by an outreach police-mental health team. *Psychiatric Services, 46*(12), 1267–1271.

Lamb, R. H., Weinberger, I. E., & Reston-Parham, C. (1996). Court intervention to address the mental health needs of mentally ill offenders. *Psychiatric Services, 47,* 275–281.

Lambie, I. & Randell, I. (2013). The impact of incarceration on juvenile offenders. *Clinical Psychology Review, 33,* 448–459.

Lanes, E. C. (2009). Identification of risk factors for self-injurious behaviors in male prisoners. *Journal of Forensic Sciences, 54,* 692–698.

———. (2011). Are the "worst of the worst" self-injurious prisoners more likely to end up in long-term maximum-security administrative segregation? *International Journal of Offender Therapy and Comparative Criminology, 55*(7), 1034–1050.

Langley, S. (1991). Lifeline suicide prevention program. In D. Lester (Ed.), *Suicide '91* (pp. 141–143). Denver: American Association of Suicidology.

Larney, S., Topp, L., Indig, D., O'Driscoll, C., & Greenberg, D. (2012). A cross-sectional survey of prevalence and correlates of suicidal ideation and suicide attempts among prisoners in New South Wales, Australia. *BMC Public Health, 12,* 14–20.

Latessa, E. J., Listwan, S. J., & Koetzle, D. (2014). *What works (and doesn't) in reducing recidivism.* London: Routledge.

La Vigne, N. G., Visher, C., & Castro, J. (2004). *Chicago prisoners' experiences returning home.* Washington, DC: The Urban Institute.

Leese, M., Thomas, S., & Snow, L. (2006). An ecological study of factors associated with rates of self-inflicted death in prisons in England and Wales. *International Journal of Law & Psychiatry, 29,* 355–560.

Lester, D. (1991). *Psychotherapy for suicidal clients.* Springfield, IL: Charles C. Thomas.

———. (2000). *Why people kill themselves.* Springfield, IL: Charles C. Thomas.

———. (2009). *Preventing suicide: Closing the exists revisited.* New York: Nova Publishers.

Lester, D. & Yang, B. (2008). Calculating jail suicide rates. *American Jails, 21,* 45–47.

Levinson, R. B. (2017). Kingsley breathes new life into substantive due process as a check on abuse of government power. *Notre Dame Law Review, 93*(1), 357–392.

Levinson, R. B. (1999). *Unit management in prisons and jails.* Lanham, MD: American Correctional Association.

Lewis, L. M. (2007). No-harm contracts: A review of what we know. *Suicide and Life-Threatening Behavior, 37*(1), 50–57.

Lewis, S. J. & Harrison, D. M. (2005). Crisis intervention with HIV positive women. In A. R. Roberts (Ed.), *Crisis intervention handbook* (pp. 682–702). New York: Oxford University Press.

Liebling, A. (1994). Suicide amongst women prisoners. *Howard Journal of Criminal Justice, 33*(1), 1–9.

———. (1999). Prisoner suicide and prisoner coping. M. Tonry & J. Petersilia, *Crime and Justice (Vol 26.)* (pp. 283–358). Chicago: University of Chicago Press.

Liebling, A. & Ludlow, A. (2016). Suicide, distress, and the quality of prison life. In Y. Jewkes, B. Crewe, & J. Bennett (Eds.), *Handbook on Prisons* (pp. 224–245). London, UK: Routledge.

Linehan, M. M. (1993). *Cognitive-behavioral treatment of borderline personality disorder*. New York: Guilford.

Lohner, J. & Konrad, N. (2006). Deliberate self-harm and suicide attempt in custody: Distinguishing features in male inmates' self-injurious behavior. *International Journal of Law & Psychiatry, 29,* 370–385.

Loucks, N. (1997). *Research into drugs and alcohol, violence and bullying, suicides and self-injury and backgrounds of abuse.* Edinburgh, Scotland: Scottish Prison Service.

Lowenkamp, C. T., Latessa, E. J., & Smith, P. (2006). Does correctional program quality really matter? The impact of adhering to the principles of effective intervention. *Criminology & Public Policy, 5*(3), 575–594.

Lutze, F. E., Rosky, J. W., & Hamilton, Z. K. (2014). Homelessness and reentry: A multisite outcome evaluation of Washington state's reentry housing program for high risk offenders. *Criminal Justice & Behavior, 41,* 471–491.

Lyneham, M. & Chan, A. (2013). *Deaths in custody in Australia to 30 June 2011.* Canberra: Australian Institute of Criminology.

MacKain, S. J. & Messer, C. E. (2004). Ending the inmate shuffle: An intermediate care program for inmates with a chronic mental illness. *Journal of Forensic Psychology Practice, 4*(2), 87–99.

MacKenzie, N., Oram, C., & Borrill, J. (2003). Self-inflicted deaths of women in custody. *British Journal of Forensic Practice, 5*(1), 27–35.

Magun, K. (2017). A changing landscape for pretrial detainees? The potential impact of *Kingsley v. Hendrickson* on jail-suicide litigation. *Columbia Law Review, 117*(8), 2059–2101.

Manchak, S. M., Skeem, J. L., Kennealy, P. J., & Louden, J. E. (2014). High-fidelity specialty mental health probation improves officer practices, treatment access, and rule compliance. *Law & Human Behavior, 38*(5), 450–461.

Mandracchia, J. T. & Smith, P. N. (2015). The interpersonal theory of suicide applied to male prisoners. *Suicide & Life-Threatening Behavior, 45*(3), 293–301.

Mann, B., Bond, D., & Powitzky, R. J. (2011). Collaborating for success in interagency correctional mental health reentry. *Corrections Today, 73*(5), 30–33.

Maruschak, L. M. (2006). *Medical problems of jail inmates.* Washington, DC: United States Department of Justice, Office of Justice Programs, Bureau of Justice Statistics.

Marzano, L., Adler, J. R., & Ciclitira, K. (2015). Responding to repetitive, non-suicidal self-harm in an English male prison: Staff experiences, reactions, and concerns. *Legal & Criminological Psychology, 20,* 241–254.

Marzano, L, Ciclitira, K., & Adler, J. (2011). The impact of prison staff on self-harming behaviours: Prisoners' perspectives. *British Journal of Clinical Psychology, 51*(1), 4–18.

Marzano, L., Fazel, S., Rivlin, A., & Hawton, K. (2010). Psychiatric disorders in women prisoners who have engaged in near-lethal self-harm: Case-control study. *The British Journal of Psychiatry, 197,* 219–226.

Marzano, L., Hawton, K., Rivlin, A., Smith, E. N., Piper, M., & Fazel, S. (2016). Prevention of suicidal behavior in prisons. *Crisis, 37*(5), 323–334.

Matsumoto, T., Tsutsumi, A., Izutsu, T., Imamura, F., Chiba, Y., & Takeshima, T. (2009). Comparative study of the prevalence of suicidal behavior and sexual abuse in delinquent and non-delinquent adolescents. *Psychiatry & Clinical Neurosciences, 63,* 238–240.

Matsumoto, T., Yamaguchi, A., Asami, T., Okada, T., Yoshikawa, K., & Hirayasu, Y. (2005). Characteristics of self-cutters among male inmates. *Psychiatry & Clinical Neurosciences, 59,* 319–326.

McDonagh, D., Taylor, K., & Blanchette, K. (2002). Correctional adaptation of dialectical behaviour therapy (DBT) for federally sentenced women. *Forum on Corrections Research, 14*(2), 36–39.

McKenna, B., Skipworth, J., Tapsell, R., Madell, D., Pillai, K., Simpson, A., Cavney, J., & Rouse, P. (2015). A prison mental health in-reach model informed by assertive community treatment principles: Evaluation of its impact on planning during the pre-release period, community mental health service engagement and reoffending. *Criminal Behaviour & Mental Health, 25,* 429–439.

McMullan, E. C. (2011). Seeking medical and psychiatric attention. In L. Gideon & H. E. Sung (Eds.), *Rethinking Corrections* (pp. 253–278). Los Angeles: Sage Publications.

McNeil, D. E., & Binder, R. L. (2007). Effectiveness of a mental health court in reducing criminal recidivism and violence. *American Journal of Psychiatry, 164,* 1395–1403.

McVey, C. (2001). Coordinating effective health and mental health continuity of care. *Corrections Today, 63*(5), 58–62.

Meltzer, H., Jenkins, R., Singleton, N., Charlton, J., & Yar, M. (2003). Non-fatal suicidal behavior among prisoners. *International Review of Psychiatry, 15,* 148–149.

Menninger, K. (1938). *Man against himself.* New York: Harcourt, Brace & World.

Metraux, S. & Culhane, D. P. (2004). Homeless shelter use and reincarceration following prison release. *Criminology & Public Policy, 3(2),* 139–160.

Miller, H. V. & Miller, J. M. (2010). Community in-reach through jail reentry: Findings from a quasi-experimental design. *Justice Quarterly, 27*(6), 893–910.

Minino, A. M., Heron, M. P., Murphy, S. L. & Kochanek, K. D. (2007) *A national vital statistics report. Deaths: Final data for 2004* (Vol. 55, Issue 19). Washington, DC: United States Department of Health and Human Services.

Ministry of Justice (2018). *Safety in custody statistics, England and Wales: Deaths in prison custody to June 2018 assaults and self-harm to March 2018.* London, UK: Ministry of Justice.

Minton, T. D. (2003). *Jails in Indian country, 2002.* Washington, DC: United States Department of Justice, Office of Justice Programs, Bureau of Justice Statistics.

———. (2015). *Jails in Indian country, 2015.* Washington, DC: United States Department of Justice, Office of Justice Programs, Bureau of Justice Statistics.

———. (2016). *Jails in Indian country, 2016.* Washington, DC: United States Department of Justice, Office of Justice Programs, Bureau of Justice Statistics.

Molleman, T., & van Ginneken, E. F. J. C. (2015). A multilevel analysis of the relationship between cell sharing, staff-prisoner relationships, and prisoners' perceptions of prison quality. *International Journal of Offender Therapy & Comparative Criminology, 59*(10), 1029–1046.

Moore, E., Gaskin, C., & Indig, D. (2015). Attempted suicide, self-harm, and psychological disorder among young offenders in custody. *Journal of Correctional Health Care, 21*(3), 243–254.

Moran, M. (2014). AMA votes to oppose solitary confinement of juveniles. *Psychiatric News.* Retrieved from http://sychnews.psychiatryonline.org/doi/full/10.1176/appi.pn.2014.12b13#.v9yu7afb17y.email.

Morgan, J. & Hawton, K. (2004). Self-reported suicidal behavior in juvenile offenders in custody: Prevalence and associated factors. *Crisis, 25*(1), 8–11.

Muehlenkamp, J. J. (2005). Self-injurious behavior as a separate clinical syndrome. *American Journal of Orthopsychiatry, 75*(2), 324–333.

Mumola, C. (2005). *Suicide and homicide in state prisons and local jails.* Washington, DC: United States Department of Justice, Office of Justice Programs, Bureau of Justice Statistics.

Mundt, A., Kastner, S., Mir, J., & Priebe, S. (2015). Did female prisoners with mental disorders receive psychiatric treatment before imprisonment? *BMC Psychiatry,* DOI: 10.1186/s12888-015-0387-z.

Murrie, D. C., Henderson, C. E., Vincent, G. M., Rockett, J. L., & Mundt, C. (2009). Psychiatric symptoms among juveniles incarcerated in adult prison. *Psychiatric Services, 60*(8), 1092–1097.

National Commission on Correctional Health Care (2015). *Standards for mental health services in correctional facilities.* Chicago, IL: National Commission on Correctional Health Care.

National GAINS Center (2004). *What can we say about the effectiveness of jail diversion programs for persons with co-occurring disorder?* Delmar, NY: The National GAINS Center.

National Institute of Justice (2004). Can screening be culturally sensitive? *Corrections Today, 66*(3), 30–31.

Nee, C. & Farman, S. (2005). Female prisoners with borderline personality disorder: Some promising treatment developments. *Criminal Behavior & Mental Health, 15*(1), 2–16.

Nelson, R. (1983). New generation jails. *Corrections Today,* 108–112.

———. (1988). The origins of the podular direct supervision concept: An eyewitness account. *American Jails, 2*(1), 8–16.

Nelson, M., Dees, P., & Allen, C. (1999). *The first month out: Post-incarceration experiences in New York City.* New York, NY: Vera Institute of Justice.

Nelson, W. R. & Davis, R. M. (1995). Podular direct supervision: The first twenty years. *American Jails, 9*(3), 11–22.

Newbold, G. & Eskridge, C. (1994). Penal innovation in New Zealand: He Ara Hou. *Journal of Offender Rehabilitation, 20*(3/4), 21–35.

Newcomen, N. (2014a). *Learning from PPO investigations: Risk factors in self-inflicted deaths in prisons.* London, UK: Prisons and Probation Ombudsman.

———. (2014b). *Learning from PPO investigations: Self-inflicted deaths of prisoners on ACCT.* London, UK: Prisons and Probation Ombudsman.

———. (2016). *Learning from PPO investigations: Mental health.* London, UK: Prisons and Probation Ombudsman.

Newman, O. (1972). *Defensible space.* New York: Collier Books.

New South Wales Corrections (2005). *Discussion paper: Suicide prevention strategic framework.* Retrieved from http://www.csa.nsw.gov.au/downloads/Discussion13.9.05.pdf.

Nguyen, T. Q., Weir, B. W., Des Jarlais, D. C., Pinkerton, S. D., & Holtgrave, D. R. (2014). Syringe exchange in the United States: A national level economic evaluation of hypothetical increases in investment. *AIDS & Behavior, 18*(11), 2144–2155.

Niedzwiedz, C., Haw, C., Hawton, K., & Platt, S. (2014). The definition and epidemiology of clusters of suicidal behavior: A systematic review. *Suicide & Life-Threatening Behavior, 44*(5), 569–581.

Nock, M. K. & Kessler, R. C. (2006). Prevalence and risk factors for suicide attempts versus suicide gestures: Analysis of the National Comorbidity Survey. *Journal of Abnormal Psychology, 115*(3), 616–623.

Noonan, M. E. (2007). *Deaths in custody statistical tables.* Washington, DC: United States Department of Justice Bureau of Justice Statistics. Retrieved from https://www.bjs.gov/content/dcrp/tables/juvtab2.cfm.

———. (2016a). *Mortality in state prisons, 2001–2014—statistical tables.* Washington, DC: United States Department of Justice, Office of Justice Programs, Bureau of Justice Statistics.

———. (2016b). *Mortality in local jails, 2000–2014—statistical tables.* Washington, DC: United States Department of Justice, Office of Justice Programs, Bureau of Justice Statistics.

Noonan, M. E. & Ginder, S. (2013). *Mortality in local jails and state prisons, 2000–2011—statistical tables.* United States Department of Justice, Office of Justice Programs, Bureau of Justice Statistics.

Noonan, M. E., Rohloff, H., & Ginder, S. (2015). *Mortality in local jails and state prisons, 2000–2013—statistical tables.* Washington, DC: United States Department of Justice, Office of Justice Programs, Bureau of Justice Statistics.

Normand, J., Vlahov, D., & Moses, L. E. (Eds.), (1995). *Preventing HIV transmission*: *The role of sterile needles and bleach.* Washington, DC: National Research Council.

O'Toole, M. (1997). Jails and prisons: The numbers say that they are more different than generally assumed. *American Jails, 11*(2), 32–39.

Opitz-Welke, A., Bennefeld-Kersten, K., Konrad, N., & Welke, J. (2013). Prison suicides in Germany from 2000 to 2011. *International Journal of Law & Psychiatry, 36,* 386–389.

Orrick, E. A., Worrall, J. L., Morris, R. G., Piquero, A. R., Bales, W., & Wang, X. (2011). Testing social support theory: A multilevel analysis of recidivism. *Journal of Criminal Justice, 39,* 499–508.

Osher, F. C. (2007). Short-term strategies to improve reentry of jail populations: Expanding and implementing the APIC model. *American Jails, 20*(6), 9–18.

Osher, F., D'Amora, D. A., Plotkin, M., Jarrett, N., & Eggleston, A. (2012). *Adults with behavioral health needs under correctional supervision: A shared framework for reducing recidivism and promoting recovery*. New York, NY: Council of State Governments Justice Center.

Osher, F., Steadman, H. J., & Barr, H. (2003). A best practice approach to community reentry from jails for inmates with co-occurring disorders: The APIC model. *Crime & Delinquency, 49*, 79–96.

Packman, W. L., Marlitt, R. E., Bhangar, B., & Pennuto, T. O. (2004). A comprehensive and concise assessment of suicide risk. *Behavioral Sciences & the Law, 22*, 667–680.

Pare, P. P. & Logan, M. W. (2011). Risks of minor and serious violent victimization in prison: The impact of inmates' mental disorders, physical disabilities, and physical size. *Society & Mental Health, 1*(2), 106–123.

Patterson, R. F. & Hughes, K. (2008). Review of completed suicides in the California Department of Corrections and Rehabilitation, 1999 to 2004. *Psychiatric Services, 59*(6), 676–682.

Payne J. & Gaffney A. (2012). How much crime is drug or alcohol related? Self-reported attributions of police detainees. *Trends & issues in crime and criminal justice No. 439*. Canberra: Australian Institute of Criminology.

Pearce, M. (2017). Timeline: The rise and fall of Arizona Sheriff Joe Arpaio. *LA Times*. Retrieved from http://www.latimes.com/nation/la-na-arpaio-timeline-20170801-story.html.

Penn, J. V., Esposito, C. L., Schaeffer, L. E., Fritz, G. K., & Spirito, A. (2003). Suicide attempts and self-mutilative behavior in a juvenile correctional facility. *Journal of the American of Child & Adolescent Psychiatry, 42*, 762–769.

Perry, A. E., Marandos, R., Coulton, S., & Johnson, M. (2010). Screening tools assessing risk of suicide and self-ham in adult offenders: A systematic review. *International Journal of Offender Therapy & Comparative Criminology, 54*(3), 803–828.

Perry, A. E. & Olason, D. T. (2009). A new psychometric instrument assessing vulnerability to risk of suicide and self-harm behaviour in offenders. *International Journal of Offender Therapy & Comparative Criminology, 53*(4), 385–400.

Pizarro, J. M. & Narag, R. E. (2008). Supermax prisons: What we know, what we do not know, and where we are going. *The Prison Journal, 88*(1), 23–43.

Policy Research Associates (2005). *Brief Jail Mental Health Screen*. Delmar, NY: Policy Research Associates. Retrieved from http://www.prainc.com.

Pollard, J. M., Schuster, J., Lin, H., & Frisman, L. K. (2007). Evaluation of a gender and trauma specific jail diversion program for female offenders, Part II. *American Jails, 21*, 53–61.

Pompili, M., Lester, D., Innamorati, M., Del Casale, A., Girardi, P., Ferracuti, S., & Tatarelli, R. (2009). Preventing suicide in jails and prisons: Suggestions from experience with psychiatric inpatients. *Journal of Forensic Sciences, 54*(5), 1155–1162.

Power, K. G. (1997). *Evaluation of the Scottish Prison Service suicide prevention strategy*. Edinburgh, Scotland: Scottish Prison Service.

Power, J., Gobeil, R., Beaudette, J. N., Ritchie, M. B., Brown, S. L., & Smith, H. P. (2016). Childhood abuse, nonsuicidal self-injury, and suicide attempts: An exploration of gender differences in incarcerated adults. *Suicide & Life-Threatening Behavior, 46*(6), 745–751.

Pratt, D., Piper, M., Appleby, L., Webb, R., & Shaw, J. (2006). Suicide in recently released prisoners: A population-based cohort study. *The Lancet, 368,* 119–123.

Pratt, D., Tarrier, N., Dunn, G., Awenat, Y., Shaw, J., Ulph, F., & Gooding, P. (2015). Cognitive behavioural suicide prevention for male prisoners: A pilot randomized controlled trial. *Psychological Medicine, 45*(16), 3441–3451.

Prins, S. J. (2014). The prevalence of mental illnesses in U.S. state prisons: A systematic review. *Psychiatric Services, 65*(7), 862–872.

Rabe, K. (2012). Prison structure, inmate mortality, and suicide risk in Europe. *International Journal of Law & Psychiatry, 35,* 222–230.

Radeloff, D., Lempp, T., Herrmann, E., Kettner, M., Bennefeld-Kersten, K., & Freitag, C. M. (2015). National total survey of German adolescent suicide in prison. *European Child & Adolescent Psychiatry, 24, 219–225.*

Radeloff, D., Lempp, T., Kettner, M., Rauf, A. Bennefeld-Kersten, K., & Freitag, C. M. (2017). Male suicide rates in German prisons and the role of citizenship, *PLoS ONE, 12*(6), 1–11.

Ray, R. (2014). Long-term recidivism of mental health court defendants. *International Journal of Law & Psychiatry, 37,* 448–454.

Reeves, R. & Tamburello, A. (2014). Single cells, segregated housing, and suicide in the New Jersey Department of Corrections. *Journal of the American Academy of Psychiatry & The Law, 42*(4), 484–488.

Reiter, K. (2016). *23/7 Pelican Bay Prison and the rise of the long-term solitary confinement.* New Haven, CT: Yale University Press.

Rhine, E. E., Mawhorr, T. L., & Parks, E. (2006). Implementation: The bane of effective correctional programs. *Criminology & Public Policy, 5(2),* 347–358.

Ribeiro, J. D. & Joiner, T. E. (2009). The interpersonal-psychological theory of suicidal behavior: Current status and future directions. *Journal of Clinical Psychology, 65*(12), 1291–1299.

Rivlin, A., Ferris, R., Marzano, L., Fazel, S., & Hawton, K. (2013). A typology of male prisoners making near-lethal suicide attempts. *Crisis, 34*(5), 335–347.

Roberts, L. (2018). Roberts: Joe Arpaio just cost Arizona taxpayers another $7 million. *AZCentral.* Retrieved from https://www.azcentral.com/story/opinion/op-ed/laurieroberts/2018/03/05/joe-arpaio-just-cost-arizona-taxpayers-another-7-million/397695002/.

Roberts, A. R. & Bender, K. (2006). Juvenile offender suicide. *International Journal of Emergency Mental Health, 8,* 255–266.

Robertson, J. E. (1993). Fatal custody: A reassessment of section 1983 liability for custodial suicide. *University of Toledo Law Review, 24,* 807–830.

———. (2004). The impact of *Farmer v. Brennan* on jailer's personal liability for custodial suicide: Ten years on. *Jail Suicide/Mental Health Update, 13*(1), 1–5.

Rodgers, L. N. (1995). Prison suicide: Suggestions from phenomenology. *Deviant Behavior, 16*(2), 113–126.

Rohde, P., Jorgensen, J. S., Seeley, J. R., & Mace, D. E. (2004). Pilot evaluation of the coping course. *Journal of the American Academy of Child & Adolescent Psychiatry, 43,* 669–676.

Roma, P., Pompili, M., Lester, D., Girardi, P., & Ferracuti, S. (2013). Incremental conditions of isolation as a predictor of suicide in prisoners. *Forensic Science International, 233,* e1–e2.

Roskes, E. (2001). Professional collaboration to effectively manage offenders with mental illness in the community. In G. Landsberg & A. Smiley (Eds.), *Forensic mental health* (pp. 9.2 –9.7). Kingston, NJ: Civic Research Institute.

Ross, S. & Heath, N. L. (2003). Two models of adolescent self-mutilation. *Suicide & Life Threatening Behavior, 33*(3), 277–287.

Rothman, D. J. (1971 [2002]). *The discovery of the asylum.* New York: Aldine de Gruyter.

Rotter, M. & Steinbacher, M. (2001). The clinical impact of "doing time"—mental illness and incarceration. In G. Landsberg & A. Smiley (Eds.), *Forensic Mental Health* (pp. 16.1–16.6). Kingston, NJ: Civic Research Institute.

Rudd, M. D., Berman, A. L., Joiner, T. E., Nock, M. K., Silverman, M. M., Mandrusiak, M., Van Orden, K., & Witte, T. (2006). Warning signs for suicide: Theory, research, and clinical applications. *Suicide & Life-Threatening Behavior, 36*(3), 255–262.

Rudd, M. D., Joiner, T., & Rajab, M. H. (2001). *Treating suicidal behavior.* New York: Guilford Press.

Ruiz, G., Wangmo, T., Mutzenberg, P., Sinclair, J. & Elger, B. S. (2014). Understanding death in custody: A case study for a comprehensive definition. *Bioethical Inquiry, 11,* 387–398.

Sanchez, F. C., Fearn, N., & Vaughn, M. G. (2018). Risk factors associated with near-lethal suicide attempts during incarceration among men in the Spanish Prison System. *International Journal of Offender Therapy & Comparative Criminology, 62*(6), 1452–1473.

Sapers, H. (2008). *A preventable death.* Ottawa, ONT: Office of the Correctional Investigator of Canada.

Sarchiapone, M., Mandelli, L., Iosue, M., Andrisano, C., & Roy, A. (2011). Controlling access to suicide means. *International Journal of Environmental Research and Public Health, 8,* 4550–4562.

Schaefer, K. E., Esposito-Smythers, C., & Tangney, J. P. (2016). Suicidal ideation in a United States jail: Demographic and psychiatric correlates. *The Journal of Forensic Psychiatry & Psychology, 27*(5), 698–704.

Schlanger, M. (2003a). Inmate litigation: Results of a national survey. In National Institute of Corrections (Ed.), *Large jail network, annual exchange* (pp. 1–12). Longmont, CO: National Institute of Corrections Jails Division.

———. (2003b). Inmate litigation. *Harvard Law Review, 116,* 1555.

Schlosar, H. & Carlson, L. W. (1997). Befriending in prisons. *Crisis, 18,* 148–151.

Sellings, D., Solimo, A., Lee, S., Horne, K., Panove, E., & Venters, H. (2014). Surveillance of suicidal and nonsuicidal self-injury in the New York City jail system. *Journal of Correctional Health Care, 20*(2), 163–167.

Senese, J. D. (1997). Evaluating jail reform: A comparative analysis of podular/direct and linear jail inmate infractions. *Journal of Criminal Justice, 25*(1), 61–73.

Serin, R. C., Motiuk, L., & Wichmann, C. (2002). An examination of suicide attempts among inmates. *Forum on Corrections Research, 14*(2), 40–42.

Severson, M. (2004). Mental health needs and mental health care in jails: The past, the present, and hope for the future. *American Jails, 18*(3), 9–18.

Shames, A., Wilcox, J., & Subramanian, R. (2015). *Solitary confinement: Common misconceptions and emerging safe alternatives.* New York, NY: Vera Institute of Justice.

Shapiro, D. M. (2016). To seek a newer world: Prisoners' rights at the frontier. *Michigan Law Review First Impressions, 114*, 124–138.

Sharkey, L. (2010). Does overcrowding in prisons exacerbate the risk of suicide among women prisoners? *The Howard Journal, 49*(2), 111–124.

Shaw, J., Appleby, L., & Baker, D. (2003). *Safer prisons: A national study of prison suicides 1999–2000 by the National Confidential Inquiry into Suicides and Homicides by People with Mental Illness.* Manchester, UK: National Confidential Inquiry.

Shaw, J., Baker, D., Hunt, I. M., Maloney, A., & Appleby, L. (2004). Suicide by prisoners: National clinical survey. *British Journal of Psychiatry, 184*, 263–267.

Shaw, J. & Turnbull, P. (2009). Suicide in custody. *Psychiatry, 8*(7), 265–268.

Shea, S. C. (2002). *The practical art of suicide assessment: A guide for mental health professionals and substance abuse counselors.* New Jersey: Wiley.

Sheridan, E. P. & Teplin, L. A. (1981). Police-referred psychiatric emergencies: Advantages of community treatment. *Journal of Community Psychology, 9*, 140–147.

Sickmund, M. & Puzzanchera, C. (2014). *Juvenile offenders and victims: 2014 national report.* Pittsburgh, PA: National Center for Juvenile Justice.

Skeem, J., Johansson, P., Andersheed, H., Kerr, M., & Louden, J. E. (2007). Two subtypes of psychopathic violent offenders that parallel primary and secondary variants. *Journal of Abnormal Psychology, 116*(2), 395–409.

Skeem, J. L., Manchak, S., & Peterson, J. K. (2011). Correctional policy for offenders with mental illness: Creating a new paradigm for recidivism reduction. *Law & Human Behavior, 35*(2), 110–126.

Skeem, J. L., Winter, E., Kennealy, P. J., Louden, J. E., & Tartar, J. R. II. (2014). Offenders with mental illness have criminogenic needs, too: Toward recidivism reduction. *Law & Human Behavior, 38*(3), 212–224.

Skogstad, P., Deane, F. P., & Spicer, J. (2005). Barriers to help-seeking among New Zealand prison inmates. *Journal of Offender Rehabilitation, 42*(2), 1–24.

Slade, K., & Forrester, A. (2015). Shifting the paradigm of prison suicide prevention through enhanced multi-agency integration and cultural change. *The Journal of Forensic Psychiatry & Psychology, 26*(6), 737–758.

Slate, R. N. (2009). Seeking alternatives to the criminalization of mental illness. *American Jails, 21*(1), 20–28

Slate, R. N., Buffington-Vollum, J. K. & Johnson W. W. (2013). *The criminalization of mental illness (2nd ed).* Durham, NC: Carolina Academic Press.

Sloan, B. L. & Efeti, D. E. (2017). Taking care of the mentally ill. *Corrections Today, 79*(3), 42–44.

Smith, H. P. & Kaminski, R. J. (2010). Self-injurious behavior in state prisons: Findings from a national study. *Criminal Justice & Behavior, 38*(1), 26–41.

Smith, P. N., Selwyn, C., D'Amato, D., Granato, S., Kuhlman, S., & Mandracchia, J. T. (2016). Life experiences and the acquired capability for suicide in incarcerated men. *Death Studies, 40*(7), 432–439.

Smith, P., Selwyn, C. N., Wolford-Clevenger, C., & Mandracchia, J. T. (2014). Psychopathic personality traits, suicide ideation, and suicide attempts in male prison inmates. *Criminal Justice & Behavior, 41*(3), 364–379.

Smith, P. N., Wolford, C., Mandracchia, J. T., & Jahn, D. R. (2013). An exploratory factor analysis of the Acquired Capability for Suicide Scale in male prison inmates. *Psychological Services, 10*(1), 97–105.

Snell, T. L. (2013). *Capital punishment, 2011—statistical tables.* Washington, DC: United States Department of Justice, Office of Justice Programs, Bureau of Justice Statistics.

Snow, L. (2002). Prisoners' motives for self-injury and attempted suicide. *The British Journal of Forensic Practice, 4*(4), 18–29.

Snow, L. & McHugh, M. (2002). The aftermath of a death in prison custody. In G. Towl, L. Snow & M. McHugh (Eds.), *Suicide in prisons* (pp. 121–134). Leicester, UK: The British Psychological Society.

Spittal, M. J., Forsyth, S., Pirkis, J., Alati, R., & Kinner, S. (2014). Suicide in adults released from prison in Queensland, Australia: A cohort study. *Journal of Epidemiology & Community Health, 68*, 993–998.

Stack, S. (2000). Suicide: A 15-year review of the sociological literature: Part I: Cultural and economic factors. *Suicide & Life-Threatening Behavior, 30,* 145–162.

Stahl, E. & West, M. (2001). Growing population of mentally ill offenders, redefines correctional facility design. *Corrections Today, 63*(5), 72–74.

Stanley, B., Brown, G., Brent, D., Wells, K., Poling, K., Curry, J., Kennard, B. D., Wagner, A., Cwik, M., Barnett, S., Daniel, S., & Hughes, J. (2009). Cognitive behavior therapy for suicide prevention (CBT-SP): Treatment model, feasibility and acceptability. *Journal of the American Academy of Child Adolescent Psychiatry, 48*(10), 1005–1013.

Steadman, H. J., Davidson, S., & Brown, C. (2001). Law and psychiatry: mental health courts: Their promise and unanswered questions. *Psychiatric Services, 52*(4), 457–458.

Steadman, H. J., Morris, S. M., & Dennis, D. L. (1995). The diversion of mentally ill persons from jails to community-based services: A profile of programs. *American Journal of Public Health, 85,* 1630–1635.

Steadman, H. J., & Naples, M. (2005). Assessing the effectiveness of jail diversion programs for persons with serious mental illness and co-occurring substance use disorders. *Behavioral Sciences & the Law, 23,* 163–170.

Steadman, H. J., Osher, F. C., Robbins, P. C., Case, B., & Samuels, S. (2009). Prevalence of serious mental illness among jail inmates. *Psychiatric Services, 60,* 761–765.

Steadman, H. J., Robbins, P. C., Islam, T., & Osher, F. (2007). Revalidating the brief jail mental health screen to increase accuracy for women. *Psychiatric Services, 58*(12), 1598–1601.

Steadman, H. J., Scott, J. E., Osher, F., Agnese, T. K., & Robbins, P. C. (2005). Validation of the Brief Jail Mental Health Screen. *Psychiatric Services, 56*(7), 816–822.

Stohr, M. K., Jonson, C. L., & Cullen, F. T. (2014). Lessons learned. In F. T. Cullen, C. L. Jonson & M. K. Stohr (Eds.), *The American prison: Imagining a different future* (pp. 257–268). Thousand Oaks, CA: Sage.

Stoliker, B. (2018). Attempted suicide: A multilevel examination of inmate characteristics and prison context. *Criminal Justice & Behavior, 45*(5), 589–611.

Stone, G. (1999). *Suicide and attempted suicide.* New York: Carroll and Graf Publishers, Inc.

Stone, D. M., Simon. T. R., Fowler, K. A., Kegler, S. R., Yuan, K., Holland, K. M., Ivey-Stephenson, A. Z., & Crosby, A. E. (2018). Vital signs: Trends in state suicide rates—United States, 1999–2016 and circumstances contributing to suicide—27 states, 2015. *Centers for Disease Control and Prevention, 67*(22), 617–624.

Substance Abuse and Mental Health Services Administration (2017). *SAMHSA syringe exchange program studies.* Rockville, MD: SAMHSA.

Suicide Prevention Resource Center (2017). *Racial and ethnic disparities.* Waltham, MD: Suicide Prevention Resource Center.

Suto, I. & Arnaut, G. L. Y. (2010). Suicide in prison: A qualitative study. *The Prison Journal, 90(3),* 288–312.

Swartz, M. S. (2010). Advancing research at the intersection of two systems. *Psychiatric Services, 61*(5), 431.

Swooger, M. T., Walsh, Z., Maisto, S. A., & Conner, K. R. (2014). Reactive and proactive aggression and suicide attempts among criminal offenders. *Criminal Justice & Behavior, 41*(3), 337–344.

Sykes, G. (1958). *Society of captives.* Princeton: Princeton University Press.

Taheri, S. A. (2016). Do crisis intervention teams reduce arrests and improve officer safety? A systematic review and meta-analysis. *Criminal Justice Policy Review, 27*(1), 76–96.

Tanney, B. L. (2000). Psychiatric diagnoses and suicidal acts. In R. W. Maris, A. L. Berman, & M. M. Silverman (Eds.), *Comprehensive textbook of suicidology* (pp. 311–341). New York: Guilford.

Tartaro, C. (1999). Reduction of suicides in jails and lockups through situational crime prevention. *Journal of Correctional Health Care, 6*(2), 235–263.

———. (2000). *The impact of facility design and supervision strategies on jail violence.* Ann Arbor, MI: University Microfilms International.

———. (2002). Examining implementation issues with new generation jails. *Criminal Justice Policy Review, 13,* 219–237.

———. (2003). Suicide and the jail environment: An evaluation of three types of institutions. *Environment & Behavior, 35,* 605–620.

———. (2004). Inside the jail: A look at building design and inmate supervision. In R. Muraskin (Ed.), *Key correctional issues* (pp. 192–204). Upper Saddle River, NJ: Prentice Hall.

———. (2006) Watered down: Partial implementation of the new generation jail philosophy. *Prison Journal, 86*(3), 284–300.

————. (2015). An evaluation of the effects of jail diversion and reentry for mentally ill offenders. *Journal of Offender Rehabilitation, 54*(2), 85–102.

Tartaro, C. & Lester, D. (2016). Suicide on death row. *Journal of Forensic Sciences, 61*(6), 1656–1659.

Tartaro, C. & Levy, M. P. (2008). Predictors of suicide in new generation jails. *Justice Research & Policy, 10*(1), 21–37.

Tartaro, C. & Ruddell, R. (2006). Trouble in Mayberry: A national analysis of suicide attempts in small jails. *American Journal of Criminal Justice, 31*(1), 81–101.

Taylor, C. (2016). The family's role in the reintegration of formerly incarcerated individuals: The direct effects of emotional support. *The Prison Journal, 96*(3), 331–354.

Teplin, L. & Swartz, J. (1989). Screening for severe mental disorder in jails. *Law & Human Behavior, 13*(1), 1–18.

Thomas, J., Leaf, M., Kazmierczak, S., & Stone, J. (2006). Self-injury in correctional settings: "Pathology" of prisons or of prisoners? *Criminology & Public Policy, 5*(1), 193–202.

Thompson, M. (2008). *Gender, mental illness, and crime.* Washington, DC: United States Department of Justice.

Toch, H. (1992a). *Mosaic of despair: Human breakdowns in prison (2nd ed).* Washington, DC: American Psychological Association.

————. (1992b). *Living in prison: The ecology of survival.* Washington, DC: American Psychological Association.

————. (2016). Providing sanctuary in New York prisons. *The Prison Journal, 96*(5), 647–660.

Torrey, E. F. (2016). The dearth of psychiatric hospital beds. *Psychiatric Times, 33*(2). Retrieved from http://www.psychiatrictimes.com/psychiatric-emergencies/dearth-psychiatric-beds.

Torrey, E. F., Kennard, A. D., Eslinger, D., Lamb, R., & Pavle, J. (2010). *More mentally ill persons are in jails and prisons than hospitals: A survey of the states.* Arlington, VA: Treatment Advocacy Center.

Towl, G. J. & Crighton, D. A. (1998). Suicide in prisons in England and Wales from 1988 to 1995. *Criminal Behavior & Mental Health, 8*, 184–192.

Towl, G. & Crighton, D. (2002). Risk assessment and management. In G. Towl, L. Snow & M. McHugh (Eds.), *Suicide in prisons* (pp. 66–92). Leicester: The British Psychological Society.

Travis, J., Solomon, A., & Waul, M. (2001). *From prison to home: The dimensions and consequences of prisoner reentry.* Washington, DC: Urban Institute.

United States Bureau of Justice Statistics (1981–2001). *Correctional populations in the United States.* Washington, DC: United States Department of Justice, Office of Justice Programs, Bureau of Justice Statistics.

————. (2002). *Reentry trends in the United States.* Washington, DC: United States Department of Justice, Office of Justice Programs, Bureau of Justice Statistics.

————. (2007). *Key facts at a glance: Number of persons under correctional supervision.* Washington, DC: United States Department of Justice, Office of Justice Programs, Bureau of Justice Statistics.

———. (2018a). *Data collection: Mortality in correctional institutions (MCI) (formerly Deaths in Custody Reporting Program (DCRP))*. United States Department of Justice, Office of Justice Programs, Bureau of Justice Statistics. Retrieved from https://www.bjs.gov/index.cfm?ty=dcdetail&iid=243.

———. (2018b). *Drug and crime facts*. Washington, DC: United States Department of Justice, Office of Justice Programs, Bureau of Justice Statistics.

United States Census Bureau (2000). *Statistical abstract of the United States, 2000*. Washington, DC: Census Bureau.

United States Department of Health and Human Services (2007). *National GAINS Center*. Retrieved from http://gainscenter.gov/html.

United States Department of Justice (2016). *U.S. Department of Justice report and recommendations concerning the use of restrictive housing*. Washington, DC: United States Department of Justice. Retrieved from https://www.justice.gov/restrictivehousing.

Vadini, F., Calella, G., Pieri, A., Ricci, E., Fulcheri, M., Verrocchio, M. C., De Risio, A., Sciacca, A., Santilli, F., & Parruti, G. (2018). Neurocognitive impairment and suicide risk among prison inmates. *Journal of Affective Disorders, 225*, 273–277.

Van Ginneken, E. F., Sutherland, A., & Molleman, T. (2017). An ecological analysis of prison overcrowding and suicide rates in England and Wales, 2000–2014. *International Journal of Law & Psychiatry, 50*, 76–82.

Van Orden, K. A., Witte, T. K., Cukrowicz, K. C., Braithwaite, S. R., Selby, E. A., & Joiner, T. E. Jr. (2010). The interpersonal theory of suicide. *Psychological Review, 117*(2), 575–600.

Van Orden, K. A., Cukrowicz, K. C., Witte, T. K., & Joiner, T. E. (2012). Thwarted belongingness and perceived burdensomeness: Construct validity and psychometric properties of the Interpersonal Needs Questionnaire. *Psychological Assessment, 24*(1), 197–215.

Verdolini, N., Murru, A., Attademo, L., Garinella, R., Pacchiarotta, I., del mar Bonnin, C., Samalin, L., Pauselli, L., Piselli, M., Tamantini, A., Quartesan, R., Carvalho, A. F., Vieta, E., & Tortorella, A. (2017). The aggressor at the mirror: Psychiatric correlates of deliberate self-harm in male prison inmates. *European Psychiatry, 44*, 153–160.

Veysey, B. M., Steadman, H. J., Morrissey, J. P., Johnsen, M., & Beckstead, J. W. (1998). Using the referral decision scale to screen mentally ill jail detainees: Validity and implementation issues. *Law & Human Behavior, 22*(2), 205–215.

Victor, S. E. & Klonsky, E. D. (2014). Correlates of suicide attempts among self-injurers: A meta-analysis. *Clinical Psychology Review, 34*, 282–297.

Victoria Department of Justice Correctional Services Task Force (1998). *Review of suicides and self-harm in Victorian prisons*. Melbourne, Australia: Victorian Government Printer.

Visher, C. A. & Courtney, S. M. E. (2007). *One year out: Experiences of prisoners returning to Cleveland*. Washington, DC: Urban Institute Justice Policy Center.

Visher, C. A. & Travis, J. (2003). Transitions from prison to community: Understanding individual pathways. *Annual Review of Sociology, 29*, 89–113.

Voulgaris, A., Kose, N., Konrad, N., & Opitz-Welke, A. (2018). Prison suicide in comparison to suicide events in forensic psychiatric hospitals in Germany. *Frontiers in Psychiatry, 9,* doi.org/10.3389/fpsyt.2018.00398.

Wallace, H. & Roberson, C. (2000). *Legal aspects of corrections.* Incline Village, NV: Copperhouse Publishing.

Walsh, B. W. & Rosen, P. M. (1988). *Self-mutilation.* New York: Guilford.

Wang, E. W., Rogers, R., Giles, C. L., Diamond, P. M., Herrington-Wang, L. E., & Taylor, E. R. (1997). A pilot study of the Personality Assessment Inventory (PAI) in corrections. *Behavioral Sciences & the Law, 15,* 469–482.

Way, B. B., Kaufman, A. R., Knoll, J. L., & Chlebowski, S. M. (2013). Suicidal ideation among inmate-patients in state prison: Prevalence, reluctance to report, and treatment preferences. *Behavioral Sciences & the Law, 31,* 230–238.

Weinrath, M., Wayte, T., & Arboleda-Florez, J. (2012). *The final report of the independent review committee into federal deaths in custody 2010–2011.* Ottawa, ONT: Correctional Services Canada.

Welch, M. & Gunther, D. (1997). Jail suicide and prevention: Lessons from litigation. *Crisis Intervention, 3,* 229–244.

Wener, R. E. (2012). *The environmental psychology of prisons and jails.* New York, NY: Cambridge University Press.

Wener, R., Frazier, F. W., & Farbstein, J. (1985). Three generations of evaluation and design of correctional facilities. *Environment & Behavior, 17,* 71–95.

———. (1993). Direct supervision of correctional institutions. In National Institute of Corrections (Ed.), *Podular direct supervision jails* (pp. 1–8). Longmont, CO: NIC Jails Division.

White, M. D., Saunders, J., Fisher, C., & Mellow, J. (2012). Exploring inmate reentry in a local jail setting: Implications for outreach, service use, and recidivism. *Crime & Delinquency, 58*(1), 124–146.

White, T. W. & Schimmel, D. J. (1995). Suicide prevention in federal prisons. In L. M. Hayes (Ed.), *Prison suicide,* (pp. 48–59). Washington, DC: U.S. Department of Justice.

Wichmann, C., Serin, R., & Abracen, J. (2002). *Women offenders who engage in self-harm: A comparative investigation.* Ottawa, Canada: Correctional Service of Canada.

Wichmann, C., Serin, R. C., & Motiuk, L. (2000). *Predicting suicide attempts among male offenders in federal penitentiaries.* Ottawa, Canada: Correctional Service of Canada.

Wicks, R. J. (1974). *Correctional psychology.* San Francisco: Canfield Press.

Willis M., Baker A., Cussen T., & Patterson E. (2016). Self-inflicted deaths in Australian prisons. *Trends & issues in crime and criminal justice.* No. 513. Canberra: Australian Institute of Criminology. Retrieved from https://aic.gov.au/publications/tandi/tandi513.

Wilson, J. A. & Davis, R. C. (2006). Good intentions meet hard realities: An evaluation of the Project Greenlight reentry program. *Criminology & Public Policy, 5*(2), 303–338.

Winfree, L. T. (1988). Rethinking American jail death rates: A comparison of national mortality and jail mortality, 1978, 1983. *Policy Studies Review, 7*(3), 641–659.

Wingate, L. R., Joiner, T. E., Walker, R., Rudd, M. D., & Jobes, D. A. (2004). Empirically informed approaches to topics in suicide risk assessment. *Behavioral Sciences & the Law, 22,* 651–665.

Wobeser, W. L., Datema, J., Bechard, B., & Ford, P. (2002). Causes of death among people in custody in Ontario, 1990–1999. *Canadian Medical Association Journal, 167*(10), 1109–1113.

Wolff, N., Bjerklie, J. R., & Maschi, T. (2005). Reentry planning for mentally disordered inmates: A social investment perspective. *Journal of Offender Rehabilitation, 41*(2), 21–42.

Wood, S. R. (2013). Dual severe mental and substance use disorders as predictors of federal inmate assaults. *The Prison Journal, 93*(1), 34–56.

World Health Organization (2007). *Preventing suicide in jails and prisons.* Geneva, Switzerland: Department of Mental Health and Substance Abuse, World Health Organization.

———. (2018). *Suicide rate estimates, crude estimates by country.* Retrieved from http://apps.who.int/gho/data/view.main.MHSUICIDEv?lang=en.

World Health Organization Collaborating Centre for Training and Research in Suicide Prevention (1986). *Definition of parasuicide.* University of Padua, Italy: WHO Collaborating Centre for Training and Research in Suicide Prevention.

World Prison Brief Data (2018). *Switzerland.* Retrieved from http://www.prisonstudies.org/country/switzerland.

Wortley, R. (1998). A two-stage model of situational crime prevention. *Studies in Crime & Crime Prevention, 7*(2), 73–188.

———. (2001). A classification of techniques for controlling situational precipitators of crime. *Security Journal, 14,* 63–82.

———. (2002). *Situational prison control.* Cambridge, UK: Cambridge University Press.

Wright, K. A., Pratt, T. C., Lowenkamp, C. T., & Latessa, E. J. (2012). The importance of ecological context for correctional rehabilitation programs: Understanding the micro- and macro-level dimensions of successful offender treatment. *Justice Quarterly, 29*(6), 775–798.

Yeager, K. R. & Gregoire, T. K. (2005). Crisis intervention: Application of brief solution–focused therapy in addictions. In A. R. Roberts (Ed.), *Crisis intervention handbook* (pp. 566–601). New York: Oxford University Press.

Zeng, Z. (2018). *Jail inmates in 2016.* Washington, DC: United States Bureau of Justice Statistics.

COURT CASES

A. H. v. St. Louis County, Missouri, No. 17-1198 (8th Cir. 2018)

Balla v. Idaho State Bd. of Corrections, 595 F. Supp. 1558 (D. Idaho 1984)

Bame v. Iron County, Utah, No. 13-4044 (10th Cir. 2014)

Bearden v. Anglin, 543 Fed.Appx. 918 (11th Cir. 2013)

Bell v. Wolfish, 441 U.S. 520 (1979)

Bowring v. E. Godwin, 551 F.2d 44 (1977)

Brad H. et al., v. City of New York, 185 Misc. 2d 420 (2000)

Cagle v. Sutherland, 344 F.3d 980 (11th Cir. 2003)

Castro v. County of Los Angeles, 833 F.3d 1060 (9th Cir. 2016)

Cavalieri v. Shepard, 321 F.3d 616 (7th Cir. 2003)

City of Revere v. Massachusetts General Hospital, 463 U.S. 239 (1983)

Comstock v. McCrary, 273 F.3d 693 (6th Cir. 2001)

Cox v. Glanz, 800 F.3d 1231 (10th Cir. 2015)

Darnell v. Piniero, 849 F.3d 17 (2nd Cir. 2017)

D.M. v. Terhune, 67 F. Supp. 2d 401 (DNJ 1999)

Estate of Belden v. Brown County, 46 Kan. App. 2d 247 (2011)

Estelle v. Gamble, 429 U.S. 97 (1976)

Farmer v. Brennan, 511 U.S. 825 (1994)

Frake v. City of Chicago, 210 F.3d 779 (7th Cir. 2000)

Grabow v. County of Macomb, 580 Fed.Appx. 300 (6th Cir. 2014)

Gregoire v. City of Oak, Harbor, 170 Wash 2d. 628 (2017)

Grenning v. Miller-Stout, 739 F.3d 1235 1241 (9th Cir. 2014)

Hale v. Tallapoosa County, 50 F.3d 1579 (11th Cir. 1995)

Harlow v. Fitzgerald, 457 U.S. 800 (1982)

Harvey v. County of Ward, 352 F.2d 1003 (D.N.D. 2005)

Harvey v. Nichols, 581 S.E.2d 272 *(Ga. Ct. App. 2003)*

Heflin v. Stewart County, 958 F.2d 709 (6th Cir. 1992)

Hill v. Jackson, 336 Ga., App 679 (Ga. Ct. App. 2016)

Holland v. City of Atmore, 168 F. Supp. 2d 1303 (S.D. Ala. 2001)

Hott v. Hennepin County, 260 F.3d 901 (8th Cir. 2001)

Hyatt v. Thomas, No. 15-10708 (5th Cir. 2016)

Jacobs v. West Feliciana Sheriff's Department, 228 F.3d 388 (2000)

Jones v. Davis, 806 F.3d 538 (9th Cir. 2015)

Jones 'El v. Berge, 164 F. Supp. 2d 1096 (WD Wis. 2001)

Kingsley v. Hendrickson, 135 S.Ct. 2466 (2015)

Luckert v. Dodge County, 684 F.3d 808 (8th Cir. 2012)

Madrid v. Gomez, 889 F.Supp. 1146 (ND Cal. 1995)

Martin v. Somerset County, 387 F. Supp. 2d 65 (D. Me. 2005)

McGill v. Duckworth, 944 F.2d 344, 351 (7th Cir. 1991)

Miranda v. County of Lake, 900 F.3d 335 (7th Cir. 2018)

Monell v. Department of Social Services, 436 U.S. 658 (1978)

Pretty on Top v. City of Hardin, 597 p. 2d. 58 (Mont.1979)

Rapier v. Kankakee County, Ill., 203 F. Supp. 2d. 978 (CD Ill. 2002)

Ruiz v. Estelle, 503 F. Supp. 1265 (S.D.Tex.1980)

Salter v. Mitchell, 711 Fed. Appx. 530 (2017)

Serafin v. City of Johnstown, 53 Fed.Appx. 211 (3rd Cir. 2003)

Settlement Agreement: D.M. v. Terhune, United States District Court for the District of New Jersey, D.M v. Terhune 67 F. Supp. 2d 401 (DNJ 1999)

Sisk v. Manzanares, 262 F. Supp. 2d 1162 (D. Kan. 2002)

Smith v. Atkins, 777 F. Supp. 2d 955 (E.D.N.C. 2011)

Stewart v. Waldo County, 350 F. Supp. 2d 215 (D. Me. 2004)

Terry v. Rice, WL 19221818 (2003)

Thomas v. County of Commissioners of Shawnee County, 40 Kan.App.2d 946 (Kan. 2009)

Turney v. Waterbury, 375 F.3d 756 (8th Cir. 2004)

Wade v. Tompkins, 73 Fed.Appx. 890 (2003)

Wever v. Lincoln County, 388 F.3d 601 (8th Cir. 2004)

Williams v. Lee County, AL, 78 F.3d 491 (11th Cir. 1996)

Witney v. City of St. Louis, Missouri, 887 F.3d 857 (8th Cir. 2018)

Wood v. Strickland, 420 U.S. 308 (1975)

Woodward v. Correctional Medical Services, 368 F.3d 917 (7th Cir. 2004)

Yellow Horse v. Pennington County, 150 F.3d 1209 (8th Cir. 2000)

Index

Page references for figures are italicized.

263

About the Author

Christine Tartaro, Ph.D. (M.A./Ph.D. Rutgers University) is a professor of criminal justice at Stockton University. She has a Ph.D. in criminal justice from Rutgers University. She has worked as a researcher for the New Jersey Department of Corrections and the Police Foundation and as a research consultant for the New Jersey Juvenile Justice Commission. She does consulting and expert witness work in the area of suicide in custody. Her research interests include new generation jails, suicide in correctional facilities, mental health, and prisoner reentry.